Secrets to Successful Events

How to Organize, Promote and Manage Exceptional Events and Festivals

Lynn Fuhler

all my best!
Lynn Fuhler

Flying Compass Press
Winston-Salem, North Carolina

This publication is presented for informational purposes only. The publisher and the author are not offering any legal, tax, accounting, financial, insurance or other professional service or advice. If readers desire such services or advice, please consult a competent professional. Content contained herein may be affected by relevant laws which vary from state to state. Please consult an attorney before using any sample documents. The contents contained herein are not guaranteed or warrantied to produce any particular results.

No warranty is made with respect to the accuracy or completeness of the information contained herein, and both the publisher and author specifically disclaim any responsibility for any liability, loss or risk, personal or otherwise which is incurred as a consequence – directly or indirectly – of the use of any of the contents of this publication. Any descriptions are fictional and any likeness to actual persons, either living or dead is strictly coincidental.

For information about special discounts for bulk purchases, please contact: Flying Compass Press, P.O. Box 24305, Winston-Salem, NC 27114 or publisher@flyingcompass.com.

Manufactured in the United States of America.

Publisher's Cataloging-in-Publication
(Provided by Quality Books, Inc.)

Fuhler, Lynn, author.
  Secrets to successful events : how to organize,
promote and manage exceptional events and festivals /
Lynn Fuhler. -- First edition.
    pages cm
    Includes index.
    LCCN 2016914380
    ISBN-13: 978-0-9979807-0-7 (print)
    ISBN-10: 0-9979807-0-2 (print)
    ISBN-13: 978-0-9979807-1-4 (eBook)
    ISBN-10: 0-9979807-1-0 (eBook)

    1. Special events--Planning--Handbooks, manuals, etc.
    2. Special events--Management--Handbooks, manuals, etc.
    3. Meetings--Planning--Handbooks, manuals, etc.
    4. Congresses and conventions--Planning--Handbooks,
    manuals, etc. 5. Special events industry--Vocational
    guidance--Handbooks, manuals, etc.   I. Title.

GT3405.F84 2016   394.2068
                         QBI16-1443

Contents

To Steve with Love

Introduction

To some, organizing a festival or an event can appear to be an easy task. To others, it may seem to be a massive undertaking. Regardless of whether you are a first-time event planner or a seasoned professional, the contents of this book are designed to provide a realistic point of view of what can be expected – the good, the bad and the ugly.

After reading this book, some may shrug their shoulders and walk away from any involvement in organizing a festival or an event. The purpose is not to discourage anyone but, rather, to illustrate what it takes to put on a well coordinated event. Understanding the possibilities allows an Event Chairman and Organizing Committee members to hope for the best and prepare for the worst.

Because every event is different in size, scope and level of volunteer experience, this book focuses on the various functions needed to build an event versus developing timelines for each committee and layering one on top of the other to create a master calendar. Timelines are fluid; functions usually remain constant. While not every festival or event will benefit from the entire book in a given year, over time it's likely various sections will prove useful.

If you are an Organizing Committee member, I would encourage you to read the book in its entirety. You may be surprised how much your part impacts others and how much others rely on you and your committee. As Aristotle noted, the whole is greater than the sum of the parts. Besides, someday you may work your way to the top to become the Event Chairman.

Because music and food are key components of many festivals, they serve as the foundation for this publication. While the event theme may vary – music, a wine tasting, an air show, food festival, film fest, book festival or a craft beer event – the underlying organizational elements are much the same for each. The unique qualities of non-musical events are addressed also.

The chapters flow in sequence starting with the Event Chairman finding volunteers to serve on the Organizing Committee. Simultaneously, efforts are made to produce sponsorship packages and line up sponsors while the Treasurer gets the business and finance areas in order. Various committees start to get comfortable with their role and responsibilities; others slowly gain momentum.

Marketing Services, for instance, needs to lay the groundwork for many other committees, so it should be the first out of the gate to get things in place. Public Relations and Publicity will follow shortly behind, because considerable lead time is needed to build its toolkit. The Entertainment Committee will be itching to book talent. However, they will need to patiently wait until sponsorship dollars are locked in and are committed or in hand to offset these expenses.

With the budgeting process complete, fellow Organizing Committee members now have time to better understand the number and types of volunteers they will need. With this information, Volunteer Services can establish volunteer job descriptions and begin to solicit sponsors and others to help at the event. Once talent is booked, the Stage Manager's work begins. Merchandise has been quietly working behind the scenes, like Marketing and Public Relations, to come up with the perfect theme for this year's poster or tee shirt. Come the event, it will be all hands on deck to push merchandise and bring in additional revenue.

All along, Site Services has been in contact with the venue to prepare for everything needed come load-in day ... time for them to do some heavy lifting. As planned, the concessionaires will easily take their place at the venue, but only after the Concession Committee has spent months reviewing applicants, coordinating with government agencies and meeting with the finalists.

If you're fortunate enough to have an office and staff, your event has a safety net, providing they have event experience. The final chapter addresses topics related to events and activities for seasoned organizers.

Ralph Waldo Emerson once wrote, "Life is a journey, not a destination." This book is a road map to a destination – to your festival or event. So enjoy the journey. Have fun. Make lasting friends and memories. Take photos. Laugh. Sit back and watch the event like everyone else. Or stand in line and experience the event as your patrons do. You've worked hard and earned the chance to enjoy it, if only for a minute or two.

Getting Started

It's always interesting to learn how an event was born – the story that explains a specific point in time when an idea morphs from a possibility into a reality. The most basic feasibility study I've heard goes something like this: "Tom is the guy in our town who everyone knows and respects. If Tom endorses the project, it's a go. We just happen to run into Tom where he breakfasts every day and brought up the idea of a community celebration. 'Our civic club is thinking about organizing a downtown festival. What do you think? Would you be interested in your company being a sponsor? My company is in and Susie and Gary said they'd support it, too.'"

In some communities, the feasibility question is skipped. Sometimes, the organization's need is so dire that they move forward without thinking it through completely. As an example, one downtown development group's executive director shared, "We have to draw people back downtown." A chamber of commerce sought to drive business into restaurants during a traditionally slow time and so evolved "Restaurant Week." In other cases, a festival is a natural progression.

When a few vineyards and craft beer makers turn into many and as members move out of the infancy stage, they begin focusing on gaining more exposure and sales. Wine and beer festivals and tasting events are a logical next step to achieve those goals. Downtown agencies interested in creating a more vibrant destination are more than willing to partner by providing the venue.

SELECTING THE EVENT'S MISSION AND THEME

For many organizers, the event's mission is established by its presenting organization – to raise funds and friends in support of its mission. Alternately, a group of volunteers advocating a common cause or interest can join together to create and produce an event. In either situation, before considering organizing an event, all parties involved should thoroughly research and then discuss the type of event, the event theme, and the intended participants or attendees.

Your audience will be determined by the theme of your event. Community festivals are usually free and draw residents. A variety of events can fall under its umbrella such as a walk or a run, a car show, beauty pageants, sporting events, food contests, a parade and musical performances.

Food, beer, wine, music, film and air fests, among many others, tend to attract residents as well as visitors. When determining the type of event you want to produce, carefully research if you have or will have access or interest from your potential talent – headliners, artists, speakers, musicians, pilots, performers, winemakers, authors, chefs, entertainers, brewmasters, etc. You may have interest but may not have the budget to afford talent fees and/or to handle travel costs. Your local government and community may have issues with alcohol and, therefore, may not be receptive to a wine or beer event in a city park or on a downtown street. Perhaps noise complaints, lack of parking and expensive infrastructure or maintenance needs have plagued a local airport. Are these obstacles too big for air show organizers to overcome?

SELECTING AN EVENT DATE

Event planners should always do a competitive analysis before creating an event and adding it to a crowded community calendar. Find out which events have traditionally occurred on specific dates or weekends on or about the same time frame of your proposed event. In some cities, the public library (officially) or local hospital's foundation (unofficially) maintains the community calendar. They want and need to know what events and activities are held that may compete with their efforts to raise funds. Take the time to make a quick phone call to see if such a foundation maintains a calendar or can refer you elsewhere.

Local destination management organizations (DMOs) – chamber of commerce, convention and visitors bureau or state tourism agency – also maintain online calendars of events. These may be for events open to the general public and, as such, do not include fundraisers.

More importantly, if your event is going to need hotel rooms, double check to assure a national convention or a college or university homecoming, graduation or athletic event is not scheduled in your region. These types of events can draw upon hotel rooms from the entire area.

It may seem unimaginable that your event hasn't even begun and this discussion is about it already being over. Play it forward. The crowds were low or attendance counts were less than expected, although weather was terrific. Some on the Organizing Committee complain how "all those other events were held on the same weekend." Don't be surprised if those other events have been held on the same weekend for numerous years. Crying over low turnout, lack of parking or traffic congestion created by other events means one thing. The Organizing Committee did not do its homework. Do a little research before investing time and energy in planning an event.

As the years go by, updating the competitive analysis is important because the terrain can change.

NEXT THINGS NEXT

Every event impacts traffic so getting the blessing of local government or elected officials is usually one of the first steps in organizing any festival or event. A revolving door of idea men frequent City Hall presenting projects claiming to be "the best thing since sliced bread." If an Event Chairman pitches City Hall on an event that is too pie-in-the-sky with unrealistic expectations, don't be surprised if the result is a quashed event and a vote of no confidence. If the same Event Chairman brings a proposal requesting use of a city park and estimates staying within the park's capacity limits, the event may still be met with skepticism. However, a lot of hurdles laid before the Event Chairman by City Hall may be overcome.

Few realize how much an event can impact a city's infrastructure either directly or indirectly. Because of extensive experience with events including organizing city festivals and events, City Hall typically knows what is practical and feasible. For more details, see SPONSORS, SITE and CONCESSIONS/VENDORS chapters.

City Hall needs to feel its good name will not besmirched by being associated with the Event Chairman, the Organizing Committee or anything related to the proposed event whether it's an official sponsor or not. The Event Chairman needs to be prepared to present a full-blown written presentation so as to convey that the event has been fully thought through.

The process is much like asking a bank for a mortgage to buy a house – you must meet all the criteria in order for City Hall to agree to underwrite the event. Even if you are not securing cash from the city, each city service and employee labor hour has a dollar value. City Hall needs to be able to justify to its constituents – residents and businesses – that the event is worthy of diverting taxpayer dollars to support the project.

FINDING THE RIGHT COMMITTEE MEMBERS

You Can't Do It All Yourself

An Event Chairman will need a number of skill sets to pull off an event. The top three are planning, organizing and sales.

The first two are obvious, but you may be wondering, "Why sales?" The answer is simple. When trying to organize an event, especially a first-time event, the Event Chairman needs to sell a variety of audiences and convince them to support the event. These can include sponsors, volunteers, vendors and patrons.

To move through the planning and organizing stages of an event, the Event Chairman has to persuade manager-level volunteers, with their own requisite skill sets and personal and professional commitments, to jump on board and become members of the Organizing Committee. This grass-roots team should stand united behind the event, and, collectively, they will add credibility to the event or festival. Finding this group of people takes considerable thought and effort.

Committee Make-Up

Listed below is an overview of committees relevant to many different types of events. Because each event or festival has its unique theme, the make-up of the Organizing Committee may need to adjust or adapt to meet those specific requirements.

In general, here's a list of committees or positions worth considering:

- Sponsors

- Site or Venue

- Talent and Entertainment

- Marketing and Public Relations

- Grant Writing

- Merchandise

- Concessions or Vendors (food and beverages)

- Volunteers

- Staging

- Security

- Vice Chairman

- Treasurer and Ticket Sales

- Secretary

In general, most committees will interact with one another and need to communicate with each other. For instance, a sponsors committee will closely work with marketing and volunteers. Site will affect concessions or vendors. Marketing will promote tickets and merchandise, concessions and entertainment. Staging will work hand-in-hand with talent and entertainment, security and concessions. Why concessions? The Stage Manager will give a five-minute warning to concessions, advising that the talent or entertainer is wrapping up. Get ready for an onslaught of people.

Volunteers touch every committee. Security and crowd control will communicate with marketing when an incident may draw media attention. The Treasurer will need to know exactly how much money each committee has spent or plans to spend and make sure enough funds are available. They will also establish proper procedures for bank drops and payments.

The Secretary will handle all correspondence for the Event Chairman and prepare thank-you letters post event. If the Vice Chairman traditionally ascends to Event Chairman the following year, they handle duties delegated by the Event Chairman and are there to assist as needed while being exposed to all aspects of the event. This year is a practice run and next year they will be in charge.

The Importance of Writing Job Descriptions

One of the most difficult challenges of any Event Chairman, and especially if an all-volunteer event, is delegating. As the old expression goes, "you don't know what you don't know." So without a clear understanding of what it takes to put on an event, how can an Event Chairman ask others to do that unknown something?

This is a chicken versus egg kind of question. An Event Chairman can't just go plucking people off the streets and say "Hey, wanna do this great event with me?"

Before an Event Chairman can ask people to assist in building an enormous event, they need to know exactly what each committee member needs to do. The Event Chairman will need to understand the underpinnings of an event – all the pieces that it takes to make the event tick.

An Event Chairman, who will lead the Organizing Committee, has to take the time to create job descriptions for each area, starting with the objective of a given committee. Some may think this exercise is trivial or beneath them, but it forces the Event Chairman to think through the entire event. Does developing job descriptions take a long time? Yes, but it also will allow the Event Chairman to quickly respond to questions as to what a particular committee's responsibilities entail. A good leader – potential committee chairman – is going to ask that question upfront anyway, so why not be prepared?

Walking through the various scenarios will also ensure jobs are not duplicated and turf wars do not ensue. Clearly define who is responsible. When all else fails, pull out the offending party's job description and ask them where it reads they should be doing X, Y and Z.

The opposite holds true. By defining what needs to happen, it's much easier to let a volunteer go when action items and tasks are not being completed in a timely manner. The adage "you can't get fired for doing nothing" may work in some situations; the act of nothingness just delays the inevitable termination. It's tough to let a volunteer go, but it's not impossible if the Event Chairman has clearly defined the volunteer's goals and responsibilities. Dismissal during the early stages of event planning is usually better because it provides more time to find and bring on a substitute team member or transfer the duties to the Vice Chairman.

Potential committee members should ask three questions: 1) what specifically do you want me to do; 2) how much of a time commitment will be involved; and 3) is a financial commitment required? Those questions demonstrate their understanding of the magnitude of what's involved in putting on an event. When those questions aren't asked, it may signal to the Event Chairman these individuals are more likely to be followers and not leaders but still prove to be valuable team players as members of one of the many committees.

Once You Have Job Descriptions ...

When an Event Chairman knows what tasks need to be assigned, it's much easier to seek someone who has those skill sets. In order not to drive yourself crazy, seek out individuals who are self-reliant, organized, polite, professional, happy and budget-minded and then delegate. For some, this is an innate leadership skill – the ability to organize and motivate people. Having the good fortune to find self-starters with requisite experience and talking them into taking on the volunteer job relies on luck and the size of the Event Chairman's network.

Here are some ideas as to the types of backgrounds that match the committee's needs:

- Sponsors – A sponsor of another event, an influencer, someone with a large network in the community, and/or someone known for keeping confidences.

- Site – Insurance experience, loan officer, public administration, parks and recreation background, landscape architect and/or civic or service club involvement.

- Talent or Entertainment – A lawyer/mediator/negotiator; humanities teacher; performing arts venue program director; non-egomaniac musician; bar or club owner; radio station program director who specializes in a particular music genre; a pilot or someone with airport or military background; a chef, caterer, local food company or restaurant manager; a librarian, book club member or book store owner; a craft brewery owner; and/or a winery marketing department or wine store.

- Marketing – Marketing, communications, social media, public relations and/or website development or maintenance.

- Signature Merchandise – Retail background, design (computer and production), printer, arts organization, online store and/or graphic designer.

- Tickets – Online store, social media, technology, website development and maintenance, marketing, communications, public relations and/or front-end developer*. (* In its simplest definition, a front-end developer is a person who designs graphically pleasing interactive websites that adapt to multiple viewing platforms or devices. This person understands and uses the latest technology, software and code, but is usually not a computer programmer.)

- Concessions or Vendors (food and beverages) – Member or past member of a civic or service organization, (for example, Jaycees, Sertoma, Rotary or Kiwanis), restaurant manager, restaurant supply vendor and/or refrigeration.

- Volunteers – Volunteer coordinator, people person and/or connections within the community.

- Staging – Theater experience, musical background, music store employee, performing arts degree and/or a nurse.

- Security – Those with military service, transportation company manager and/or bank personnel.

- Vice Chairman – Civic or service organization, marketing, sponsors and/or communications.

- Treasurer – Bank, financial institution, accountant, bookkeeper and/or CPA.

- Secretary – Executive secretary, administrative assistant or office support staff.

When asking an Organizing Committee member to serve, make sure they are available for meetings as well as during the event. Unfortunately, key people you'd like to participate may not have the time available. Realize upper and mid-level management and those who are self-employed usually have more control over their schedules and can leave the office during the day for meetings. However, their workload may not permit the luxury of disappearing for several hours.

Lower level personnel most likely won't be able to leave for Organizing Committee meetings during the day. Late afternoon or evening meetings may result in better attendance for all levels of volunteers.

Committee Volunteer Types

For those who have managed events for a while, it's likely you've already discovered some of the most generous, kind and delightful Organizing Committee members. Unfortunately, for every 10 warm-hearted souls, you'll encounter one or two interesting characters which can push the limits and make an Event Chairman question why they ever agreed to serve. While some readers may think a few of the personality types described below are less than flattering, they are in fact real life examples.

Not everyone who signs on to volunteer does so for the same altruistic reasons. Yes, this information could have been excluded. However, when an Event Chairman is so focused on the event, they may not recognize these types in the early stages of planning. When a nagging something's-not-right feeling starts to emerge, it's difficult to pinpoint until the full-blown personality appears. Before the event kicks off, this person distracts from what should be a good thing and frustrates those who have worked so hard. This section is nothing more than to provide a heads-up, or a sampling, of the type of people (good and bad) you may encounter.

Dynamic Duos – The co-chair leadership style occurs when neither person is willing to serve independently. Be careful because when one goes, most likely the other will go, too. Sadly, when this happens, the committee is left without an heir-apparent.

The Lifers – These folks are the heart and soul of the event. They enjoy the event, as well as the deep friendships developed as a result of this common bond. They may not actually like the event theme, be it beer, wine, food or music, but they enjoy the camaraderie.

The Ego – Until the event is finished, The Ego will have the talent or sponsors thinking he or she is the Event Chairman. Thought to be impossible to be replaced, this person stretches the limits in many ways. They are too important to do paperwork and may tie up a volunteer supervisor for hours by calling and interrupting for the purpose of updating them on the latest news or activities rather than saving the information for a scheduled meeting or sending details in an email. Because "The Ego" can't be bothered to file required reports, the supervisor sometimes can assume the role of personal secretary and enabler in order to document the conversation.

Be wary of letting them negotiate talent fees or sponsorship agreements alone, as they can "give away the farm" at the expense of the event to curry favor. Come the event, this person's only self-appointed job will be to schmooze with the talent or sponsors. In doing so, they perpetuate the myth; this is their event, going so far as to even ask for recognition from the stage. They appear to suggest few on the Organizing Marketing appreciate all they do. Rumor has it this person has even had plaques made which are on display at home or office for talent and friends to see honoring their contributions to the event.

Organized Socializers – These are the folks you want schmoozing with your sponsors, VIPs and entertainers. They know how to put on a party, make people feel at ease and anticipate needs better than anyone else. They can school everyone else on how to say please and thank you, paving the way to ask a sponsor to remain on board next year, too.

The Corporate Volunteer – These are volunteers who come to you because they work for one of your corporate sponsors. It's difficult to turn them away and, if you're lucky, your needs match their talents. In many cases, they are a perfect fit with one small hitch. While one would think they know their role within the company's organizational chart, this person can become confused when it comes to the event. This person may throw around their company name for personal or professional gain, doesn't see the big picture or doesn't understand when something isn't politically correct.

Pull-It-Together At the Last Minute – They always get things done, but that late-to-the-table style puts a kink in things for planner types. It's best if this volunteer works in an area that doesn't impact others.

The Delegator – Don't we love those volunteers who assume everyone else has support staff too, not realizing the burden some requests create? Can you drop that in the mail so I can have it tomorrow?

The Lead Generator – Out of the blue, someone will step forward and volunteer to serve on the Organizing Committee. No arm-twisting is involved. No prior relationship exists with anyone involved. At a glance their background and skill set appear to match a need. You agree to bring them aboard although your gut says something doesn't add up. Later you find out they are one of those, "can I come to your house Thursday evening and meet with you for an hour" people but refuses to tell you the topic of conversation. Go with your gut. They are selling something and trying to gain access to your network and the event's various lists.

"Mom" – This delightful person thinks of others before herself, brings goodies to the committee meetings and worries that everyone has brought a sweater or sweatshirt to wear in the evening when the temperature gets cooler. You'll be so busy during the event, "Mom" will do all the worrying for you and make sure all of her kids are taken care of, plus she won't get in your way or usurp anyone's position of authority.

The Closest Distance Between Two Points – This is the guy who doesn't read anything. Organizational charts were meant for the other guys. If I want to speak directly to the Event Chairman, I'll simply bypass my immediate volunteer boss, as well as their boss. Let's get the answer now rather than following chain of command. It won't take long to figure out who this is. This person also speaks directly to the media and will commit to things before the budget is approved.

A Past Chairman falls into three distinct categories:

Moved On – Many community leaders are highly sought after and involved in many community activities. They join the event and some move up the ranks to become chairman. They serve and then quickly move on, leaving the event better than they inherited it and also passing along their files and returning "Can you help me?" calls when needed.

Tell Me What You Want Me to Do – A few enjoy the event and stay involved. Some can easily adapt to no longer being in charge. They roll up their sleeves and do as asked. This person understands their new role as just one of the Organizing Committee members.

The Meddler – Disguised as a "Tell Me What You Want Me to Do" volunteer, they are unable to truly give up the power and prestige of their former position. They do not truly want to accept a less authoritative role and can't resist the opportunity to stick their nose into any number of issues outside their committee's purview.

Don't be surprised if the media call him or her. This person will gladly oblige by providing a quote but fails to let anyone know of the contact until the Event Chairman or Public Relations and Publicity Committee Chairman read it in the daily newspaper. It comes across that their goal is to make sure no event is as perfect as the year they served as chairman. The Event Chairman or Public Relations and Publicity Committee Chairman may spend extra time doing damage control.

Here's one real life meddling experience.

A sponsor hotel always wrote into its contract/agreement that should a business opportunity come its way, then talent accommodations could be shifted to one of its other properties within its family of hotels. One year this occurred. A major film production crew came to town to film nighttime scenes at the local marina, a block from the official host hotel. As the Event Chairman, I knew this was a substantial piece of business for the hotel. While pleased for them, the change in hotel location required re-working the transportation schedule; but, overall, it didn't hamper the event. However, on event set-up day, a former chairman just happened to be positioned at the "substitute hotel" for no apparent reason. During check-in, one entertainer commented she was expecting to be staying at the beach as she had in the past. "The Meddler" entered the conversation, and rather than deferring to the volunteer in charge of talent, told a fictional story. Instead of diffusing the situation, she made it worse.

The Organizing Committee

Serving with a group of people focused on a common mission can bring everyone together. While not everyone gels (information needed by one can hold up another and cause friction), the team as a whole learns to adapt to the shortcomings of a few and overall should be closer than when the journey began. Over time, they will develop a special bond. For some, friendships will endure for years to come.

If the Organizing Committee members have accepted their roles and assumed the responsibility and been given the authority to run their areas, the Event Chairman has the unique perspective of watching all members of the team and seeing them in action – how they work together, address obstacles and support each other. If the Event Chairman has assembled a good team, they aren't in the trenches. They can simply manage.

The challenges of event management are considerable, but nothing is more frustrating than when a member of the Organizing Committee or a volunteer on one of the committees won't get moving. The number of days to the event keeps clicking away.

Here are things that can be done in an attempt to jump-start activities:

1. Find out how the person came to serve. Did they volunteer? Did they volunteer but not understand the magnitude of the commitment? Did their boss volunteer the subordinate? Did the boss understand their existing workload? Did they work their way up the ladder within the event? Was it an ego-driven desire to serve? Was the assumption that "staff did it all" and the position was more honorary than functionary? Are their expectations of the task at hand realistic? Do they have the ability to bow out politely?

2. See if someone can delicately talk to his or her boss to ask if this person's regular workload is the cause. More than likely the supervisor can adjust the workload if this is an event worthy of the company's involvement. The volunteer may be completely unaware of the event's requirements and/or not

support the cause. The individual's job performance may have been in question before and this may make things worse. The individual may not be the person the company would have wanted out in the community and internal politics have made this even messier.

3. Staff or other affected Organizing Committee members may desire to start soliciting a replacement volunteer, suggesting to potential candidates that they may wish to contact the Event Chairman or Organizing Committee Chairman directly and express interest in serving on a given committee. The poor performing volunteer is never discussed outside the Organizing Committee. Often, it is easier to fire a volunteer when a replacement is readily at hand.

4. The Event Chairman or the Organizing Committee Chairman should review the calendar from the event date backward including milestone activities and due dates with the offending party. A volunteer who wants to be in total control may or may not welcome the input, but the Event Chairman or the Organizing Committee Chairman should remind him or her that much needs to be done to get the event back on schedule.

5. The Event Chairman should pull out the job description and review it with the under-performing Committee Chairman or the Committee Chairman should similarly present it to the under-performing committee member. Again, the job description will or should reinforce how much work needs to be done in a short amount of time.

6. Never underestimate the competitive nature of a volunteer. They may simply not like, know or trust his or her volunteer boss. Rather than doing their volunteer job, this person does nothing when they should resign.

7. An Organizing Committee member needs to quickly understand all volunteers strive to make the event and their fellow event organizers look good. Like the line from the movie "Jerry Maguire," "Help me ... help you. Help me help you."

ON YOUR MARK, GET SET, MEET!

Getting the Timeline Set

Some may disagree, but I believe it takes 11 months to put on the next event. This excludes lost time for vacations and holidays.

Pull together a schedule of committee meeting dates including a wrap-up session. For more details, see POST EVENT – Post-Event Wrap-Up.

Monthly meetings initially are all that are needed, providing target dates for key action items and other pertinent Organizing Committee deadlines are met, for example, securing event sponsors. About three months out, schedule twice a month meetings. As the event nears, various committees will set their own meetings. For instance, the Volunteer Services Committee Chairman will set an all-volunteer meeting for the week before the event. The Merchandise Committee will meet to organize inventory.

As your event is shutting down, pull out the calendar and circle next year's date. Typically, the date would always be reserved three years out in order to control the event's destiny and not risk another event taking your coveted spot on the calendar or booking your venue. Allow one month following your event for all wrap-up activities to be completed, like sending thank-you notes and requesting all expenses or invoices be received by the Treasurer for prompt payment.

The First Meeting

The first time the Organizing Committee meets, the Event Chairman should provide a framework or context for the group to operate within. This should include:

- A list of proposed meeting dates and locations.

- The event's mission statement.

- A review of how proceeds, if any, will be used.

- The organizational chart – see example in this chapter or go to: www.festivalexperts.org/essential-tools

- Policies and procedures

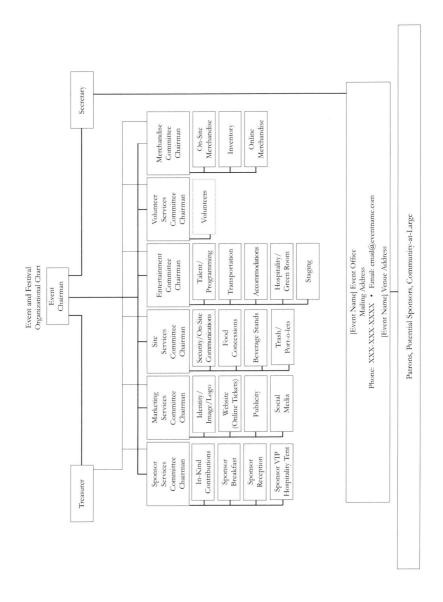

Event and Festival
Organizational Chart

Secretary

Treasurer

Event Chairman

Sponsor Services Committee Chairman
- In-Kind Contributions
- Sponsor Breakfast
- Sponsor Reception
- Sponsor VIP Hospitality Tent

Marketing Services Committee Chairman
- Identity/Image/Logo
- Website (Online Tickets)
- Publicity
- Social Media

Site Services Committee Chairman
- Security/On-Site Communications
- Food Concessions
- Beverage Stands
- Trash/Port-o-lets

Entertainment Committee Chairman
- Talent/Programming
- Transportation
- Accommodations
- Hospitality/Green Room
- Staging

Volunteer Services Committee Chairman
- Volunteers

Merchandise Committee Chairman
- On-Site Merchandise
- Inventory
- Online Merchandise

[Event Name] Event Office
Mailing Address
Phone: XXX-XXX-XXXX • Email: email@eventname.com
[Event Name] Venue Address

Patrons, Potential Sponsors, Community-at-Large

- Job descriptions – these help define expectations.

- A biographical (bio) request form for the Public Relations and Publicity Committee Chairman.

- Proposed budgets for each Committee Chairman – this provides a starting point to say "I need more" or "I don't need dollars for X, Y or Z" or a deadline for budgets to be provided to the Treasurer.

- A list of unavailable dates from Organizing Committee members – work conferences, vacations, etc. This will aid in re-scheduling Organizing Committee meeting dates if few members are available to attend. Once all out-of-pocket dates are added to the master calendar, it's easy to see which committee members are available and why some aren't responding.

During this meeting, review the mission statement to assure everyone fully understands, agrees with and supports the event. If not, now is the time to head for the parking lot. It's surprising how many get partway into planning an event and then start to grumble about where the proceeds are going. Get buy-in from the start.

In a similar fashion, allow time on the agenda for each Organizing Committee member to review the organizational chart and individual job descriptions. As mentioned earlier, make sure they fully understand what they are committing to do and agree to their role and how it relates to the overall framework, and then ask them to endorse their role.

When to Panic

As the Event Chairman, you have a head start on the Organizing Committee. You've got everything laid out in your head or on paper – the event's flight plan or ingredient list, if you will. You've either created or reviewed all the job descriptions, set the committee meeting dates and added them to your calendar, and found or are seeking qualified individuals to serve with you and lead the event forward. You can see the end goal – the event.

Fast forward. The Organizing Committee is in place and everyone has attended the event's first three meetings. It seems every member of your organizing team is just floating along aimlessly. Don't panic! This is known as event lag. You're worried but don't want anyone to know you're panicking. You start to wonder if you've chosen the right people. Will the event even happen? The sponsor you've been courting for months just said yes. A little cartoon bubble over your head reads, "Hold firm the rudder. Steer straight ahead and just stay the course. No need to panic. The Organizing Committee is alive. They just haven't started kicking yet."

Remember, it took you awhile to get up to speed in order to get everything organized. They're in a similar position; and, while they may not catch up with you in the planning process, they will soon start to dig in and get moving. So there's no need to panic. If a committee member seems short on results-driven reports, glance at the job descriptions and start to ask questions about this and that. Ask when or if they can take specific action and update you in the next seven days.

Like a miracle, at the fourth meeting everyone comes to the table with evidence of activity and now seems fully engaged. You take a deep breath and sigh in relief, because you finally feel you aren't going to carry this entire event alone. You have to remember: every team member gets settled into their role differently. For some, other personal and professional commitments need to pass before they can add another to their plates.

Those volunteers who love a deadline or love to pass a deadline before they get too excited are those who drive Event Chairmen to the brink – to lose their hair or make it turn gray.

The most valuable player at the table is the Vice Chairman because they are the confidant of the Event Chairman and whom the Chairman will ask to ready a Plan B just in case Tom or Susie drops the ball. These two will spend countless early-morning breakfasts at the local diner reviewing the event's progress.

Always expect at least one of the Organizing Committee members to have an off year. This provides the Event Chairman the unique opportunity to begin finding a replacement for the dispassionate volunteer. If the Vice Chairman's position is a rising one, it will be to their benefit to serve as the silent partner to the now flailing volunteer. It provides the opportunity to learn the ins and outs of this job and allows them to better describe the duties to potential replacement candidates. In the worse case, the Vice Chairman will jump in and fill this position when vacated.

After years of doing festivals and events, I've learned one thing: when someone isn't showing up for meetings and/or asking questions, it's because they are not doing anything.

A volunteer should be treated no differently from an under-performing employee. Sit down and have a face-to-face with them. Because most events are planned and occur within a 12-month window, the amount of time necessary to see action taking place is limited. Give the underachiever a near-term specific deadline to meet three goals. Advise them that failure will leave you no choice but to replace them.

Some volunteers will readily admit they have too much going on in their lives and welcome the chance to bow out, especially if they've been strong-armed to participate. Some will be relieved and use the sit-down meeting as a chance to resign. Others will start performing.

Paid Support Staff

While each member of the Organizing Committee should have a job description, it's important they understand the role of paid support staff. Typically, this person's primary job related to the event is to support the Event Chairman and whisper in their ear when something is not on schedule or within budget. This person's job is not to do everyone else's job. Don't be surprised if this event is just one of the paid staffer's many responsibilities.

Sponsors

Two of the most important things an Event Chairman needs to do after getting the Organizing Committee in place is to begin creating sponsorship packages and soliciting sponsors. Whenever possible, turn a challenge into an opportunity.

A popular downtown craft beer festival was plagued with inconsistent Wi-Fi service. They were unable to operate an on-site ticket office, even though the community touted free Wi-Fi downtown. The solution: secure a meeting with the general manager of the local cable provider and present them with an in-kind sponsorship package. All the sponsor needs to do is assure the Wi-Fi transmission is strong from event start to finish. With the cable provider's name and logo everywhere, it's a sure-fire way to guarantee Wi-Fi service.

A LITTLE RESEARCH GOES A LONG WAY

Do Your Homework Before You Begin Soliciting Sponsors

1. Much like getting a job, sponsorships are about whom you know and what you know — relationships. Who can open a door for you? Do your homework first.

2. Competitive analysis, a marketing term, is an excellent way to discover all the events held in a community and identify the sponsors. If possible, find sponsorship packages (values or

pricing levels) on their respective websites. Guesstimate the financial commitment of the various sponsors. This will provide an overview of dollars flowing into the community and the "norm" for sponsorship requests.

3. How many business headquarters are located in your community or within your region or state? These businesses have a natural connection and typically want to be good corporate citizens. If no headquarters are based in your city, are regional offices housed in your community?

4. Before soliciting someone to be a member of the Organizing Committee, spend time researching the person, as well as their employer. Having a team member also serving as an "inside man" and making the request or "ask," should assure the company its sponsorship dollars are in good hands.

5. Some corporations have donation request applications. If this is the process, find out when due and how much funding is available.

6. What type of presence does a potential sponsor already have in the community? Does it already sponsor events? If not, why doesn't it? Do its employees volunteer for various community events, meaning the company gives time and money? Is there a thread you can tug on that might draw you close to someone to learn more about how this business supports the local community?

7. A company's organizational chart may help you better understand the value of sponsorships. Department names and titles to watch for are community affairs, marketing, public relations and/or corporate affairs. Having staff members readily available to serve as a point person and support the event makes it much easier to be a sponsor. The website LinkedIn® is a valuable resource for this type of information.

8. In previous days, the local media – newspapers, radio and television – were a great source for sponsorships. Because circulation, listeners and viewers have diminished, so have advertising dollars. They may still be viable sponsors, but cash may not be an option as much as bartering ads and airtime for event exposure. Radio and

TV stations can often make on-air personalities available to serve as masters of ceremonies (MCs) and DJs. I personally steer towards radio staffers who tend to work well in an unscripted environment. These folks are quite helpful in keeping the event on track and the crowds engaged when things are running behind schedule.

9. Find out if a company is planning to expand into your area. Sponsorship of a key event can provide immediate exposure to a new name. Once moved in and unpacked and involved elsewhere in the community, it may move on. Watch for newspaper stories by setting search engine alerts for key words: your city, your state, move, relocating.

10. Alternately, while most economic development agencies keep leads tightly under wraps, a government agency may fall under the Freedom of Information Act – public information can be accessed. Nonprofit or chamber of commerce personnel who service economic development inquiries and solicit businesses to move are worth contacting and meeting. Remember, cultural events are the quality-of-life activities they promote as part of a relocation package.

Like City Hall, a sponsor needs to feel being associated with an Event Chairman, the Organizing Committee or anything related to the event will not tarnish its good name. Soliciting sponsors requires the ability to sell corporations on the concept of not only an event but a *particular* event.

How to Secure Sponsors – It's Much Like Dating

Everyone wants to know the secret to finding sponsors. It's much the same as dating and finding the perfect one to marry. Not everyone you think is sponsor material will be the slightest bit interested in your event. ... not the tall leggy building you pass by every day or the company with the big logo smile.

First, understand no one owes your event anything, least of all a business to sponsor your event. Budgets are thinner than they used to be. Corporate dollars are allocated during the budgeting process. While some discretionary dollars are available, large dollar sponsors not already earmarked are rare. You'll need to determine when the budgeting process for each potential sponsor occurs. If a formal request or submission form is required, you will need to determine possible deadlines and the type of information needed.

Here's a list of things sponsors consider when developing a relationship with an event.

- What's the word on the street about the event, the Event Chairman or Organizing Committee?

- What is the reputation of each Organizing Committee member? Are the chairman and committee members stand-up citizens and do much for the community?

- What are the work habits of the Event Chairman and Organizing Committee members? Do their bosses smile and nod approvingly when these people are mentioned?

- Are the Event Chairman and Organizing Committee members the type who are always busy but always willing to take on more?

- Do the Event Chairman and Organizing Committee have a reputation for follow-through?

- Are they people everyone knows, likes and trusts?

- Is the Event Chairman always punctual and appreciative of others' time?

- Do the Event Chairman and Organizing Committee find ways to make the nearly impossible possible?

- Are the event's requirements of sponsors formalized but flexible to meet individual sponsor's needs?

- Do the Event Chairman and Organizing Committee members keep promises in a timely manner?

- Is the Event Chairman dependable and do they surround themselves with others with those same qualities?

- Does the festival and its leaders have a reputation for being fiscally conservative?

- Does the Organizing Committee have a reputation of taking care of their sponsors and are sponsor departures a rarity?

- Does the event have the good fortune of having a long-time Treasurer who understands events and keeps tabs on expenses?

- Does the Treasurer make timely payment of sales tax to the state's revenue department and also submit the state and federal income tax returns in a similar manner?

- Is the person who now serves as the Treasurer respected in the community?

- Has the event been fortunate that whenever a sponsor departs for business reasons, another is waiting in the wings?

Sponsorship Thresholds

Within every company, a dollar amount or a threshold exists that an individual branch manager or mid-level manager can spend without question. It is tucked away in a discretionary budget for use in the community. It can be spent without authorization from high above. For many years, the amount in a second tier city was $500.

Need a sponsor for a related event scheduled at a local library? Send a proposal to a potential sponsor for any amount equal to or less than the threshold amount and you stand a good chance of easily obtaining a "yes" response. Anything with a higher price tag will need to be elevated up the corporate ladder.

Spend some time talking with others who do events in your community, and they can quickly clue you in to what your community's threshold is.

In-Kind Contributions Add Value

Often in-kind contributions aren't given the attention they deserve. They significantly affect the bottom line of any event, whether a donation involves products or services.

These contributions often get lost in the shuffle. Event volunteers may use these items or services for their particular area and handle "the ask" and "thanks and appreciation" directly with their contact. The larger event planning body may not even realize what transpired, only that Chris did a great job and didn't spend her budget. When Chris is no longer involved, those freebies disappear and create a hard cost to the event if it is an essential item.

Treat in-kind contributions as if they have value, but do not allow them to exceed the value of those making a cash contribution – major or contributing sponsors. Let the donor determine the value of their product or service. Designate your Treasurer or your Sponsor Services Committee Chairman as the person to maintain the completed forms and the master list. Track the quantity of products and services, the total value and the number of people or vendors making the donations.

The worst possible thing you can do is treat someone's company donation as if it has no value. Make sure thank-you notes are prepared for the Event Chairman and the person who secured the product or service to jointly sign. After all, wouldn't you like to know you could request a donation next year?

CREATING SPONSORSHIP PACKAGES THAT SELL

When creating the event's sponsorship and underwriting categories, take care to differentiate the benefits and values of each. To assure parity within each set category, do not allow any to be modified by a single person without conducting a thorough review with the Event Chairman, the Immediate Past Chairman and the Sponsor Services Committee Chairman. To be fair, all the pieces should be put on the chessboard to determine if everyone is getting equal treatment.

To save man-hours and paperwork, the basic sponsorship package contents should become part of your sponsorship contract in the form of an addendum and be attached behind the event's lawyer-approved contract. Cluster similar elements together, for example, advertising, on-site exposure, hospitality, publicity and social media. Add the unique sponsorship package components under an "Other" category at the end.

This will make it much easier for your sponsor, too. Your sponsor contact will see that the same package you brought to them during your initial meeting is now attached to the contract. It will save them time when reviewing before signing or sending up the ladder for their boss to sign.

Each year, the Event Chairman, the Immediate Past Chairman and the Sponsor Services Committee Chairman should review the contents of each level of sponsorship. No changes or adjustment should be made without the approval of this group.

Do-It-Yourself Sponsorship Package

It's possible a corporation is interested in being a sponsor; however, the standard package, while not bad, could be fine-tuned a bit. A marketing professional involved with a music festival once said, "I never met a sponsorship package I didn't rewrite to maximize my company's exposure and play more to our existing marketing efforts." For example,

- Perhaps the company has a costumed character it would like to make available to do an onstage appearance or to walk through the venue so selfies can be taken.

- Perhaps it is a major restaurant chain and would like to have its staff work in a particular area such as the information booth wearing their uniforms.

- Perhaps a sponsor has technology equipment such as a large screen for streaming the main stage act. It would like its logo to display during the breaks (commercials).

- Perhaps this retail outlet would offer a special gift with the first 100 tee shirts sold on opening night.

- Perhaps this radio station wants its on-air personalities to handle the stage announcements.

- Perhaps this food distributor wants only its products to be sold in the various concession booths.

- Perhaps this beverage distributor wants to have exclusivity allowing only its products to be sold at the venue during the event.

- Perhaps your newspaper sponsor is interested in publishing a special insert that would be delivered with its newspaper prior to the event and also be distributed at the event. Normally, newspapers will want the special insert to have value in order to sell advertising. While the event may request certain information be included (the venue's site map and details on each of the featured talent – headliners, artists, speakers, musicians, pilots, performers, winemakers, authors, chefs, entertainers, brewmasters, etc.), ultimately the newspaper controls the content.

Government Sponsors

Whenever possible, work to include your city or town as a sponsor. The unconditional support of elected officials and management will flow down to all departments.

In an ideal world, government sponsorship will also include a cash contribution but do not underestimate the cost of man-hours given to an event by city personnel. While the city may not want to have the total in-kind contribution show up in the newspaper, it would be helpful to an Event Chairman to see the extent of the city's commitment.

Below are just a few examples of city support:

- Mowing of a city park.

- Pruning of bushes.

- Spraying for mosquitoes.

- Supplemental landscape work in advance of the event, for example, watering the lawn, fountain enhancements.

- Installation and removal of barricades; re-routing traffic signage.

- Additional police on site during the public hours of the event and visits after hours.

- Traffic control surrounding the event; additional staff to man post-event traffic.

- An express permitting process for sound, electricity, signs, banners, tents, etc.

- Fee waivers for the park, power, water, signs, banners, tents, etc.

- Additional support from the parks and recreation department which handles the park application and bookings for the venue.

- City electrician to pull power for concessions including running new outlets at various intervals in the park, checking breaker boxes for sound and lighting needs and changing light bulbs using a bucket truck.

- Proclamation from the city.

- Parks and recreation staff members to meet with concessionaires to address park utilities.

- Make sure street lights are functioning.

- Additional trash dumpster pick up each morning and manual clean up of the park each day.

A Hotel Sponsorship Package – Official Host Hotel

If your event is going to need accommodations or a VIP breakfast or reception, the Event Chairman may want to consider developing a special hotel or resort sponsorship package. Hotel considerations include:

- If the hotel gives up X rooms to be a sponsor, will it still have Y rooms available to be able to house the guests coming for the event, knowing another large group may already be in-house?

- So the hotel isn't undercutting itself by being a sponsor, is the event the type or kind the hotel could never hold due to its size or physical needs?

- Is the event prestigious and is a sponsor relationship the best way to reach the event's demographics, who are also the hotel's potential customers?

- If the hotel has a higher-paying group that wants those same dates, does the hotel have an out clause or a sister hotel that could house the event's talent – headliners, artists, speakers, musicians, pilots, performers, winemakers, authors, chefs, entertainers, brewmasters, etc. – instead?

- Can the hotel or resort provide the privacy the talent needs or will it be invaded by groupies and paparazzi, creating a challenging situation for all guests?

- Which of the hotel's competitors would be interested if the hotel or resort gives up this opportunity?

- If a food function, known internally as F&B (food and beverage), what are the hotel's actual hard costs? Do those hard costs cover or exceed the value or exposure being received? How many people normally attend the event's VIP food functions? When will it be held and/or does it occur during the low season or is the hotel displacing higher revenue generating business?

- Are there other revenue generating opportunities for a sponsor hotel? Perhaps events like an after-hours jam, bar business, hosting related events, restaurant business, etc., could be considered.

- Can the hotel dictate all other paid F&B events be held at the property?

- Can the hotel be listed as the "official host hotel?"

- Would the Organizing Committee be interested in using the hotel's event space to hold its regular meetings?

- Can the hotel offer special rates or packages during the event to major sponsors? Perhaps the hotel has been courting the event's corporate sponsors for group functions and this may provide the perfect opportunity to visit the hotel.

- Would the hotel like to receive copies of any group inquiries, and/or would the hotel negotiate it be promoted, as the official host hotel, in all electronic communication sent to those buying tickets or subscribing to receive event updates by email?

- Would the hotel like to bring lunch to the venue the day of the set up? This would further enhance the hotel's relationship with the Event Chairman and various Organizing Committee members, creating a bridge should there be a change in leadership.

An Airline Sponsorship Package

The airline industry has changed much since deregulation with mergers, low cost start-ups serving a narrow list of destinations, higher fuel prices, squeezing more seats into smaller spaces, online travel agencies (OTAs), baggage fees, open boarding (no assigned seats) and booking tickets online directly with an airline.

Most airlines currently offer group or corporate client ticketing but a minimum number of travelers are needed to qualify, and they must travel as a group. That can pose challenges when talent is flying in from various locations on different days and times. While the number of tickets needed may meet the minimums, nothing else applies.

Research the locations where your talent is flying from, or anticipated to fly from, and determine which airline offers the best service or connections. An airline that seasonally flies to and from your destination during peak demand is not likely to offer service in the low season when your event is scheduled.

Most airline websites list a contact for group or corporate clients. Start there first.

While rare these days, it may be possible to work with an airline account representative. They will know the ins and outs of their industry and may be able to find a special U or Y coach seat rate versus a Q coach seat rate.

A well-connected airline account executive or former airline employee will also know how to address challenges of traveling with equipment like cookware, books or an upright bass – "an extra ticket please, because my baby doesn't travel with the luggage!" They may also know who to contact within the company and within the airport when a delayed flight may mean a delayed performance. See how much power they wield in holding a plane when a connection is tight.

The dollar amount needed for an air carrier to qualify for a major or contributing sponsorship package may not match the in-kind value received. However, airline personnel more than likely can take care of your event and your talent by serving as the event's personal travel agent. Perhaps the airlines in-kind contribution can be recognized to provide it some exposure.

As a Plan B, a local travel agency can also assist in coordinating travel because its staff books air travel on a daily basis and understands the industry. However, some airlines do not offer commission rates. For this reason, they might not be one of the travel agency's preferred air carriers. Also, some airlines now charge a service fee to those who book using a travel agency's GDS (global distribution system) rather than making a reservation on the airline's website.

GETTING YOUR FOOT IN THE DOOR

... and a Meeting with a Potential Sponsor

It may sound simple, but sometimes trying to find the right person to open a door takes a bit of time and networking. Knowing the right person to put in a good word is key. This needs to be an individual with a credible reputation. You are asking them to call on a friend or business associate, to use one of their chits or social capital and to vouch for a yet-to-be-held or fairly new event. Not everyone is willing to give of their time and to provide access to their contacts.

As the event matures and builds its own reputation, that alone can open the door or result in phone calls and emails being returned to schedule a meeting with a potential sponsor.

Unlocking this door is what allows the Event Chairman to call a potential sponsor and for the call to be returned and a meeting to be scheduled. At the appointed hour, show up on time dressed like a professional, shake this person's hand, make your presentation, leave your contact information in the form of a business card and express thanks again using the individual's name. Write a brief thank you either by email or sent in a mailed note. Then follow-up when promised.

Sponsor Presentations

All sponsors should be given the courtesy of a formal presentation. No self-presentations should be permitted by any Organizing Committee member on behalf of the event. As a courtesy, the Event Chairman and the Sponsor Services Committee Chairman should to be advised more than 48 hours in advance that a meeting is being planned with a potential sponsor. Each sponsor call should be made with at least two event representatives present. For the purpose of continuity, it is recommended they be the Event Chairman or Sponsor Services Committee Chairman or Immediate Past Chairman. A written report shall be submitted at each Organizing Committee meeting updating the status of sponsorship calls.

THE SPONSOR PAPER TRAIL

The Difference Between a Sponsorship Package and a Sponsor Contract

A sponsorship package describes all the ways a potential sponsor will be able to participate in an event, and all the exposure the sponsor will receive in return for their contribution. It answers the "what's in it for me" question. The package is considered to be all-inclusive and typically presented during the meeting with the potential sponsor. As explained in SPONSORS – Do-It-Yourself Sponsorship Package, it is the baseline from which additions, enhancements or subtractions can be made, provided they are reviewed and approved by the Event Chairman or Sponsor Services Committee Chairman or Immediate Past Chairman.

Major and contributing sponsorship packages, or whatever name your event desires to give to the various sponsor levels, can be almost identical in content, except the "Major" level contains the maximum benefits, while the "Contributing" features a lesser quantity of items and/or removal of certain elements. For each smaller dollar amount a sponsor gives, they should receive less value.

The sponsor contract is a legal document that obligates the event to provide the means by which the sponsor can participate and guarantees exposure to the sponsor in exchange for the contribution. While it is possible to insert the sponsorship package into the sponsorship contract, it's easiest to avoid unnecessary paperwork and, instead, wrap the package into the contract or agreement by making the package an addendum to the contract.

Sponsorship Contracts

Now why on earth would you need a contract? These are good corporate citizens. Stop thinking this way. The event is a business and it needs to operate like a business. Try and take a handshake into the courtroom and have a judge side in your favor. No one ever hopes it comes to that, but the XYZ Company vice president you made the deal with can be terminated tomorrow; so you need a paper trail and a legally binding one at that.

If an event is going to commit to spending dollars for talent, sound, lighting, port-o-lets, permits, etc., you've got to have a signed sponsorship agreement indicating this is guaranteed revenue to cover your expenses.

Far too many Event Chairmen "count" a promise as a signed and contracted sponsor. When the formal commitment and signature doesn't come, the sponsor disappears like smoke. Only count on a sponsor once the sponsorship contract is signed by the authorized person at the company (confirming a budget exists), and the event's authorized contract signer – the Event Chairman.

A legal document is designed to protect both parties. It should clearly address rain, tornadoes, acts of God, hurricanes, floods, fires, etc. Clarify the sponsor's ability to demand a refund due to inclement weather when the pre-event publicity and exposure has already occurred. Once a sponsor is in, it should be in come rain or shine.

While a legal agreement is necessary, it should be drafted in such a manner that a potential sponsor, upon receipt, does not feel compelled to send it off to its legal department to comb through the document. These become delays and unnecessary pain points. From my perspective, the actual agreement should be short, clean and contain minimal legalese. If presented to a supervisor for signature, it should take no more than five minutes to read it and sign it. Anything longer has the potential to be interrupted by a phone call, an email or underlings. Make it easy for your sponsors to sign on the dotted line.

The sponsor contract most likely will be reviewed in depth by the person who was presented the sponsorship package and/or someone else in the department or others on a committee if the decision is made by an employee group. For this reason, it's important that the Sponsorship Package be incorporated into the contract.

Each type or level of sponsorship may have its own separate contract.

The original, fully executed contract should be provided to the Treasurer along with payment in full, if applicable. A copy of this fully executed agreement should be sent to the sponsor for its files by the Sponsor Services Committee Chairman. Copies should also be distributed to the Event Chairman and publicity-relevant details of the contract shared with the Public Relations and Publicity Committee Chairman.

Sponsor Contract vs. Invoice

The sponsor has signed off on the contract, but why won't it send the money? Because a business requires an invoice be submitted in order to make a payment. Did you send one?

Unless otherwise arranged, within 30 days of the contract being fully executed an invoice should be generated by the Treasurer and sent requesting funds. What's the company name that should appear on the invoice? Don't assume if your corporate sponsor's public name is ABC Bank that the name on the invoice is the same. It may be ABC Bank Holding Corporation. Also, make sure the invoice has the correct mailing address – which may not be the physical address – of the formal named organization. Don't be surprised if the invoice needs to be sent to your event's sponsor contact for processing.

Part of your agreement may be that the payments may need to be broken up over several months. Let your event Treasurer know if this is the case, so they can adjust the event's forecast or budget. Find out what dates your sponsor contact would like put on the invoices. Make it easy on yourself. If needed, create all invoices at the same time. Ask the sponsor if you can send all now, or if your contact would like them mailed separately. The Sponsor Services Committee Chairman should put a tickler note on their calendar and have the Treasurer do the same.

As stated before, following the signing of the contract, the Sponsor Services Committee Chairman should provide a copy of the fully executed agreement to the sponsor along with a thank-you letter.

The Sponsor Checklist

The checklist is a communication tool that provides a sponsor specifics on what each corporate sponsor needs to do and when. This single document allows the company the ability to efficiently allocate time and resources to the event. It also eliminates multiple last-minute phone calls or emails from the Sponsor Services Committee asking for materials. With the checklist both parties know what is expected of the other and by what deadline.

TAKING CARE OF YOUR SPONSORS

Sponsor Communication is Key

To keep everyone looped in and avoid any embarrassing situations, all correspondence with sponsors should be copied to the Event Chairman and the Sponsor Services Committee Chairman.

Delivering on Promises Made to Sponsors

The Event Chairman is likely to be one of the people involved in soliciting sponsors. However, as chairman, they have much to do to orchestrate an event. A smart chairman delegates the responsibility of hand-holding sponsors soon after each has signed on the dotted line… that's not to say they won't be hovering to make sure their sponsors are being pampered.

The Event Chairman should select a multi-talented volunteer to be in charge of sponsor services – someone they consider an extension of him or herself and someone they trust. This person should have diplomatic people skills, be well organized, readily accessible, capable of making decisions on the spot (also known as having common sense) and have some understanding of marketing.

Similarly, on the sponsor side, your sponsor services contact may now be working with one or more people down the corporate ladder – the administrative assistant of the decision maker, human resources for volunteers and marketing for communication, logos, banners, etc.

Come event time, it's highly likely the Event Chairman and the individual first presented the sponsorship package will meet again. All involved personnel, including the sponsor's decision makers will most likely make an appearance at the event. If the relationship was cemented and promises kept and in a timely manner, these sponsors will be the ones smiling from ear to ear.

Ask the Sponsor Services Committee Chairman to maintain a master list of all sponsors – major, contributing and in-kind. Also include contact information – names, title, physical address and mailing address for each, plus phone and email addresses. Make copies available to the Marketing Services Committee, Volunteer Services Committee and Public Relations and Publicity Committee.

Sponsor Events – Nametags and Noise

Nametags and noise are two small things that can make and break a sponsor event. Please use nametags for sponsor events held before or outside of the event venue. This will help in identifying sponsors. Be less concerned with the event logo being on the nametag and more concerned with the person's first and last name and company name being large enough and bold enough to read from three feet away. Stay away from the artsy fonts. Go for the clean san serif versions. This saves the embarrassment of those not wearing their reading glasses to see the name easily and know to whom they are speaking.

Avoid holding an event where the noise bounces off the walls with nothing to absorb it. Rooms with carpeting help deafen sound. This makes it easier for conversations to be heard versus every third word being caught. What did they say? Rooms with bad sound quality can get you into embarrassing situations, too. More than once, I've observed someone who didn't get the gist of the conversation find it necessary to send someone else in to gather intelligence. The hope was both could piece together the information. Was that meeting set for Thursday at four o'clock?

INFLUENCERS & REVENUE SOURCES

Community VIPs

Events are not created in a vacuum. They touch many areas of the community and, together, these various groups and individuals help weave the fabric of event support. These are also known as influencers, evangelists, important people within local economic development efforts (chambers of commerce, tourism, and business and industry), elected officials (city, county and state) and power brokers. These community VIPs can affect your event and should not be excluded. They most likely have busy schedules and your event may not even be on their calendars. In some cases, they may not be perceived to wield power but, in reality, they do.

Make sure your Sponsor Services Committee Chairman also creates a master community VIP list. Build it, then pass it around to the entire Organizing Committee to add, subtract and discuss. In some way, all of these VIPs should be aware of the event and thus have the potential to positively influence the event or make a direct or indirect impact. This category would also include potential sponsors previously solicited that said no, as well as future, potential sponsors. While they may not be invited to your poster unveiling breakfast or your opening reception, they may be people you would send a personal invitation (not a flier or an email) for your kick-off party.

Finding Money Via Grants

The more appropriate term should not be grants but rather octopi. Some grants have numerous tentacles (requirements) needing to be strictly monitored and reported. It's easy to get yourself tangled up if not in compliance.

Grants may be perceived to be easy money, except if you're the person submitting the paperwork. If your event is going to seek grant money, make sure one person is coordinating this effort and is responsible from beginning to end. They will be most familiar with the multi-page grant application, its requirements and stipulations.

Some convention and visitors bureaus (CVBs) offer grants for events. However, the event usually has to have a track record (not be a first-time event). Fund requests may need to be specifically aligned with the CVB's purpose – to fill hotel rooms to further generate resort tax dollars. A magical multiplier formula is used to then determine the economic impact for a destination. For more details, see MONEY MATTERS – Placing a Value on Your Event.

What grant opportunities are available? Check with the local chamber of commerce, CVB, state tourism agency, local and state arts organizations and performing arts venues. Reach out to and cultivate individuals – hospitals, colleges and universities – tasked with generating grant monies from non-competing grant resources. Ask if they can keep you in mind if they see an opportunity.

On-Site Donations

Always look for ways to raise money but avoid appearing to be desperate or begging at every turn. It can get wearisome and also raise questions, whether your event is financially sound or make your sponsors think twice before jumping on a sinking ship. A fine line exists between the two.

Loose change is a wonderful thing. In an area where people stand in line for concessions and where they will walk back to their seats, place a donation station. If your patron's hands are full, give them a small space to re-shift what's in their hands. Give them an excuse not to put the change in their pocket or purse but drop it in the jar instead.

Donation containers work best if bolted down to a larger object so someone can't just walk off with it and its contents. An empty donation container will likely net you zero at the end of the day. A donation jar should be stocked each day with a starter set of coins and dollar bills.

Perception is the key. A "stocked" jar suggests a successful event, and people wish to donate to and be a part of such. This is known as the bandwagon effect.

Have fun with the vessel (jar). Perhaps involve your poster or tee shirt designer in the project. If the props used in creating this year's artwork are no longer functional for their intended purpose, perhaps they can be showcased within or on the donation box.

If an air show, for instance, raises funds to support aviation scholarships, consider placing a child's toy airplane inside. Plant a seed for how the funds will be used or include a small placard explaining. A wine event may use a floor fountain in its decor, and this could become a wishing well. A food event could fabricate a kitchen cabinet with antique objects sitting on floating acrylic shelves. An oversized beer stein may serve the purpose for a beer festival; have a little fun with it. Take a non-functioning beer tap with the event logo/artwork featured on the handle as if pouring money into the donation container.

Allow for the removal of the cash and coins each night. Two people should be required to remove the funds and one should be the Treasurer or a member of their cash handling team and a volunteer with a deposit slip being witnessed or signed by both parties.

Money Matters

One bluegrass festival chairman needed to fill one last slot on the organizing committee – the Treasurer. He asked a well-respected and well-connected member of the banking industry for a referral. Rather than a referral, the banker volunteered himself because he loved bluegrass music and relished the chance to be involved.

If this is a first-time event, the Treasurer will be instrumental in creating the framework of the business and its finances. If the event is under the wing of an existing organization, the Treasurer will need to determine the parent organization's fiscal policies and procedures. If an existing, stand-alone event, it may require a review of past financials, as well as the event's policies and procedures.

CREATING THE FINANCIAL FRAMEWORK

Getting Started – Year One

A series of things are needed to create a credible event. First, establish a nonprofit corporation or operate under the wing of one such organization. A new nonprofit organization typically requires that Articles of Incorporation be filed with the Secretary of State's Office (or similar) within your state. A fee is normally required. Thereafter, each year an annual report may need to be submitted along with the requisite filing fee.

Some events are housed under the umbrella of an existing organization and later, as it grows, the event may be spun off to operate independently.

Federal Employer Identification Number

The Federal Employer Identification Number is known as a FEIN or an EIN. It is used to pay withholding taxes for an employee. You may not have any employees, but the FEIN is required for other reasons.

Setting Up a Bank Account

In order to set up a bank account, a FEIN number is needed or a social security number is required. Establishing a corporation (an entity vs. a person) adds a degree of checks and balances, especially as it relates to the event's monies. A copy of the Articles of Incorporation filed with the Secretary of State's Office (or similar) is also required to establish a bank account. The nonprofit Board of Directors will need to vote on a resolution authorizing a bank account be set up and define who is designated as authorized check signers. For additional security measures, checks written over a specific dollar amount should require two signatures. This requirement can be printed on the checks.

Sales Tax

If you plan to sell merchandise, you should collect sales tax. Check with local and state taxing agencies to assure the correct amount is being collected and to find out when and where the funds need to be sent with the proper paperwork. For ease in cash handling and making change, some events sell merchandise with tax included and rounded up to the nearest dollar or 50 cents. It may take a bit to determine the product sales price when combined with the amount of tax to make this happen. However, once at the event with the volume of transactions and change passing hands, volunteers will appreciate this time saving effort.

Resale Number

This number is kept on file, as an example, with the poster printer and tee shirt or sweatshirt vendor. With this completed form, the event indicates they are selling merchandise and the end purchaser will be paying the sales tax. Once sold, the event becomes responsible for paying the sales tax collected from the purchaser to the appropriate government agency.

CREATING A BUDGET FOR YOUR EVENT

If, as the Event Chairman, you've been doing events for a while, you'll have a pretty good idea what things cost to do an event. If you're a first-timer, find yourself a numbers guy – an accountant or bookkeeper – to serve as Treasurer. Find someone who has strong analytical skills; it will be a huge bonus when it comes to budget projections and forecasting.

For first-timers, a good starting point is the job descriptions. Every responsibility may have a product or service tied to it. Each of these has an associated expense. For the bigger expenses, a city's parks and recreation department might be able to provide some estimates.

You've got to be able to put numbers on paper so you can get a sense of how much money it will take to organize an event and how much money from sponsors and in-kind contributions you'll need.

When putting a budget together, separate it into two columns. You'll want to list the things you'll need cash to buy and things you may be able to get donated – paper cups, printing, etc.

If this is your first year, developing a budget will be like pulling numbers out of thin air. Zero-based budgeting, a budget created from scratch with most line items being researched to justify the numbers, is your starting point and will force the Event Chairman, Treasurer and each committee chairmen to think through their needs in advance. Year two will obviously be much easier.

WHY ONLINE TICKETS?

First, the Event Chairman and Treasurer should both recognize selling the event's tickets online would make the Organizing Committee's life much easier and much better. Yes, the term better is subjective and this is why the word was intentionally used.

Many first-time Festival Chairmen or Treasurers gravitate to a ticket vendor's name found on other local event websites or tickets without doing much hard research. It's important to discover what other options are available. Spend time doing a bit of soul searching first to discover what the event really needs and wants. Consider these questions:

Would you like all the tickets sold from one system? When all of your ticket sales are reported in one place, you'll know exactly where the event stands from one minute to the next, providing the ticketing system offers real-time reporting.

Do you want your patrons driving around town to local stores or businesses within limited hours to purchase a cash-only ticket (no checks please)? Yes, we understand this does drive customers to local businesses, perhaps the event sponsors. However, your Treasurer will need to be involved to implement off-site "cash" security measures and the local business will need to be willing to accept those conditions.

This scenario requires volunteer time, mileage, phone calls and emails to check off-site inventory, replenish tickets and make sure pre-event ticket sales match revenue. Who wants to deal with awkward situations when ticket sales and ticket revenue don't match?

1. Would you like your tickets to be available 24 hours a day?

2. Would you like to accept credit cards, and in some cases, e-checks?

3. Would you prefer online tickets because PCI compliance provides the event added security precautions? For more details, see MONEY MATTERS – PCI Compliance.

4. Would you prefer to reduce the amount of on-site cash handling created when tickets are purchased in advance?

5. Would you like to have the ability to accept checks by mail and record them within the online ticket service (ticket office)?

6. Would you like to also sell merchandise online along with your event tickets?

7. Would you like your patrons to arrive at the event wearing this year's tee shirt?

Second, like anything, getting set up will require a bit of effort, but short-term effort for long-term convenience is well worth the time and energy. Your Treasurer most likely can provide or will have the information required to set up online ticketing, including the event's legal name, bank account information – where ticket sales revenue need to be deposited, if a for-profit or nonprofit, type of business, the Federal Employee Identification Number (FEIN or EIN), etc.

Third, realize the event will be paying more to an online ticketing service when it acts as the event's bank, meaning less money goes into the event's coffers. Get the true picture. While the percentage rate and transaction fee at first glance may appear to be less than the competitors, play out the scenario. Start with your ticket price and then factor in all the extra fees or additional percentages added to the ticket or registration price to determine your full costs.

Fourth, if your web developer is pushing a particular online ticketing vendor, do a little research. Do a quick online search to see if that ticketer offers an affiliate program. Will your web developer receive a percentage of your event sales the first year after setting your event up with this company?

Finally, one more thing needs to be added into the equation if your online ticket service is also serving as your bank. When do you get your money? An online ticketing service may offer to release some of your dollars before the event, but this amount can be a relatively small percentage. For more details, see MONEY MATTERS – How the Online Payment Processing Piece Works.

But My Event is Free, Do I Still Need a Ticket?

Even if your event is free, requiring an online ticket may be a valuable tool. It provides a gauge as to the number of people who will attend. It allows an Organizing Committee to prepare accordingly for the anticipated crowd size, since it affects volunteer staffing, parking, trash containers, food supplies, security, etc. It also gives you a verifiable attendance count which will come in handy when soliciting sponsors. Additionally, this information is important data for your Marketing Services and Public Relations and Publicity committees.

Online Ticketing – Deciding What's Important to Your Event

For many, online ticketing provides a convenient place for consumers to purchase tickets as well as a way to automatically create a database of patrons for continued communications and future event solicitation.

Seasoned Event Chairmen and Treasurers understand better their specific needs and typically do considerable research to narrow down their ticketing service choices. The first step in processing payments online is to find out what your event needs and wants. These are two different things. Event organizers should then prioritize these lists. Then and only then can you begin to research all the viable options and make a selection accordingly.

It's possible no one ticketing service is a perfect match. Here's a list of questions to ask:

1. Why do we want to move to online ticketing or why do we want to move away from our current online ticketing vendor?

2. What are our costs for credit card processing – the percentage rate and fee? What is the gateway payment processor fee, for example, Authorize.Net® if using a traditional bank? What are the cost and/or fees for an online ticketing service if also serving as your bank?

3. If we hold multiple events, how does that work? Can we promote multiple events at one time? Can we sell tickets to multiple events at one time? Are our patrons required to purchase one event at a time or can they place a single order?

4. Can we offer different levels of pricing for members and non-members?

5. Can we accept donations?

6. Can we insert the ticket buying process into our website so it appears as if we're selling the tickets and not using an outside vendor?

7. Do we want our logo to be more prominent than the online ticketing system's logo?

8. Do the payments flow directly to us?

9. When does the event money flow into our checking account?

10. Do we pay extra for the online ticketing service to serve as our bank?

11. Can we use our existing Authorize.Net® account?

12. Can we sell merchandise online? Do our patrons need to order each attendee's ticket and merchandise individually, so each ticket applies to specific merchandise or can they order all their tickets and then all the merchandise as a group, for example, 3 posters, 1 large sweatshirt and 4 large tee shirts?

13. How much design and content flexibility do we need – colors? pre-set email messages and reminders?

14. Can we sell tickets on Facebook?

15. What type of reporting does it have?

16. Can we process refunds online?

17. Can we offer paper and mobile (QR codes on smartphone) tickets?

18. Can we scan tickets at our gates?

19. Does the ticket service offer a ticket office feature we can use at the event or in our office?

20. Does the ticket service offer scanner or credit card swipe rentals?

21. What type of customer support is available – email, phone, chat and how quickly before a response is received?

22. How does the online ticketing vendor get paid?

23. Does the system also offer a registration feature for sponsor events, concessions, vendors and/or exhibitors?

24. Can our sponsors also sign up for other events like the sponsor luncheon? If yes, can the order allow them to select a food preference or indicate an allergy? Can our sponsors also place their tee shirt and poster orders online?

Why Online Ticketing Might Not Be The Answer

Know your market and demographics. If an event is geared toward a more mature market, these long-time cash customers may be reluctant to buy tickets online.

Recognize that some of your patrons may not have a computer or feel comfortable making a purchase over the Internet. However, most likely these same individuals have flown on an airplane in the recent years. Someone in their family would have made their online reservations. It's possible that they can reach out to this same person and ask them to assist in the online ticket purchase.

Demographics may show your younger patrons live with the latest technology but only have checking accounts, not credit cards. They may be receptive to buying tickets online and paying by e-check. For more details, see MONEY MATTERS – Check This Out – E-checks.

You may feel your ticket price is too low to warrant online tickets. Remember that many tickets are not purchased individually but rather are sold as pairs or groups. A combined purchase may merit further research.

Your Treasurer or those handling your accounting function may not be comfortable with technology or the thought of someone depositing money into your checking account as online ticket sales occur. Offer this reminder: while they may not personally do this, this is done every day as a normal course of business. Every day bank customers use their online accounts to transfer funds for payments to accounts for their utility companies; mortgage holders; car lease holders; car, home, life and health insurance vendors; government taxes; etc.

With this in mind, the Event Chairman and/or Treasurer may want to consider bringing someone with more tech experience onto the finance team or transitioning to leadership someone that may be more receptive to using the latest technology.

Pricing and Fees

We read about it every day. Consumers despise fees. Most notorious are Ticketmaster, hotels and resorts, airlines and phone service providers. Yet, some festivals and events, rather than raising their prices, tack on fees for a myriad of things, like parking, handling (when the tickets are emailed to ticket buyers) and the cost of credit card processing.

Event organizers should note events tacking on fees might likely find many negative comments on social media and blogs. Here's a common social media post, "Avoid buying tickets online. Fees are ridiculous. Buy tickets at the door. They are cheaper there."

If you add fees to your ticket price, play out that move at least six places forward on the chessboard to see fuller implications:

1. Yes, the event organizer can pass the additional fees (credit card percentages and rates where allowed by law) to its patrons plus the online ticket service charge.

2. Customers – smart consumers – will not buy online, thereby significantly reducing presale revenue which may be needed to cover expenses before the gates open.

3. Advance sales can be a predictor as to how popular the event will be.

4. More cash customers showing up at the gate means more security concerns on site – local law enforcement, bank runs to make deposit, increased possibility of robbery, etc.

5. If your event offers on-site credit card processing, this line will likely be longer than a cash only line.

6. The event's reputation can be affected by social media comments.

7. Overall attendance can drop if consumers suspect they are being gouged.

8. The media will jump on board and the news story will not be about the entertainers or the scholarships being given with the proceeds but rather interviews of customers who have paid the fees once and promise never to come back.

9. If you must charge additional fees, do the math. Analyze it from different perspectives, such as a family of four. If the tickets costs $10 each and added fees are $5 per ticket. That's $20 more per order. The order total is $60 and one-third of the total price is fees. Probably too high a fee. If the ticket costs $12 each and added fees are $3 per ticket. That's only $12 per order or one-fifth the total price.

After thinking it forward, wouldn't it be better to raise your ticket price within reason? Consumers will quickly let you know if your pricing is too high or a fair value. Recovery from an overpriced event, excessive fees and a bad reputation takes a considerable amount of work and time.

To better understand pricing, seek an online ticketing and registration system that takes a straightforward approach. A flat price per ticket allows the event organizer to know exactly what the event's costs are. Curiously, some ticket vendors additionally charge a percentage of the ticket price. If the same ticketing service resources are used per sale, this appears to penalize higher priced tickets.

Here are a few examples illustrating consumer annoyance with fees:

In a story on Newser.com, (Go to: http://www.newser.com/story/98833/ticketmaster-we-know-you-hate-our-fees.html) "Ticketmaster has finally acknowledged the seemingly obvious: that its service fees are annoying and cause some people to abandon the ticket-buying process entirely." Consumerist.com, a blog affiliated with "Consumer Reports," annually reveals the Worst Companies in America. Ticketmaster was named to their top four (2013, 2011, 2010), top eight (2012) and top 16 (2014).

In 2008, the airlines started charging a checked baggage fee that has grown to include carry-ons and in-flight food. In April 2011, the U.S. Department of Transportation announced new airline passenger protection regulations to include full disclosure of additional fees. In a survey conducted in March 2015 for the U.S. Travel Association by Research Now, the most frustrating costs associated with flying, according to respondents, were fees for: 1) flight changes or cancellations, 2) seat assignments, 3) checked bags and 4) priority boarding.

The Federal Trade Commission (FTC) warned 22 hotel operators in November 2012 that their online reservation sites may violate the law by providing a deceptively low estimate of what consumers can expect to pay for their hotel rooms. "Consumers are entitled to know in advance the total cost of their hotel stays," said FTC Chairman Jon Leibowitz. "So-called 'drip pricing' charges, sometimes portrayed as 'convenience' or 'service' fees, are anything but convenient, and businesses that hide them are doing a huge disservice to American consumers."

How the Online Payment Processing Piece Works

Answers to questions in MONEY MATTERS – Online Ticketing – Deciding What's Important to Your Event will help guide you in researching viable options for online payment processors.

An online payment processor is needed if you want to bank your own monies. Some online ticketing services offer banking services; however, you will pay for the privilege. While the costs may seem inexpensive, create a matrix to play out a variety of scenarios to see just what the real costs would be.

Here are a variety of options should you elect to be your own bank:

Stripe

This is a new generation payment processor funded by some of PayPal's initial investors. It was designed by tech people who desired a cleaner, simpler way to process online transactions. As a side benefit, users won't find Stripe's logo splattered everywhere, like PayPal does with its endless commercials and self-promotion. The monies Stripe processes go immediately into your Stripe account. Earnings are then transferred to your bank's checking account on a two-day rolling basis after the initial deposit which may take a few days longer.

As of this writing, Stripe charges a per transaction fee and a flat percentage fee. The good news, unlike many payment processors, when issuing a refund, Stripe's fees are refunded, resulting in zero cost to the event organizer. With Stripe you take control of collecting your money, and it is available to you before your event starts, when you need it the most – not after the event is over.

Setting up a Stripe account takes about five minutes. It asks some basic questions because it needs to know about your organization and what you plan to do. You won't need to complete a lengthy application process. Stripe also wants to know if you are tethered to this earth in some way. You agree not to be a business in any of its "we do not accept" categories. Stripe will continue to review your account, allowing you to set up your event immediately and begin selling tickets.

Stripe offers the ability to be seamlessly integrated into online ticketing services. For the event organizer and the consumer purchasing tickets, there won't be any barriers, hurdles or logging in or out. Transactions are smooth and shouldn't generate questions or be a cause for concern. Reconciling reports between Stripe and your online ticketing service should be a breeze.

An event organizer doesn't get dinged more when someone uses a business credit card (if you opt to accept it) or for the higher fee rewards/affiliate credit cards. It's a simple flat rate. Stripe has thought through the entire process. Your event name can be the name appearing on the credit card charge because Stripe offers the event the ability to set the statement descriptor. This is perfect for an Event Chairman holding more than one event.

Still wonder about Stripe? Visit its website; you'll see a short-list of its customers – Internet-based businesses. The list is obviously much longer. Remember when Sony Pictures was hacked delaying the release of "The Interview"? After much debate, the movie was made available for streaming; Stripe handled the payment processing.

PayPal

PayPal is a well-known payment processor. It has always been a bit clunky, but it is getting better. Patrons won't need a PayPal account in order to purchase tickets online. However, it will require users to manually click from PayPal to return to the online ticketing service, whereas others like Stripe automatically make that happen.

Consumers will still find PayPal's logos and commercials throughout the transaction process.

Until recently PayPal forced all events to automatically accept e-checks. Fortunately, preferences can now be adjusted to opt out. For more details, see MONEY MATTERS – Check This Out – E-checks.

Payment Gateways – Authorize.Net® and Others

If you have a bricks and mortar establishment with a retail operation and/ or work with a traditional bank, you may want to continue using that merchant services relationship. You may be accustomed to the fees and transaction charges. Most banks will be able to work with Authorize.Net®, one of the biggest, and any of a number of others who handle online transactions. Check with your bank about setting up an Authorize.Net® payment gateway and the associated costs.

For those who are unfamiliar, a payment gateway is needed to process information between the credit card reader and the financial institution. The schedule of rates and fees for credit cards is rather complex, so you may want to ask your merchant account rep to walk you through how it works.

Payment gateways offer two types of fee for services: 1) bricks and mortar retail operations which may be appropriate for an event's merchandise booth and 2) Internet sales (online ticket sales and online merchandise sales). Each type of use requires a different set-up. Usually your bank can help you establish a traditional merchant account or payment gateway, although you may want to shop around for the best rates and fees.

If you plan to maintain an existing payment gateway (like Authorize.Net®) and banking relationship, check to see if the payment gateway is seamlessly integrated into your online ticketing service in order to reduce hurdles for your patrons, like requiring extra clicks to return to the online ticketing service, like PayPal requires.

Traditional payment processors or merchant service accounts charge a transaction fee plus a percentage. If a refund or cancellation occurs, it will charge you again for the refund or cancellation. Stripe, for instance, simply reverses the original charge.

Most ticketing systems support a handful of payment processors, but not all options are available from each.

Check This Out – E-checks

E-checks are great for products when payment can be held and delivery occurs after funds are confirmed.

For those patrons who do not have credit cards, e-checks provide a viable payment resource or option. For events (a service, not a product) desiring to sell ticketing before and during the event, this can prove challenging. E-checks are much like real checks. The possibility exists that funds may not be available to cover a purchase.

If your online payments are processed through PayPal, you may elect not to accept e-checks. Here's why: when an event sells tickets before and during the event, it is possible a ticket can be bought and paid for using an e-check. The ticket could be presented for entry, and later, after the event is over, the event organizer learns the check bounced.

Private or White Label Ticketing – Full or Quasi

Are you sick and tired of your online ticketing vendor's logo and name being more predominant than yours? Would you like your event logo to be showcased instead?

Before I share how to get around this, learn why you're getting less name recognition:

1. The event patron's ticket monies are paid directly to the ticket vendor and not to the event. When the credit card statement comes at the end of the month, the ticket vendor's name needs to be readily connected to the name on the credit or debit statement so the chance of a chargeback is reduced.

    Payment processors typically assess a chargeback fee when a charge is called into question. That inquiry requires ticket service man-hours to respond to calls asking questions like, who are you? Why did you charge me? Labor intensive staffing comes into play when chargebacks occur.

    Those fees can get quite hefty when consumers refute credit card payments simply because they don't recognize a name on their statement. If a ticket vendor's charge goes throughout without a hitch, decreasing staff needs and credit card chargebacks, its profits increase.

If the online ticketing vendor is acting as your bank, it's likely it will be the one dealing with chargebacks when "its name" pops up on the credit card statement and your patron doesn't recognize the name. With your event name etched in the ticket buyer's mind, wouldn't chargebacks be reduced?

2. Does the online ticketing service truly assume all the risk because it is serving as the bank and collecting the monies? Indirectly, isn't the event also sharing the risk? While the direct hit is made to the ticket service, the ensuing transaction impacts the event, too. How much more risk is there if the event serves as its own bank?

3. If your customers have a question about the event or tickets, are your customers more likely to contact the vendor with the biggest logo or you? Before you make a decision regarding an online ticketing service, check its Contact Us page to see what mechanisms are available for your customers to connect with them. Is it by phone, email or chat, and what hours are they available? How accessible is your ticket vendor to your customers if questions arise about the transaction? Accessible customer support can be the difference between a smooth event and a frustrating one.

4. The same question holds for you as the event organizer. Check its Contact Us page to see what mechanisms are available for you to reach out to them. Is it by phone, email or chat, and what hours are they available? How accessible is your ticket vendor to you for any number of reasons? Accessible customer support can be the difference between a smooth event and a frustrating one.

5. Promotion. Promotion. Promotion – Is your event being used to promote your online ticketing vendor's services to your customers? Check those emails being sent out to your patrons with their tickets and reminders to determine if at every turn your ticket vendor's services are being heavily promoted.

If you want the money to flow directly to you and want the online ticket vendor's name and endless commercials to disappear, you have two options:

Full Private Label Ticketing

It will take a period of time to arrange as the service will need to set up your personalized domain name and purchase a secure certificate for you tied to your use of its system. This is at a cost to the event. You may be required to commit to a multi-year contract to go this route.

Check to make sure your credit card transaction fee and percentage rate aren't higher than the street price and you aren't locked in for the duration of the contract. This will, however, guarantee your name and logo are front and center. If you have staff already handling customer inquiries – phone, email or chat – and have established hours of operation, you should be in good shape.

Quasi-Private Label Ticketing

It can be set up immediately if inserting the auto-generated programming code into your existing website. The only evidence of the ticketing vendor's name will be in the domain name – http:// www.eventname.online-ticket-vendor-name.com. As before, if you have staff already handling customer inquiries, have various methods to stay in contact and hours posted, this set up will work. If the event webpage is maintained by the online ticketing service or an event is free, this feature may not be available.

Other Considerations

Investigate the depth and flexibility of a private or white label ticketing service. Feature rich options providing the most versatility in the long run are a big plus. Seek a provider with a full range of features from customizable forms to add-on merchandise to built-in sponsor exposure and social media tie-ins, like being able to sell your tickets on Facebook. Is it staying current with demands and continuing to add enhancements? As an event's needs change and grow, working with a service with beginner to advance-level offerings, should allow the event to continue with the same service.

When converting to private label, one goal should be to make the ticketing blend into your event's website, so the end user will feel you and the ticketing service are one and the same. If your website was designed with a very specific color palette and font, the more color and font selections the better. If you can change other design aspects too – like background colors – all the better.

With private label ticketing, an event is able to remove an outside ticket vendor's commercials from its website and take control of its revenue stream. If you are a new event, search for a white label vendor with features you can use today, but also one that has considerable depth so you can grow into it moving forward.

Options: Tickets, Wristbands, RFID or Cashless?

These options vary from the very simple to the sophisticated.

Simplest

Buy a ticket online, then present your paper ticket or smartphone with QR code at the event and gain entrance. What was the purpose of the online purchase? If the event desired to drive revenue in advance of the event and minimize cash handling at the event for safety and security, it worked.

Simple with an Added Cost – Wristbands

Buy a ticket online, then present your paper ticket or smartphone with QR code at the event and exchange it for a wristband. What was the purpose of the online purchase? As stated earlier, if the event desired cash flow before the event and to lessen the demands for on-site handling of cash, it did the trick. If the goal was to eliminate lines near the gate, this may or may not be the answer. It all depends on the event's ability (staff and/or volunteers) to quickly handle the exchange.

With moderate crowds and a balanced pace, it may be an easy exchange – present the ticket and receive a color-coded wristband. The wristband's color determines which area(s) a patron, volunteer or sponsor can enter. In some cases, pre-event communication directs different types of patrons to different gates and only those specific color wristbands are available.

The challenge occurs when a paid guest takes on a different role. A sponsor is a volunteer and then wants to access VIP corporate seating later in the day. Do they take off one wristband and put on another? Or do they wear dual wristbands? How do you take the other one away later?

On the backside, volunteers need to know how to properly affix a wristband so the fit is correct. Security needs to be trained to know what colors provide access to which areas.

But you have to ask, "Once someone's inside the event, what's the point of a wristband?" Go to a baseball or a basketball game, present the ticket to the usher, walk through the turnstile and you're done. If your event is a multi-day event, wristbands may be of benefit, providing they cannot be removed and given to someone else and are durable enough to withstand everyday activities.

Above all, remember wristbands are an expense to an event. They are an extra layer that may not be necessary. It all depends on the size of your event. Yes, they will require manpower before and during the event to address any issues.

If, according to Mary Meeker of Kleiner Perkins Caufied Byers, 40 percent of the population has smartphones, why wouldn't you allow your patrons to just present their smartphones or paper tickets for ingress/egress. For more details, see MARKETING – Websites – Mobi.

Not As Simple and a Bit More Work – RFID

Many know the term RFID (radio frequency identification) from the company selling blocking devices to stop the transmission of credit card data from a wallet. As such, RFID may be perceived to be a bad thing but in reality, it can be a good thing for festivals and events. Because of what's involved RFID is sometimes only cost effective for larger events.

RFID is a sophisticated wireless electronic tracking chip – and typically incorporated into a wristband so it cannot be used by more than one person. RFID can be activated and de-activated. When someone reports not having received their wristband or advises it's been stolen, it can be de-activated. If a wristband was put on too tightly, it can be removed, de-activated and a new one affixed in its place.

A festival needs to have a few important things in place to make sure the a RFID experience is good:

1. Require a wristband with a quality chip or work with a wristband vendor whose chip supplier is reputable. Anyone can find a cheap price for a wristband, but the difference between quality and cheap could be 1,500 unhappy guests at your gate with a defective chip unable to get inside.

2. A quality fulfillment house is capable of sending/mailing each

wristband to each purchaser in a timely manner. Because each wristband/ticket has a value, it should be treated as currency. Like any online store, checks and balances need to be put in place to assure every transaction is being properly fulfilled and shipped.

3. The event Treasurer should be involved to assure security measures are in place and have answers for the "what ifs." If using wristbands being shipped in advance, plan on the event charging a shipping and handling fee to recover those hard costs.

4. Instructions should accompany the wristband and clearly explain: a) where and how to activate the wristbands online or using an app before the event; b) what steps to take if the buyer believes the wristband cannot be activated (defective); c) how to properly put on a wristband – which arm and for a correct or best fit; perhaps include a link to a demonstration video; and d) what to do if the wristband was installed and is too large or too tight.

   Expect follow-up questions, emails and phone calls. Also, anticipate the need for patrons to activate wristbands at the event. This would occur if a wristband is found to be defective, deactivated and replaced, or ticket sales occur at an on-site ticket office.

5. Staff must be available to monitor and analyze gate activity/ RFID check-ins – heavy use, poor wireless transmission, Internet service drops, etc. – and to have a Plan B and tech staff available to respond immediately with appropriate measures.

RFID can tackle the challenges associated when a patron serves multiple roles. With RFID, a patron can show up for a volunteer shift in the Sponsor VIP Hospitality Tent and be given access via their RFID chip for a limited number of hours only. Security will need to be trained to understand how multiple layers of access can be given from a single wristband and how to communicate with their volunteer or paid supervisor if anyone has a question about technology – a scanning device, the wireless transmission is low or drops, etc.

If the event is a multi-day event, RFID wristbands may be of benefit providing they cannot be removed and given to someone else and are durable enough to withstand everyday activities. It will depend on economies of scale – the total number of attendees, event demographics, ticket costs, gate traffic and security costs – as to when or if RFID wristbands make sense for an event.

The actual wristbands, shipping, handling and scanners or automatic scanning gates are an expense to an event. They will require trained individuals on site to deal with issues should they arise. That too will be a hard cost. As before, if, according to Mary Meeker of Kleiner Perkins Caufield Byers, 40 percent of the population has smartphones, wouldn't it be easier for the event's patrons to just present their phone and eliminate this extra layer?

Sophisticated and Usually Expensive – Cashless

The term cashless can be applied to wristband technology and/ or products like ApplePay. (Go to: http://www.apple.com/apple-pay). Because of what's involved cashless works best and is more cost effective for large events.

Cashless is typically RFID technology linked with a credit card (limit or a ticket purchase). Think of a cashless wristband as a gift card that has been loaded with a spending limit into a wristband. This requires all vendors to have a cashless point of sale (POS) device. Patrons make purchases by simply presenting their wristband.

One of the leading providers handles purchases of food, beverages and merchandise simply by double tapping the wristband. An app on a smartphone, or authorized on-site locations, allows the credit card owner to load or reload funds onto the wristband. At the end of the day the account is settled. What happens with unspent funds? Check it out because there may a charge to refund the balance on the wristband.

Some cashless wristband systems allow a master account with a spend limit for the group. Each person, say a family member, can spend on the account. So send Evan or Megan to the concessions to buy mom and dad something to eat. When doing this, it's like giving them a gift card. Will they spend it all or come back with "change" on the wristband?

Cashless may be the ultimate answer, but it's best not to jump in feet first unless you know the event can handle this technology leap and that your event's demographics will be receptive. Take those 1,500 unhappy customers mentioned in the RFID option above and multiply them many times over if a glitch occurs or the event is not prepared for a worse case scenario.

Cashless is a popular technology already used by waterparks. Unlike a festival environment, this is a fixed location with wireless infrastructure, fixed ticket booths with activation devices and RFID readers in their outlets.

If offering ApplePay as the cashless payment option, all vendors need to be able to accept this form of payment. Know your audience. Are they one of the 40 percent of people, according to Mary Meeker of Kleiner Perkins Caufield Byers, who have smartphones?

Is it necessary for an event to add another layer and additional costs with a wristband when patrons could just present their phone for payment?

HOW MUCH IS THE EVENT INTO THE BANK?

If your event has been in existence for a while and it has built up a healthy cash balance in the bank, it may be possible to temporarily borrow those funds to cover some of the pre-event expenses until revenue from the sale of tickets or merchandise can pay back the funds. Your Treasurer will be the one to let you know how much should or can be borrowed. Usually the Event Chairman and the Treasurer will know who needs to authorize the use of the reserves and how those dollars can be accessed.

Throughout the course of the event, you plan to sell tickets and merchandise, providing the weather cooperates. At some hour, the event should replace all the borrowed money and begin to generate profit.

It may seem like a difficult thing to calculate, but if your event has kept good records and receipts for tickets and merchandise, it will be easy to compare hour by hour historical data, weather conditions being equal, and know the approximate hour when the funds you used to buy tee shirts will be put back into the coffers.

First-time events don't have the luxury of historical data or a cash balance to serve as a cushion. Consider using an online ticket service and payment processor where the funds are released to the event as tickets are sold. Why work with a ticket vendor that won't release your event's funds until after the event is over when most of your expenses are in advance or need to be paid during the event? For more details, see MONEY MATTERS – Why Online Tickets? and Online Ticketing – Deciding What's Important to Your Event. Finding a flexible online ticketing services just takes a little time and research.

It's important to note that each event's goal should be to add to its cash cushion. It should always be easier to add to the fund than to pull money out. Unfortunately, those rainy days can happen and that's when the cash balance will be needed most.

ON-SITE MONEY HANDLING

On-Site Event Office

Your Treasurer will need to create instructions for handling cash, how to process credit card purchases, cash register operations and how to make deposits. For security purposes, separate each of these instructions so no one sees all processes in one place, except the Treasurer and their committee. De-compartmentalize each function, so each person only knows his or her individual job. Perhaps the Treasurer can review these with a local financial institution to check if anything is missing or if any further safeguards can be put in place.

Making bank deposits during a busy event can be a challenge, especially if the event and vendor's financial institutions are not close by. Check with the closest bank to the event venue (and in a perfect world, it will be one of your sponsors) to see if it can accept night deposits from its customers and non-customers alike during the event. Various members of the Treasurer's committee, and not the well-publicized Treasurer, can possibly walk with local police officer escorts to make bank deposits at staggered times throughout the event if conveniently nearby.

Some of the best folks to work on the Treasurer's team are bank employees because they have been prescreened before being hired. Certified Public Accountants (CPAs) and bookkeepers may understand the process, but it's the people who physically count money on a daily basis who have some of the best working knowledge.

If concerned about the volume of cash being handled, the event may want to run a silent alarm into the on-site office. In this way, it can be activated should it be needed.

On-Site Ticket Office

Your event's on-site ticket office is where you'll sell tickets and process cash and credit card transactions. To keep the lines moving, many events have more than one ticket window. In some cases each window will handle both types of transactions or some will handle one or the other. Some will also serve as a will-call or pick-up window if payment was done over the phone or if the individual was unable to print out their ticket. The latter can be verified by checking the online ticket office by your volunteers given admin level access.

Your Treasurer can select from one of the following ways to handle the transaction – cash register, drawer or box. Whichever method is selected, checks and balances need to be in place to make sure numbered tickets match cash or credit card sales.

For those using an online ticketing office, many such services offer a ticket office for use by the staff or the Treasurer's committee prior to the event as well as during the event. The ticket office may not require that the full depth of information be entered as it does when the general public purchases tickets. In this way, purchases made using the ticket office can adapt, reducing long lines during peak demand.

The greatest advantage to using an online ticketing office is all transactions are recorded in a single location. At any point the Treasurer can log into the dashboard and see exactly how many tickets are sold. There should be numerous other reports, too, providing as much or as little detail as desired.

For the online ticket office, your Treasurer may elect to use laptop computers (with or without a mouse – tethered or wireless requiring batteries), tablets or even smartphones. Some may need to be tethered to electricity or make sure they are fully charged or back-up batteries are available. After use for some time, cooling fans on certain laptop computer models are activated making for a noisy unit which can make it difficult to hear customers.

To provide your event the most flexibility and to minimize ergonomic challenges for the user, consider online ticketing services that can be used on touch pad screens, providing Wi-Fi is available. Remember to double check with your insurance provider regarding liability coverage for devices or computer equipment should they be lost or stolen.

Playing this forward, check to make sure the online ticket office's buttons for "numbers" of tickets selected and spacing between each are large enough in size in order to lessen your cash handlers re-doing orders again and again simply because they are unable to make the correct selections.

If you are not interested in manually entering those 16 digit credit card numbers, several options are available:

1. A credit card swipe that can be tied via a USB device (regular or mini connection) to a laptop, tablet or smartphone.

2. An all-in-one device that fits two different needs – scanning tickets at the gate and swiping credit cards.

In many cases the two functions are separate and paying for a dual function rental may not be necessary.

3.   Some online ticket service apps also incorporate credit card processing.

4.   Check reviews if you are considering using a wireless credit card swipe because they may alert you to concerns such as reliability and performance and address questions you may have. As before, some online ticketing services offer equipment rental.

After making a ticket office payment, your event patrons will proceed to the entrance to present their ticket or QR code on their smartphone to gain entry at the gate, or the ticket office can let them through immediately.

Much of the information covered in the MONEY MATTERS chapter applies here. Stand-alone ticket offices should have a secure entry for personnel or visible security.

Tickets, Please!

For those who have purchased tickets in advance, they'll proceed straight to the entry gate and present their ticket. In operating what I'll call the old-fashioned way (non-online ticket sales), a paper ticket will be presented and, assuming the ticket is perforated, it will be torn along the line with half being returned to your patron and the other being retained for the Treasurer's committee to process later.

If the event is using an online ticketing system, make sure it includes a free scanning app or rents equipment with a scanning app installed. The apps typically allow the roster of ticket holders to be downloaded. Then, as either the paper or mobile ticket (QR code displays on a smartphone) is presented, the device scans the ticket indicating if it is valid or invalid. Valid ticket holders are then admitted. The real value of a scanning app is it should also update your event's reporting at the same time since at certain increments the scanner devices sync. Usually these sync times are pre-set at intervals to stop two or more people from entering on a single ticket.

Scanning apps with check-in and check-out features are also a plus. Because they provide accurate data and attendance counts, it should eliminate challenges with someone saying they need to get back in when the roster shows the "check-in" has already taken place.

The answer to this may seem obvious, but renting equipment with a scanning app does several things:

1. Frees up your Organizing Committee members' phones for personal and event business.

2. Keeps the event rosters on event-controlled equipment for a fixed period of time. Would you really want your event roster downloaded on a phone to which you don't have login access?

3. Allows the Treasurer's committee to exchange devices when necessary to re-charge the batteries. Usually this is overnight.

4. Allows the event organizer to download rosters for any or all of the event dates. It wouldn't be the first time someone showed up on the wrong date.

For low-tech events or those with small attendance numbers, you may want to print out a paper roster and then manually check patrons in using the online ticketing system or use a barcode scanner (tethered to a computer or wireless) to scan each ticket or to scan the barcode on the roster.

The Art of the Transaction

Cash

Cash usually works for everyone. Your Treasurer will need to put security measures into place to protect the event, the volunteers and cash handlers. These safeguards should provide the ability to check for counterfeit bills. Some events and concessionaires limit the denomination or bill size to not greater than $50 or $100 to further protect themselves and to minimize risks.

Traveler's checks and money orders are not as foolproof as once thought. Ask your Treasurer to determine if the event will accept traveler's checks and/or money orders. With the advent of credit cards, fewer traveler's checks are processed. Your Treasurer will need to confer with a local financial institution to determine how to verify if a traveler's check is legitimate or fake.

Checks

Do you plan to accept checks? If yes, only local checks? If so, on only local banks? Will the Treasurer limit the amount of a check, say to $100? Will a layer be added to the approval process, requiring a member of the Merchandise Committee or cash handling team to approve a check? The event may require an ID with full address, driver's license number and phone number. You can even attempt to call the phone number on the spot to see if it works. Ask your Treasurer how to identify a forged check.

When signing off on a check, even when a member of the Merchandise Committee knows someone, it does not mean they know the amount of money in that person's checking account. This added step may deter someone from writing a bad check and then again, it might not.

Credit Cards

Your Treasurer may limit the types of credit cards accepted. If using Authorize.Net® or a similar payment gateway and a traditional bank, it's important to note some major credit cards charge lower percentage rates and fees than business credit cards and affinity cards (cards with third party logos, endorsements and rewards programs that are also under the umbrella of some major credit card companies). All of these costs affect the event's bottom line. For more details, see MONEY MATTERS – How the Online Payment Processing Piece Works.

Refunds and Exchanges

You sell it. They buy it. They bring it back.

Your Merchandise Committee Chairman in conjunction with the Treasurer will need to determine if the event will allow returns or exchanges. Some events do; some don't. If the item was obviously damaged by the buyer when worn, it may not be returned. If the item is still fully packaged in plastic with an unbroken seal, it may be returned and exchanged or refunded. As another example, they bought multiple tee shirts in the same size, but in putting the first one on discovered it was too small. Now they want to exchange these items for a larger size. The most important thing is to set a return or exchange policy.

If no refunds are permitted, post a sign in a conspicuous place with these words: "We do not accept returns," or "All sales are final." Some customers will still try to return an item.

If your event allows items to be exchanged, a sign or two stating the following should be visible in the merchandise booth: "We will exchange an item as long as it has not been worn or damaged."

If the event offers refunds or needs to give refunds, putting the money back on the original credit card is one of the easiest ways to do it. However, most payment processors will charge the event a transaction fee and a percentage rate when a refund is given.

Money Handling Procedures

The Treasurer will need to set up procedures regarding money handling at the event. These should control transactions made at the ticket office and in the event-operated food concessions, beverage stands/trailers, merchandise booth and donation container(s). These may also be helpful to other vendors, such as food concessionaires, not controlled by the event. For more details, see MONEY MATTERS – The Toolkit.

Set up at least two cash registers in your event-controlled food concessions or merchandise booth. Select cash register models that have the ability to provide data after the fact; one with a paper register tape is a bonus. Two are suggested so you have one functioning at all times and the other is a back up. This allows one register operator to take a register down to cash in or out and not impede sales. Alternately, you can also set up two cash drawers or boxes.

Common sense and general safety should come into play.

1. The volunteer cashier is required to count the cash in the register, drawer or box at the beginning and end of their shift. For ease in shift changes, ask the cashier to arrive early to count cash. It's helpful when a volunteer knows how to count change vs. just reading the amount that displays on the cash register indicating how much to return to the customer because it provides a double check. Someone with retail or bank teller experience will be advantageous for this position.

2. The volunteer cashier should be advised in advance who has the authority to skim cash in order to reduce the amount in their register, drawer or box. Don't laugh; you'd be amazed how someone appearing to be in authority could initiate the process and walk off with the event's money.

3. A receipt should be given to each cashier each time cash is skimmed so the end counts balance.

4. For safety, the cash registers, drawers or boxes should be kept away from the front counter and away from sight if possible.

5. The volunteer cashier should handle one cash transaction at a time.

6. The frontline volunteer can take the cash and say, "I'll get you change for that $XX." If that's not the amount the customer thinks they have given, that is the customer's chance to say, "Hey, I gave you a $YY."

7. When a frontline volunteer hands cash to the cashier, it should be placed across the top of the cash register, drawer or box and not inside the designated slots. More than once a customer thinks they have paid with a different denomination, only to count their change and say it's not correct. When the cashier has the money across the register, drawer or box, they can immediately confirm to the frontline volunteer the amount given. When the transaction is completed, the bills are then placed in their respective sections in the register, draw or box.

8. If an issue arises, immediately stop and bring in a volunteer supervisor. This can range from not enough money returned, to a counterfeit bill, to a customer with a behavior problem – rude, drunk or obnoxious. Depending on the level of behavior, a supervisor may ask the police to step in.

9. When the volume of cash reaches a certain level in the register, draw or box, the cashier should move it below, away from public view, as a security precaution.

10. The Treasurer will have decided in advance what denominations to accept and if traveler's checks or money orders will be accepted.

11. The Treasurer will instruct how to check bills to determine if counterfeit.

12. Limit if or which concessions will accept traveler's checks or money orders to only those where a volunteer supervisor can confirm they are or are not counterfeit.

13. In the event of a robbery or hold-up, follow pre-established procedures reviewed when the cash register, drawer or box monies were being counted at the beginning of the shift.

ATMs, Robberies, Hold-Ups and Counterfeit Money

Encourage the Treasurer to meet with a local financial institution, preferably one of your sponsors, to:

1. Learn more about automatic teller machines (ATMs) options and installation requirements and to then determine if these may be needed at the venue.

2. Determine the best way to check for counterfeit bills.

3. Ask for advice so cash handling volunteers can be instructed what to do in the event of a robbery or hold-up.

4. Review current procedures relative to robberies and hold-ups and mechanisms to track money, for example, dye packs, security cameras and silent alarms.

The Toolkit

This section applies to all the event-controlled cash or credit card transactions (ticket office, event-operated food concessions, beverage stands/trailers, merchandise booth and donation container(s)), as well as provides suggestions for other non-event controlled concessions.

The Treasurer should attend the food and beverage concessionaires pre-event meeting, whether or not these are event-controlled concessions, to review money-handling procedures. This may prove helpful to first-time concessionaires not familiar with your type of event as well as veteran concessionaires. For more details, see MONEY MATTERS – On-Site Money Handling and Money Handling Procedures.

Cash Handling Supplies

These are suggested items for the on-site ticket office, food concessions, beverage stands/trailers and merchandise booth:

- Clipboards – This should save the concessionaire from searching for a sheet of paper amid the many other items most likely stored in the concessionaire's temporary on-site office (vehicle or storage trailer). These can be used for tracking inventory, notes, phone numbers, cash, deposits, etc. Finding a clipboard is much easier than finding a piece of paper.

- Receipts – The Treasurer will provide a receipt book to the Beverage Stands Coordinator for the person delivering ice to food concessionaires and beverage stands/trailers. These can be tallied at the end of the event and presented by the Treasurer or a member of their committee for cash payment for the ice used. Place these receipts on the clipboard, too. Require the receipt, when paid, to be marked "paid in with full" with the amount paid, the date and the signature of all parties.

- Cash registers, drawers or boxes – These should allow for an easier transition between cashier shifts.

- Cash – Events still turn a fair amount of cash, especially for food and beverage sales. Cash handling lines move more quickly than credit card lines. If credit cards are accepted, newer technology will require a Wi-Fi connection. A credit card swipe can be tied in via a USB device (regular or mini connection) to a laptop, tablet or smartphone.

- Bank Deposits – If a local bank, hopefully an event sponsor, is located near the venue, ask the Treasurer to check to determine if it is receptive to accepting night deposit bags from non-customers. If this is possible, then the Treasurer should share the details as to how this can be arranged and requisite paperwork needed.

- Paper Bags – For safety, place the locked bank deposit bags in the brown paper bags when it's time to do a transfer. Local law enforcement may be willing to walk with a member of the cash handling team and concessionaires to a nearby bank to make a night deposit drop.

- Calculator – While it would be easier to use a calculator with paper tape to see what was added vs. where you stopped when you were distracted, it requires electricity – a valuable commodity at an event. Use a battery-operated version, perhaps?

- Money Straps – This will allow you to bundle money into pre-set increments from $50 to $250.

- Coin Wrappers – If you find yourself with a considerable amount of change, use wrappers.

- Cash Counting Machines, Coin Counters and Coin Scales – Depending on the number of events you do, this may or may not be a wise investment.

- Cash – The one thing you don't want to happen is to run out of change on a weekend. Better to have too much than too little. Don't be surprised if concessionaires borrow from one another during the event. While competitive rivalry is fun, being neighborly usually has its benefits.

- Starting Cash – Here's a rough idea of starter change for a beverage stand/trailer: $220 in $1 bills; $200 in $5 bills; and $200 in $10 bills.

SETTING UP SHOP
- CONCESSIONS & MERCHANDISE

Concession Tickets

Concession tickets can be used to eliminate the need for concessionaires to collect money and make change. These special tickets are purchased elsewhere at the event and used to purchase food and drinks. Concession tickets can return up to 80 percent of ticket sales to the food vendors, leaving the balance to the event. Research both sides of the fence before deciding to use concession tickets.

Pros

Some event organizers like concession tickets because of the lack of trust factor. If your non-event controlled concessions are paying the event a base cost for the booth space plus a percentage of profits, concession tickets are one way to keep vendors honest. Who says the event gets its full share otherwise?

Some view money as dirty or full of germs. Who wants to handle money and food at the same time? A designated cashier at each concession booth could be the answer, provided cash handling procedures are in place and security wanders by occasionally or has a visible presence at the event.

Some events sell food and beverage concession tickets based on 1 ticket = $X. Concessionaires then need to accept a certain number of tickets to equal the value of their product. A food concessionaire may need to adjust its product (size and/or volume) to cover its costs and make a profit. What happens when the product should actually sell for $4.50? The vendor most likely can't accept to lose 50¢ for each item sold for $4. Selling the item at $5 makes it appear overpriced and drives patrons to other vendors with better pricing.

The Treasurer or a member of their committee will collect and sign for concession tickets turned in at each concession and then pay out monies to each concessionaire using the established formula. The Treasurer will be able to track ticket spoilage or windfall revenue for the event.

Cons

Consumers hate concession tickets for a number of reasons. First, they hate to stand in line to buy the concession tickets; and, second, to stand in line again to purchase food and beverages. They hate to commit to $X worth of tickets when they don't know what it is they want. All of this amounts to wasted time and frustration by your patrons.

To get a ballpark idea of what your patrons want to eat and drink, they will need to visit every concession to figure out what it is they might want. Then do the math in their heads. Then go stand in line to purchase tickets. Then go stand in line at the concession. Oh, wait. They worked up quite an appetite going through this exercise. Even though they are still hungry, they are not going to stand in the ticket line (which by the way is not located in a convenient place) again. Kind of ironic, isn't it? Concession tickets leave a bad taste in one's mouth.

Add on another layer. Your patron didn't bring enough cash. The ticket booth won't take credit cards, so they stood at the nearby ATM before standing in line at the concession ticket booth.

I'd be curious if anyone has ever done a study to see the amount of time it takes to stand in line to buy concession tickets and then pay with them vs. standing in line once at a concession to make a purchase and pay with cash.

Now after reading both the pros and cons, decide what will work best for your event. Just remember: when people stand in line, they have time to post comments on social media about standing in line.

Domino Effect

It is to the event's benefit to secure and maintain a variety of quality food, beer or wine vendors. Be careful of this scenario: among a group of marginal food vendors are a few quality ones. Because the ratio skews more to marginal food quality, not surprisingly, sales decrease. The quality vendors see more demand for their products and sell out. The overall event makes less money. Word on the street draws more negative attention to the marginal vendors with high praise to the few quality vendors.

The real impact is seen the following year when consumers "assume" the same marginal quality will continue. So two years of declining revenue can set the event on a downward spiral.

Watch carefully if revenues go down and neither the weather nor a competing event are to be blamed. The Organizing Committee needs to recognize that the quality, or lack thereof, of their food vendors can pull down the event's reputation and profit potential.

A plan should be in place to strategically seek out quality vendors, to the point of personal visits if necessary to secure their participation. The Marketing Services Committee and Public Relations and Publicity Committee need to ramp up their efforts to assure potential ticket buyers a quality experience for their money.

Retail Sales of Merchandise

For more details, see MERCHANDISE – Merchandise Booth and MONEY MATTERS – Shopping Carts.

Selling Merchandise Online

In essence, what your event is doing is setting up a retail business online.

Just about everything an event would do to create a bricks and mortar store will be involved – inventory, display (photos and descriptions), credit cards, policies, refunds, taxes, shopping bags (shipping and handling), etc. Because many of these decisions are financial in nature, the Treasurer will play an important role. Your Merchandise Committee Chairman will be involved in placing orders, monitoring and fulfilling orders. Past event inventory can be sold online, too.

The Production Schedule created in MERCHANDISE – The Production Schedule was built for on-site sales at an event. If your event plans to sell merchandise online, the schedule will need to be adjusted.

Consider one of two ways to sell merchandise online:

1. Set up a shopping cart within your website. Use a shopping cart plug-in or module that allows merchandise to be purchased from a variety of devices. Shopping carts have traditionally only provided the ability to sell merchandise on a website, not on social media sites.

2. Select an online ticket system that allows the event organizer to sell merchandise along with event tickets. The event organizer should have the ability to: a) upload images and descriptions of the products; b) enter the different sizes and color selections; c) decide if inventory will be shipped in advance of the event to the purchaser or be available at the event for pick up.

Some online ticketing systems allow merchandise to be grouped together with a single ticket order so the full order is shipped out and not tied to a specific person while other set-ups tie each item to a particular person. Either way works, but the former allows you to send out more items in a single shipment, perhaps resulting in lower shipping and handling costs.

While funds are put out for inventory in advance, revenue can be generated before the event to help with cash flow. Because many event-goers like to come to the event sporting the current year's tee shirt, many events prefer to ship in advance. Online sales can be a predictor of the popularity of the design and may help in determining how much inventory will be needed for on-site sales.

If your Treasurer is one to watch and track the average ticket price, this is a great way to see what type of revenue is generated from every ticket holder for tickets and merchandise. It's even easier if the tickets and merchandise are sold and reported in the same system.

To be of value, a shopping cart and an online ticket service should offer extensive reporting features.

Shopping Carts

Shopping carts are an optional way to sell event tickets. Many, many shopping carts are available and most are software packages you can purchase and install in your website; some are available for a monthly fee. Before you purchase a shopping cart, realize an event is not a product; it is a service. Shopping carts are designed to sell products, and as such offer many options simply because they need to be able to adapt to the diversity of products in the marketplace.

Services, like online ticket sales, have different and unique needs. Having the capability to show photos of a pair of jeans or a sweater makes sense if you sell these types of products. Zooming in to show an enlarged view of your musician's guitar, chef's cookware, winemaker's bottle of wine, author's book or filmmaker's poster isn't necessary. What an event needs to do to sell a service or ticket is different. Using a shopping cart for an unintended purpose is like trying to make a square peg fit in a round hole.

Unlike a shopping cart, some online ticketing/registration services offer the ability to make additional selections during the purchase process. You may be able to buy one adult ticket and a tee shirt or register for a sponsor luncheon and select your meal choice – chicken, beef, seafood or vegan.

Shopping carts most likely won't let you sell your tickets on Facebook or offer an app to scan tickets as your patrons present their paper or mobile tickets.

According to a January 26, 2014, Nielsen Norman Group article, Ecommerce UX: 3 Design Trends to Follow and 3 to Avoid by Amy Schade (Go to: https://www.nngroup.com/articles/e-commerce-usability), "Our latest ecommerce research revealed user-experience improvements to shopping sites such as large product images, robust reviews, and easy discounts. New designs suffer from hidden product information, poor site feedback, and crowded customer-service areas." None of the above address ticket services needs; all are tied to products.

Merchandise Booth

For more details, see MERCHANDISE – Merchandise Booth.

Event Proceeds Benefit Local Charity or Scholarships

Events of all types name a local charity as its benefactor. Providing profits are available, this can be a big win for the community as well as the nonprofit. The Marketing Services Committee and the Public Relations and Publicity Committee should play up the beneficiary at every opportunity. For the event, it may draw others less inclined to come but wanting to support the nonprofit. The nonprofit may also prove to be a valuable resource for event volunteers.

If scholarships are awarded from the event's proceeds, take the opportunity to recognize the person or persons from the stage during the event or perhaps award the scholarship during the event.

If an event encounters a challenge — long lines, traffic congestion, lack of port-o-let timely service, computer glitches, show not running on schedule, bad news coverage — have the Public Relations and Publicity Committee push hard on the benefactor message. While it may not slow down all of the social media comments, it may make a few stop to think twice before posting a not-so-nice message. Put a face to the benefactors, too. These are the organizations and people who will be hurt the most in the end.

ACCOUNTING & ACCOUNTABILITY

Final Figures

Shortly after the event is over, the media will come calling. The Event Chairman or Public Relations and Publicity Committee Chairman will be asked how much money the event made for a wrap-up story it plans to run. The Organizing Committee will also be interested but not more than the Event Chairman or the Treasurer.

Net profit is the barometer many will use to determine if the event was successful. An event may miss the mark on the total profit but still have had an excellent turnout, fabulous mentions in the press, accolades from the talent and excellent weather.

Unfortunately, the bottom line figure is what gains the spotlight. The answer regarding profitability will take 30 days or more because all invoices will need to be processed. The event is not obligated to share this information with the media. This 30-day or longer period can be used as a stall tactic. The final figures technically can only be available after a certified audit is completed.

Forecasting

Forecasting is an art. Data from each event year moving forward helps perfect the forecast. Forecasting takes any number of factors and incorporates them into projections as to when income, revenue and expenses will occur. It will factor into the equation the following:

1. Past and predicted weather conditions – sunny, rainy, hot, cold and exact temperatures

2. Outside economic factors – a local union strike, a depressed/robust economy, high/low housing prices, high/low unemployment, the price of fuel if a drive-in event, good/poor flight connections, limited lodging options to stay overnight, etc.

3. Competitive events – college football games, a hospital fundraiser, when the school year begins or ends or when school is on break, etc.

4. Local infrastructure – are roads planned to be under construction, are parking spaces lacking or adequate, etc.

5. Event reputation – good or sour

6. Sponsor support – declining or everyone wants to be involved

7. Ticket pricing vs. perceived value

8. Quality of entertainment, food and beverage vendors

9. Event atmosphere – welcoming or restrictive

10. On-site merchandise or food – over-priced or of good value

The trick is to take the budget and then to apply each number as to when the income and expenses will actually occur. Will sponsors drag their feet or will they commit early?

Forecasting allows the event to chart its cash flow – when income and expenses occur. Is the cash flow forecast off because slow paying sponsors hinder the event's ability to write deposit checks for talent and the sound and lighting equipment? What's the drop-dead deadline talent contracts can be signed? For instance, if merchandise is being sold online, that's an upfront expense to the event. Are patrons willing to buy this year's themed merchandise ahead of time so they can wear it to the event?

Can an event's sales of merchandise be forecast by each hour of the day so the Treasurer and Event Chairman can see at exactly what hour the event will have recovered all of its costs? Will the Treasurer need to borrow from last year's profits in order to pull together enough cash before the event to prepare cash payments for talent and change for cash registers and boxes? During the event is the Stage Manager willing to allow five more minutes between acts to improve concession and merchandise sales?

1099s

In my personal experience, if your talent – headliner, artist, speaker, musician, pilot, performer, winemaker, author, chef, entertainer, brewmaster, etc. – is an individual (and not a corporation) and the event paid them at least $600, your event will need to issue to this person a 1099-MISC form (Go to: http://www.irs.gov/uac/About-Form-1099MISC) and file the appropriate copy with the Internal Revenue Service (IRS) usually by the end of January each year. For this reason, it is extremely important to require as part of each talent contract, every person's legal name, social security number and current mailing address.

What happens if your talent moves around frequently? Unfortunately, the IRS-required 1099s may not be deliverable and be returned to the event. The U.S. Postal Service forwards mail for up to six months, and it can be extended for another six months. It is possible your event's artist could be contracted to perform any time January to June, move, and by the time the 1099-MISC form is filed the following January, the forwarding order has expired. When the envelope with the form is returned for a bad address, the event can show it attempted to meet its IRS obligation. Save the returned envelope.

Audits

Take the time to understand the difference between an audit and a certified audit. In my personal experience, if you want to find any improprieties, the event will need a certified audit to catch it. The event will pay more; but when working with volunteers, it provides an added security net.

The non-certified audit compiles a statement of assets, liabilities and fund balance, along with statements for revenue, expenses paid, cash flow and fund balance. As such, a Certified Public Accountant (CPA) is only able to work with the information provided. A certified audit "audits" these same items and performs the audit to obtain reasonable assurance about whether the financial statements are free from material misstatement.

When organizing an event, the Event Chairman and the Organizing Committee are held in the public's trust to do what they promised with the funds. A certified audit sweeps up after the event to make sure finances were handled appropriately. For more details, see PUBLIC RELATIONS AND PUBLICITY – It's Not What You Say; It's What It Looks Like.

State and Federal Income Tax

Yes, everyone gets to file and pay taxes whether or not a profit is made. Hopefully, your event has secured the services of a certified public accounting firm to compile the event's year-end financial statement comprised of a balance sheet and statement of operations. The firm may also handle the preparation and distribution of the Internal Revenue Service (IRS) required 1099-MISC forms, in addition to preparing the event's annual federal and state income tax return.

PCI Compliance

The event Treasurer should be aware of online credit card security requirements (PCI Compliance) because, if not within standards, your patrons' credit card data is at risk of being stolen; and the event's ability to process payments using credit cards is jeopardized.

The Payment Card Industry Security Standards Council (PCI SSC) (Go to: http://www.pcisecuritystandards.org) is responsible for the development, management, education and awareness of the PCI Security Standards, including the Data Security Standard (PCI DSS), Payment Application Data Security Standard (PA-DSS), and PIN Transaction Security (PTS) requirements.

According to ComplianceGuide.org, (Go to: https://www.pcicomplianceguide.org), the Payment Card Industry Data Security Standard (PCI DSS) is a set of requirements designed to ensure ALL companies process, store or transmit credit card information in a specific way in order to maintain a secure environment. Essentially, any merchant's server must comply or risk not being able to process payments online.

The PCI SSC was launched on September 7, 2006, to manage the ongoing evolution of the Payment Card Industry (PCI) security standards with focus on improving payment account security throughout the transaction process. The PCI DSS is administered and managed by the PCI SSC, an independent body that was created by the major payment card brands (Visa, MasterCard, American Express, Discover and JCB).

It is important to note that the payment brands and acquirers are responsible for enforcing compliance, not the PCI Council. Legitimate online ticketing services monitor PCI compliance requirements and bring themselves up to the standards because it affects the infrastructure of its entire operation.

PLACING A VALUE ON YOUR EVENT

Knowing your event makes a difference is important but how do you illustrate this? Writing a check from the event's proceeds and presenting it to your designated charity can serve this purpose. What if you want to include quantifiable data in a sponsor package or a grant proposal? Who can help and how can you accurately compute the affect your event has on the community?

If you are interested in determining your event's direct and indirect economic impact on your community, contact your local destination management organizations (DMOs) – chamber of commerce, convention and visitors bureau or state tourism agency. Many have an economic impact multiplier for leisure visitors, meetings and conventions and sporting events.

According to Destination Marketing Association International (DMAI), formerly the International Association of Convention and Visitors Bureaus, based in Washington, D.C., its Event Impact Calculator is considered an industry standard for measuring the economic value of an event and calculating its return on investment and local taxes. In October 2016, DMAI unveiled a special Festivals and Cultural Events module in response to requests to assess the highly valued festivals and cultural events sector.

In addition to the direct impact, an indirect multiplier also affects the local economy. This occurs when tourism dollars are spent by those working in the travel, tourism and hospitality industry and in turn re-spent by those where industry employees do business.

The multiplier is specific to your destination and can change each year. The formula involves the following information:

Day Visitor Personal Spending per Day
Event Spending per Day per Visitor

Overnight Visitor Personal Spending per Day
Event Spending per Day per Overnight Visitor

Average Stay (number of nights)
Attendance
Persons per Room (for the Entire Party)
Total Number of Day Visitors

Economic Impact Multiplier =

For a new event and even an established event, paying to access this calculator once a year can be quite expensive. Many convention and visitors bureaus already pay the licensing fee and may provide an affordable mechanism to determine the event's economic impact. A total of 10 data sources are utilized when calculating an event's economic impact on a community.

The event will need to provide to the DMAI's licensee the size of the event, number of days, the dates and type of event and, if available, costs tied to the event. When the event is unable to provide information, industry averages for the local area/city are used to compute the figures.

The Greater Philadelphia Cultural Alliance provides this Economic Impact Calculator for arts organizations. (Go to: https://www.philaculture.org/research/1624/economic-impact-calculator)

Marketing

An Event Chairman remarked, "When a Marketing Committee Chairman comes to the first book festival meeting and announces they want to re-vamp all the marketing materials, rein this person in quickly (unless you coaxed them to volunteer and assigned this task). Few events have a budget and the time to tackle this AND market the event. These kinds of folks normally move on before they can finish anything anyway."

If this is your first festival or event, the list of what needs to be done is endless. In essence, the Event Chairman is setting up a business. Besides their role, probably the two most important jobs at this stage fall on the shoulders of the Treasurer who will set up the financial framework and the Marketing Services Committee Chairman. This three-legged stool and the infrastructure each establishes will serve as the event's foundation.

ESTABLISHING THE EVENT'S BRAND IDENTITY

While the Event Chairman has established the organizational framework and is busy finding volunteers to serve on the Organizing Committee, the Marketing Services Committee Chairman is working closely with him or her to turn a sea of thoughts and ideas into the event's brand identity.

Organizers of first-time events are encouraged to develop a descriptive name for their event. Often such a name incorporates the destination's name and theme type. When seeing the name, most people will easily recognize where it is held and what the event is about. If at all possible, make it obvious beyond your city's borders and regional culture and customs. Avoid using a name that is too cute or clever and needs to be explained to the masses; unless, of course, your event is directed toward a niche market that understands these terms. If the name is not clear, it may not be a good choice. Research the proposed name in other common languages to make sure it translates well for your target demographics, too.

With the event name in place and a narrowed list of ideas about the event's identity, the Marketing Services Committee Chairman is ready to begin collaborating with a graphic designer or artist to develop the logo. Once the logo is approved and finalized, other marketing tools like stationery and the website can then be created.

While an inexpensive, no-frills logo design could be used, it's important that the event convey a professional, yet pleasing image. Anything less will pose challenges when soliciting sponsors. Would you give someone money with a proposal on a piece of paper without a logo, name, address, contact information or website?

If you desire to freshen your event's existing image, it may or may not include updating the name. The change may simply involve the logo. As before, once approved, the name and/or logo can be rolled out to all marketing tools and materials.

Stationery

The letterhead, envelopes, digital letterhead template, labels, etc., should include the event logo (which may be different from the logo for a given year), the office mailing and physical address if open for walk-in traffic (not the venue address), phone number and web address. Because the event's website should have a Contact Us mechanism, it is not necessary to include an email address.

Consistent Look

The Marketing Services Committee Chairman should work with a graphics designer to set the standard font style and size the Organizing Committee members should use when sending (email and non-email) correspondence. This may seem strange to dictate this, but consistency in presentation of the event's image is extremely important.

Make it easy on your volunteers. Send each a digital template of the letterhead, creating a sample document using the standard font style and size in the set-up.

Here's an example of why consistency is so important. Imagine the Event Chairman sending a sponsorship package to a sponsor in Times New Roman® 10 point font to squeeze everything on a few pages. The Sponsor Services Committee Chairman follows up with a letter and supporting material in Lucida® Calligraphy 12 point. Later, the Volunteer Services Committee reaches out with a form in Gill Sans® Pro Light 11 point. When the Marketing Services Committee needs to ask how many tee shirts are needed, they send their form in Arial® Standard Narrow Italic 12 point. What a mishmash of information! Maintaining consistency provides a cohesive, recognizable identity for the event.

Websites – General, Mobi, Responsive Design, Dynamically Generated or Served, Updating Content, Key Components

General

Many marketers today have been involved in building several generations of websites as electronic tools are constantly changing and evolving.

At one point, marketers and website creators thought it was best to include as much information as possible in a website. The goal was also to use as much movement as possible to show off your company, its products and services. Things have done an about-face and now, less is more. It's about having the right "less" available for your patrons.

Finding a website designer is easy. In some cases, the Marketing Services Committee Chairman may do a bit of arm-twisting with someone they know or work with, especially if the budget is thin. A member of the Organizing Committee may also have a local website design contact and bring them aboard.

If these aren't viable options, outsourcing can be arranged using online freelance services with providers from around the world. Users can select which countries and cultures they desire to use and narrow down potential candidates. A word of caution, avoid open bidding on your request for proposal (RFP) because you will be quickly deluged with providers who lack understanding of your language and offer services at $2 an hour.

With a bit of research, it's possible to locate designers outside the event's home country with a strong work ethic, clear understanding of your culture, and an exceptional portfolio at a reduced project or hourly rate. Regardless if local or outsourced, the Marketing Services Committee

Chairman will need to be available and accessible on a regular basis to respond to questions in order to keep the project on track. In addition to website design, many of these online service providers also have programmers available to handle special website coding needs.

If the event plans to use a Content Management System (CMS) but no one with the event is comfortable with setting it up, consider outsourcing the initial set-up once the theme is selected. Do not let someone tackle this who "thinks" they know how to do it because it will only result in a huge headache later. Your website is your most important marketing tool. For more details, see MARKETING – Websites – Updating Content.

For the greatest flexibility, consider a CMS website theme with tons of pre-set features – multiple home page designs – portfolios, blogs, shopping and magazine style; sliders and more sliders; header choices; pre-created pages with navigation bars; grid, column and text layouts; social media icons, etc. and evidence of regular updates.

Mobi

According to mobilemarketingmagazine.com, research suggests by 2019, there will be almost 200 billion mCommerce [mobile commerce] transactions a year, up from 72 billion in 2014.

According to a December 2014 report by Dr. Windsor Holden of Juniper Research, transactions by mobile phone and tablet users are expected to reach 195 billion a year within the next five years, with the highest growth rates expected in the NFC (Near Field Communication) (Go to: http://nfc-forum.org) sector, accelerated by the launch of ApplePay and upcoming solutions from banks based on Host Card Emulation (HCE) technology.

"Storefronts that have deployed carrier billing solutions have already seen positive results across a range of indicators – higher conversion rates, higher average transactions values, higher transactions volumes," said Dr. Windsor Holden. "For the first time, they can monetize consumers who would otherwise have been excluded either because they lacked a credit card or because they were unwilling to enter card details online."

The report also observed that many mobile ticketing services had seen rapid adoption rates following their launch, suggesting a pent-up demand for these kinds of services. In the U.S., New York Waterways' mobile ticket solution accounts for 25 percent of all sales less than two years after its launch, while the Massachusetts Bay Transportation Authority's mTicket service accounted for 15 percent of sales in under nine months.

This may not come as a surprise, but smartphone usage is up. Mary Meeker with Kleiner Perkins Caufield Byers is one to follow when it comes to Internet trends, including mobile phone usage. (Go to: http://www.kpcb.com/blog/2015-internet-trends.)

Since 1995 mobile phone users have grown from 1 percent to 73 percent of the population. Of the 5.2 billion users in 2014, 40 percent of those used smartphones while the balance used a feature phone.

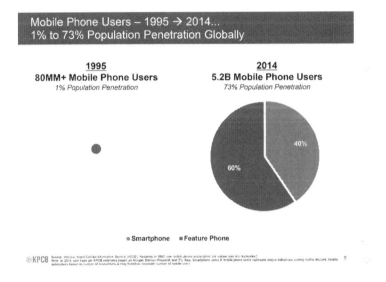

In 2008 Internet engagement was less than 1 percent and is now 11 percent year over year and mobile is at 3 hours per day per user in the USA.

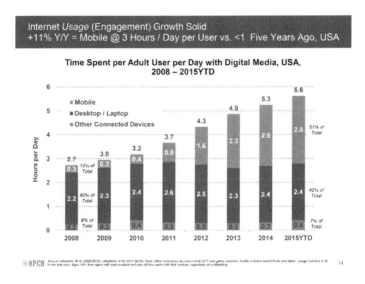

Internet impact for consumers is at 100 percent and 75 percent for businesses.

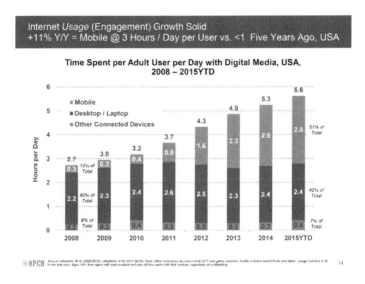

Since 1995 connectivity via the Internet has grown from 9 percent to 84 percent in the USA.

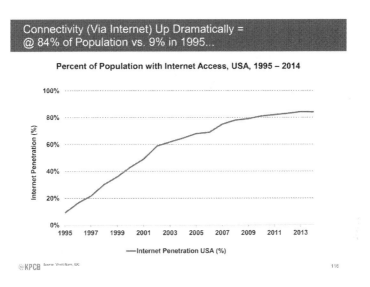

Since 2009 connectivity via mobile smartphones has grown from 18 percent to 64 percent in the USA.

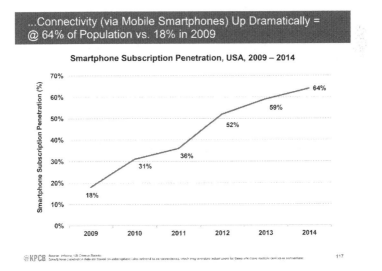

Since 1998 e-commerce has grown from 1 percent to 9 percent of retail sales in the USA.

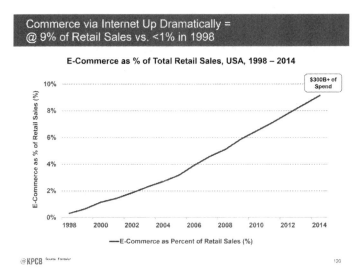

Percentage of cell phone owners who use the phone to perform at least one of the following activities in the USA.

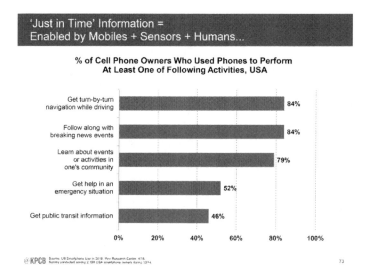

Responsive Design

The term "responsive design" has forced a new manner of thinking. Website design and navigation were simplified, automatically adjusting to the size of the device (desktop computer to smartphone and everything in between). Don't assume the back-end or programming is uncomplicated though. It can sometimes take a lot of effort to make something appear clean and simple.

If you're wondering if a website is responsive design, open one on your desktop and then narrow the viewing window. If responsive, you can see all the elements move to one side and stack on top of each other.

The predicament with a responsive design website is that it's rather difficult to illustrate how it will display without creating the website. Gone is the old-fashioned proofing step. The designer literally needs to set up three or four different page widths in final format for each different page layout – desktop computer and various sizes of tablets and smartphones.

The challenge with any type of design is it can be reviewed and/or approved by two different kinds of people who both say they are visual: those who need to see something to truly understand it and those who are visual and can envision what something will be like just by talking about it or staring at a blank sheet of paper. Clarify up front what type of visual persons are involved in the website approval process. It will save the website designer (and the event budget) from designing several websites.

It's always helpful if the key people involved in building a website find a handful of websites they like. However, they need to be VERY specific as to what they like. What some mean is they want your website to be the mirror image and function of another website. This tends to zap the creative juices of a website designer, but at least you know what pattern to follow.

For those who have experience in website development, they know how to help get the designer the answers needed. Ask the non-visual person to clarify more about the font, because they may not realize many different fonts are used for the headlines, sub-headers, body copy, photo captions, copy over photos and navigation bars. Colors and links are the same way. Do you want the link from the photo and also the words? That may require new coding from what was originally built. It would have been nice to know up front.

Start with a sit down meeting with a sample of all the "I like these websites" with the website designer, the Event Chairman and the Marketing Services Committee Chairman. Get everyone in the same room at the same time with cell phones in the "off" mode. It may be necessary to explain the "like sites" may be great but not a match to your event's experience and, therefore, difficult to match exactly although certain elements can be worked into the overall design.

Define expectations. This can only occur after the Marketing Services Committee Chairman has met with every other committee to talk through their individual needs. I say "meet" because it's much easier than being peppered with a thousand thoughts in multiple emails. The committee needs to have one cohesive list of everything they want, and a meeting provides the opportunity to explain why. In turn, the Marketing Services Committee Chairman can explain why this may or may not be possible. Every feature has a cost. Some elements may need to be put on the Phase II Website Update list.

In a perfect world, give one person (Marketing Services Committee Chairman) the responsibility and the authority to sign off on the website after all vested parties have had the chance to explain their respective needs. However, some Festival Chairmen suffer from lack of trust and/or lack of communication as to what they want in the website. Even though they say they give the responsibility and authority, a little string is attached.

How do you handle the perpetual "change" artist, especially when your website release date is quickly approaching? Remind them of the hard costs to the event to do change orders and advise those costs will be billed to the Event Chairman's discretionary account. The budget set by the Marketing Services Committee was estimated based on how the website was to be built, not for all the additional changes over the original quote.

Building a website is much like building a house with a set of architectural plans drawn that includes walls, plumbing, electricity, ductwork, location of various rooms – kitchen, bathroom, washer/dryer, etc., and the design elements (colors, cabinets, trim, flooring, etc.). As the contractor progresses through the construction of the house, if the owner decides to make changes, say to move the kitchen to another side of the house, there can be significant costs and delays. The same logic prevails with a website. You may believe the changes are minor, but each element has a cascading effect.

Dynamically Generated or Served

In October 2013, a major search engine announced search engine optimization (SEO) would take into consideration websites that were dynamically generated or served or were responsive design. In spring

2015, they drew the line in the sand and made good on its promise to impact (decrease) the volume of mobile traffic sent when a website was not dynamically generated or served for mobile or responsive design.

For those who try to tell you your website is broken because it is not responsive design, they may need to take a closer look. Some businesses responded to this new change by maintaining their standard website while creating a mobile version of the website, versus incurring the cost of a new responsive design site. Each dynamically generated or served website is sent the correctly adapted design to the appropriate device – mobile to mobile and a regular website to a desktop computer or laptop. In the end, this allowed the business not to pay for a complete re-design and to keep the search engine happy.

The drawback with responsive design is it does not always lend itself to displaying all website content. So the question is, "Is it better to toss out important elements just to develop a responsive design website, or would it be smarter to go with a dynamically generated or served website that allows important information to be retained?"

Updating Content

A seasoned marketer, a graphic designer and/or a front end developer can help set up the initial website, but it's important to realize that your website will have lots of moving arms and legs. Plan to budget for regular programming and content updates by a professional or create your website in a CMS (Content Management System) so the content can be updated internally.

Consider these CMS options – Squarespace®, Weebly®, or Wix. Each of these is a hosted service requiring your website be on their respective CMS server and a monthly fee is charged. WordPress and concrete5® work the same way – hosting and monthly fee – or the software theme can be purchased and installed elsewhere.

Some charge more for an upgraded version which allows the entire event website or data to be exported. The fees will vary depending on the design theme options. Some are much more flexible than others. A thoughtful decision making process when creating the website will assure numerous options are available at time of development as well as later.

Some CMSs have well-known names but dated technology. Of the numerous CMSs available, some are blogs. Do not confuse a blog with a website because they are different. If your website updates are minimal, you may prefer to have the website updated by a professional. A member of the Marketing Services Committee with requisite skill sets, and not just someone who wants to be a website designer or webmaster, may be able to make the updates. Anyone involved should have some basic understanding of website code and design if assigned this task.

More than once, I've witnessed a perfectly designed website destroyed by a well-intentioned individual with no design experience. Before long, the bones of the original site have disappeared and it now resembles something akin to desktop publishing quality work – clip art gone awry.

A website is your public image – your customer's first impression. If necessary, build some features into it that limit the amount of damage an individual can do. Use a preset number of fonts, in a limited color palette and with predefined font sizes. Those controls will help minimize changes.

Always, always, always maintain two levels of passwords and have an off-site back-up copy of your entire website to assure a disgruntled volunteer doesn't negatively impact your event or stop you from having access to your most important sales tool.

Watch, too, so that an event's domain name is timely renewed. When a volunteer moves on and the email address affiliated with the account is no longer valid, renewal notifications won't be received. For this reason use generic email addresses for the event. For more details, see MARKETING – Email Accounts.

Be wary of frequent mailings from slippery domain name registrars with which you have no business relationship. They will suggest it's time to renew when your registration is current and handled by a legitimate company.

Key Components

Each festival or event's website has key components: About Us, Event Schedule and Tickets, Sponsors, Visit, Directions, Shop and Contact Us.

A secondary level is for specific market segments: Related Events, News (Media), Volunteers, Concessions, Join the Mailing List, Donations, Social Media and a Privacy Statement.

Each Committee Chairman will need to be involved with their area's webpage. For instance:

> *About Us* – This section can include details about the event, the event Organizing Committee, the host or presenter of the event and/or the history of the event, or all of the above.

Event Schedule and Tickets – Publish your event calendar only after your talent – headliners, artists, speakers, musicians, pilots, performers, winemakers, authors, chefs, entertainers, brewmasters, etc. – has been contracted (signed and in writing). Tickets can go on sale immediately or at a future date. Your Entertainment Committee will be involved in this section of the site. Your Treasurer will be involved with ticket sales decisions. For more details, see MONEY MATTERS – How the Online Payment Processing Piece Works.

Sponsors – As quickly as your sponsors' agreements are executed, add their provided logos to the sponsor page with live links to their websites. Designate each sponsor's role by the size and placement of its logo or name. Make sure the event's contact information is included should someone be interested in learning more about sponsor opportunities.

Visit – While your event may be directed to the local community, it also has the ability to draw visitors from out of town. These patrons may need a place to stay, so this is the perfect place to include your official host hotel, official airline or nearby airports serving your community. If none are available, link to your destination management organizations (DMOs) – chamber of commerce, convention and visitors bureau or state tourism agency. Double check with your Sponsor Services Committee Chairman to make sure you're not leaving out a sponsor.

Directions – While so many people have mapping capability on their smartphones, this page should include not only a map of your event venue or location but also several paragraphs of written directions for those traveling from major nearby cities. The latter is for those without GPS mapping capability. Ask your Site Services Committee Chairman to confirm if any roads will be closed. If using an online map, the Marketing Services Committee may be able to add icons onto the map such as event location or venue and parking lots, decks and garages.

Shop – When you see the word "shop," the words "shopping cart" often come to mind. Remember some online ticketing services allow events to sell merchandise along with a ticket. With this in mind, you may be able to have one system support two needs – ticketing and merchandise sales. Involve both your Merchandise Committee Chairman who controls inventory, pricing, shipping and handling and your Treasurer who can address sales tax questions.

Contact Us – Does the thought of spam drive you crazy? It's possible to set up a Contact Us form incorporating a security check such as Captcha™. You know those fill-in fields where you have to enter letters or words shown in a photo or another where you move objects onto another object, for example, pizza toppings to the pizza, in order to submit an email or form.

Because many events are volunteer driven, it's easy for event history and communication to be lost. To compensate for this, set up a form on the website where the user can select, for example, from a drop-down menu where each inquiry should be routed. This removes a step from someone serving as the clearinghouse for all emails.

As a back up, you can have a second person, such as the event Secretary, be copied on every email. At each committee meeting, double check that all email inquiries or concerns have been handled. A programmer may be required to set up the form, but it will allow a "paper trail" should a volunteer disappear in the middle of the night and the Event Chairman need to re-construct committee activities.

A secondary level is geared toward more specific market segments:

Related Events – The more the merrier as they say. Some festivals require basic criteria be met in order to be a sanctioned event or to be included in a list of related events. If you have a volunteer serving as a liaison between these events, send them the schedule of events before it's published to assure no one is left out.

News (Media) – The media area provides information to the news media in a standard industry format. Some event websites require media inquiries to sign in or be reviewed to access information. Legitimate media should never balk at such a request, but only at the time delay it creates when on deadline. Many events make news releases readily available but then control access to the image library or require email requests for photos. The Public Relations and Publicity Committee should double check that all elements in this section are in place. This committee may also be enlisted to proof the entire website and make sure all links are functioning.

A wonderful programming feature, if you have the extra money, is to have custom code written which will generate a weekly email report. Its purpose is simple: indicate the page where a link is broken and list the bad link.

A helpful tool would be to create two unpublished or password protected webpages that require the specific website address to access. One page would contain the event logos and the other would contain all images available for outside use, plus B-roll footage. It's much quicker to send inquirers the links and/or user IDs and passwords than fill up outbound emails with logos and artwork.

Volunteers – Some individuals prefer to volunteer at an event rather than attend the event. This section will detail how volunteers sign up (with a mechanism to actually sign up), what areas need volunteers and when the pre-event meeting will be held. The Volunteer Services Committee should review and approve this page's content before going live. Some events set up an online registration sign-up form with reporting and data exporting features.

Concessions – Anyone and everyone interested in selling something at your event will come calling. Similar to the volunteer area, this page should detail the type of concessionaires permitted at the event – food, beverages, merchandise and miscellaneous items like glow sticks and balloons; licensing requirements; access to the application and required fees; as well as the date selected concessionaires will be announced. Some events set up an online registration sign-up form to collection applications and fees, and refund those not selected. Next year when it comes time to solicit concessions again, the contact information is readily available.

Frequently Asked Questions – Examples of types of questions here are: 1) Lost and Found – Indicate where it will be during the event as well as after the event is over; 2) First Aid – It sometimes is easier to sit in the crowd and check the event's website than it is to get up and walk through the crowd to find out an answer; and 3) General – Advise if coolers, pets and alcohol are permitted.

Join the Mailing List – If your event is in the process of gathering email addresses to send news and updates, these people need to opt-in. The federal CAN-SPAM Act prohibits mass emailing anyone without his or her consent. No valid reason exists to put your domain name at risk by being labeled as spam. Numerous email-marketing services are available at a fee. For more details, see MARKETING – Email Marketing.

Donations – Many online ticketing services allow donations. The event may want to use its existing system if it prefers to monitor a single system vs. multiple services. Because this is a financial matter, involve the event Treasurer in making decisions regarding donations.

Social Media – Some events incorporate Twitter feeds directly into their website while others simply link off of social media icons to the respective website. Make sure this opens in a new webpage to continue to keep the festival's website open. As a side note, some online ticketing services allow the event's online ticketing to integrate into the event's Facebook page, giving the event another sales outlet. Encourage your Marketing Services Committee to review how Twitter and Facebook will display on the event's website as social media feeds or icons.

Privacy Statement – Everyone includes the same basic lingo. Just make sure the Marketing Services Committee proofs this page and then adheres to what is stated.

The above covers the basic needs of just about every event. However, each event is unique. Some events may want to incorporate audio or video clips. Some may want to include newspaper clippings or the ability to take a customer satisfaction survey.

CONTROLLING YOUR ASSETS & YOUR MESSAGE

Passwords

For more details, see THE EVENT OFFICE – Passwords.

Voice Mail Recording

If event voice mails are picked up infrequently, the outgoing message should indicate when that occurs. Also suggest that if a response is not received within X days, to call back, indicate the best time to call and remind each caller to include their area code. It wouldn't be the first time incomplete information was provided, an audio file was difficult to understand or a phone message was lost.

The person picking up the messages should log them in and assign them to the Event Chairman or an Organizing Committee member to respond. The master list should be reviewed at each committee meeting to make sure everyone knows the answers and that callers received a response. When someone calls multiple times and no one has responded, it's a tip-off a volunteer is not doing his or her job.

Email Accounts

When an event has its own website, it has the ability to create emails using its domain name. It's smart to set up generic email accounts that can be forwarded to relevant volunteers and retained on the server. This will assure no one holds the event hostage when files aren't turned over. At least an email trail will allow the event to back into a part of a committee's activities.

If every major area has its own email address, so much the better:

sponsors@eventdomainname.com;
siteservices@eventdomainname.com;
entertainment@eventdomainname.com.

As time goes on, these may start to generate spam, and your tech guru can create new email addresses, if your spam filters aren't working. While your network administrator (IT) will have access to each of the addresses, have your event Secretary also maintain a copy in the files, so you know which email address forwards to whom. The event can also control the user IDs and passwords for maximum access.

Keeper of the Logo

Rightfully so, marketing and communications professionals work to assure the corporate image and message are consistent. As such, they can often be labeled as control freaks. I doubt it will bother them since they strive to assure the event speaks with one voice and to do so within the event's corporate brand standards.

Among the Marketing Services Committee's inventory is the event logo. They know the specific colors to use, the official font style and whether the horizontal or vertical version should be used. They normally have a variety of versions depending on the need – printing, web, presentations, email signatures, banners, full color or black and white.

Many marketers go to great lengths to ensure the corporate logo used on the website is not one that can easily be lifted (AKA stolen by anyone). If "borrowed" without express written permission, it will be easy to tell because the logo when embedded into the background can look odd.

When asked, the Marketing Services Committee is more than willing to share the event logo with sponsors and others with legitimate reasons.

In some cases, when a logo is provided to a third party, the Marketing Services Committee will require a production proof be provided so it can be approved prior to the final product being created. This committee's goal, after all, is to make sure the event is captured in the best light.

Here are two examples why an event wants to control who has its logo:

1. Event patrons often want a souvenir – a baseball cap, a tee shirt, a mug, a coffee cup, etc. The proceeds from those sales go to fund the event and, perhaps, go to scholarships. A street vendor who took the logo illegally and without permission, printed it on a tee shirt and is now selling it on the street corner. This takes money away from the event, putting it in the street vendor's pocket.

2. Individuals who sell professional football or baseball signature wear or college athletic gear all pay a licensing fee to the license holder for the right to reproduce the official logo within certain standards or face the wrath and financial penalties of their legal departments. As examples, the name of a U.S. national football championship event and the name of a major motion picture award ceremony are trademarked and cannot be used without permission of the owner.

Control freaks? You bet, but marketing professionals are responsible for protecting the rightful owner's logo or artwork from illegal use.

Trademarks/Service Marks/Registration Marks

Logos are the intellectual property of an event. Before a creative team develops the event's logo, the Event Chairman or Marketing Services

Committee Chairman should request the artist's rights be transferred or assigned to the event once approved and finalized. Make sure all usage rights, not just the reproduction rights are secured. When this happens, you can avoid re-negotiating rights each year and the need for ongoing payments. Buy or request all rights in perpetuity, allowing the event to use the logo at any time for any purpose. This should be done in writing. If notarized, this is all the better.

Just owning the logo isn't enough. Event organizers are urged to protect this property by securing a trademark (products) or service mark (event). These can initially be obtained by filing the proper paperwork with the appropriate agency in the state, typically for a lower fee than at the federal level (U.S. Patent and Trademark Office). For instance, in Florida and North Carolina, it's handled by the Secretary of State's Office. Successful applications have the right to then display the ™ (trademark) or ᔆᴹ (service mark) symbol behind the name or phrase.

To view a list of trademark offices by state, go to: http://www.uspto.gov/trademarks-getting-started/process-overview/state-trademark-information-links.

After or while the event is securing the state's trademark or service mark, apply with the U.S. Patent and Trademark Office (USPTO) (Go to: http://www.uspto.gov) to receive broader protection. The application and payment can be processed online with the fee normally higher than at the state level. National submissions require more research and investigative work. Be sure to apply for each appropriate category of use to protect the event's intellectual property. Successful marks bear the registered symbol (® – R in a circle in superscript) behind the name or phrase.

At the state or federal level, the mark will need to be renewed at some time in the future with the owners proving the logo is still in use.

SO YOU THINK YOU KNOW YOUR CUSTOMERS

Get To Know Your Customers. Survey Them Early On

After some research, the Marketing Services Committee will discover or reconfirm common denominators regarding the event. These will prove to be useful when making marketing decisions. This same information is also extremely helpful when soliciting sponsors. If your event is new, some of this data won't exist. To gather the information from the event's ticket holders or participants, a survey is required.

Just staring out into the crowd won't tell you the specific demographics: age, male/female, income level, type of cars driven, zip codes, etc. Know your target audience. Let them tell you who they are and what they like and dislike. Even if you don't have a research budget to do a formal survey, a very basic survey instrument can be prepped and analyzed. Take the time to have someone with marketing experience review the questions. You'll also want to make sure it's short in length but covers a range of questions or topics.

Be careful when using volunteers to solicit surveys taken at the event so the results aren't tainted. Small things can affect respondents. A volunteer wearing a sponsor's shirt with a logo and distributing a survey can subtly impact a respondent being asked to name sponsors.

These days fewer surveys may be taken using the walking around with clipboard approach. Instead, a survey taker may present a tablet or smartphone and ask respondents to touch the screen to answer questions. Younger guests will feel comfortable with technology; older patrons may beg off participating.

If your event is applying for any type of grant, this information is invaluable. More so, if the grant program is administered by a destination management organization (DMO) – chamber of commerce, convention and visitors bureau or state tourism agency. The survey results can also be incorporated into sponsorship packages as well as added to fact sheets for the media.

The Survey Instrument

Avoid leading survey questions, where respondents base their X decision upon a Y statement. Clean simple questions are best.

When asked to check one of the following, what is the correct order? The answer varies but the most important thing when using the Likert Scale is to use an odd number of responses, use the same items consistently and in the same order, unlike the example below which reverses the order, making it more difficult for a survey respondent to follow.

☐ Excellent   ☐ Very Good   ☐ Good   ☐ Fair   ☐ Poor

☐ Poor   ☐ Fair   ☐ Good   ☐ Very Good   ☐ Excellent

Can the tone of the word options drive more upbeat responses, especially when leading with the most positive word first? Yes, and that is why it's important to use a unipolar scale (measuring one dimension) of options that is balanced. In the example below, are the terms "superb" and "poor" exact opposites and equally balanced? No. The term "excellent" may be a better choice than "superb."

☐ Superb   ☐ Above Average   ☐ Average   ☐ Below Average   ☐ Poor

Online Surveys

Online survey systems make this a much simpler task nowadays. Realize if the system the event is using is free, there may be limitations to the number of questions that can be asked or the volume of data collected.

In all cases, make sure the questions, answers and reports can be exported and saved in a safe place. As your event grows and continues, you will want to compare responses from year to year. Make sure the questions are worded the same so the answers are apples to apples.

Include a link to a survey on your register receipts as well as on the event's website. When someone desires to express their opinion regarding the event, they may opt to take a survey or send an email using the Contact Us page of the website. Make stage announcements during your event to drive people to take the survey. Have an adequate number of surveys available to be taken and use a survey system with a server large enough to handle a rush of responses. If the reports allow you to pull a date and time stamp, it will be easy to see if your respondents were in attendance when the survey was taken.

Summarizing Survey Results

Here are two different examples showing how data can be summarized:

Attendees Summary Option 1

Utilizing information obtained from a representative sampling of the 20XX audience, it was determined XX percent of the attendees reside in or around the greater [City Name] area. There were attendees from every city in the [County Name] and more than XX percent from [a nearby large city]. Another XX percent reside in [list major cities and nearby counties].

Almost X percent came from other [state] counties or from out of state.

Just over XX percent were ages 22-35 with XX percent ages 36-54 and XX percent were 54 and older. Over XX percent of the audience attended at least X days and nearly XX percent attended all X days. Over X percent had attended an [Event Name] in the past and virtually every survey participant stated they planned to attend in the future.

Attendees Summary Option 2

Official survey results portrayed the average [Event Name] attendee as young, upwardly mobile and very happy with the X-day event.

The average person attended the event X.XX times in 20XX with XX percent in the XX-XX age bracket. X percent of the attendees of the total earned between $XX,XXX and $XX,XXX. Most importantly, XX percent of those polled thought the [insert event theme type] program was above average to excellent. Even parking seemed to leave the crowd undaunted with XX percent of the total rating available parking spaces as above average.

The survey was prepared and distributed by XYZ Company, a corporate sponsor, randomly polled X,XXX people attending the event.

TAKING ADVANTAGE OF EVERY OPPORTUNITY

Valuable, Valuable Airtime

Your stage – be it for a cooking competition, a wine demonstration, a panel of speakers or entertainers – provides an Event Organizer valuable airtime to promote absolutely anything you want because you control the microphone.

And while this may seem like a tedious process, in order to assure that every event sponsor receives fair and equitable air time, employ someone – preferably one of your public relations volunteers – to script the commercial stage breaks every day of your event from start to finish.

When you delegate the responsibility, give very specific instructions as to the style or tone you would like – professional yet casual, fun, short on private jokes and spoken in terms those from outside the area will understand. Avoid using very local terms to describe things.

For instance, if you are going to say "on the beach," do you mean on a particular stretch of sand or on an island with the word beach in the name? If you were to say "West End's own XYZ Company," is that a place? Is it better to provide a descriptor before it like, "Just west of downtown [city name], in the West End neighborhood is XYZ Company"? Whenever possible, be inclusive and recognize that the announcer may need to set the stage as to how something [West End] fits into the whole [west of downtown [city name]].

It's not unusual for a four-day event or festival to have a 10-page, single spaced script.

If you're lucky enough to have a radio station's on-air personalities (OAP) to handle this awesome task, welcome them with open arms. They should feel comfortable with the overall framework and know how to ad lib when necessary. For instance, you can't do an event at the same time as a major sporting event and not interject the scores or comment about a perfect full moon rising in the sky.

Providing the event's details to an OAP helps them fill the air. Provide cues too, for example, "Let's thank all of our wonderful sponsors who make this event possible." [CUE: point to logos and names on a banner above the stage]. Include content like:

- Highlights of the entertainment schedule.

- Background on upcoming artists and if this is talent's repeat visit.

- List the sponsors (and if necessary, phonetically spell out the names). If you want to know who's not from the area, just ask an OAP to pronounce Cape Girardeau or Reynolda or Buena Vista. Some computerized voice mapping systems used on smartphones and in vehicles get close sometimes, but in other instances, the pronunciations are laughable.

- An introduction of the artist or finalist who designed this year's poster.

- A special sponsor anniversary.

- Presentation of a fake sponsorship check as the real one was cashed months ago.

- Introduction of elected officials and sponsors for formal presentations by the Event Chairman.

- Brief bios on the talent – headliners, artists, speakers, musicians, pilots, performers, winemakers, authors, chefs, entertainers, brewmasters, etc.

- Pushing merchandise sales. Nothing better than the OAP modeling a snazzy signature [Event Name] tee shirt and encouraging others to buy one, too. [CUE: point to tee shirt and then the merchandise booth].

- Tease upcoming related events – children's programs, the next day's line up, etc.

- Housekeeping items, for example, lost and found location, where to go for medical assistance, general direction of the port-o-lets, reminder no audio recordings, ask assistance with trash pick-up at the end of each day.

- Promotion of the concessionaires and a mention of specific items and vendors [CUE: point to the concession tent].

- Referencing related events – How many of you attended the children's library program yesterday?

Promotional Materials for VIPs

While your Merchandise Committee members may assume 100 percent of the posters and tee shirts will be available for retail sales and budgets revenue accordingly, get ready to break their hearts. A certain number of items need to be used for promotion, goodwill and politics. It's a cost of business and the cost should be expensed to the respective committee.

It may be less expensive to do a small run of fliers or posters on a less expensive paper stock for posting in store windows. This reduces the chances they will be stolen before the event.

You can't ask your event talent – headliners, artists, speakers, musicians, pilots, performers, winemakers, authors, chefs, entertainers, brewmasters, etc. – to sign multiple copies of the event poster and then not give them one, especially since it features their name. What's the worst thing that can happen? They might frame the poster and hang it at home for family and friends to see. Make transporting each gift easy by providing a well constructed mailing tube if giving a poster to your talent. Don't be surprised if the event is asked to drop it in the mail for them though. Smile and say, "No problem."

The Media

If you want to have your local newspaper feature the event's artwork, providing a copy of the poster in paper or digital format makes that much more possible. If paper, avoid rolling it if you can. Hand carry it between two pieces of corrugated cardboard. Yours is not to question what happens to it after the fact.

While the ethics clause of most major newspapers prohibits its reporting staff from accepting gifts, don't be surprised if some "expect" to receive a poster and a tee shirt and will be so bold as to ask. Sadly, this will put the event in a precarious situation. You're darned if you do and darned if you don't. You'll be able to tell rather quickly who are legitimate reporters by how they handle things.

You may need to play a little game, indicating you are aware they aren't allowed to accept anything, and should a bag containing a poster and a tee shirt disappear later, you'll be left scratching your head wondering where you might have placed it.

Sponsors

For more details, see examples after SPONSORS – The Difference Between a Sponsorship Package and a Contract.

Other Organizations and Elected Officials

Any number of organizations can assist the event. Throughout the course of the year, you'll know who made life easier for the Event Chairman and Organizing Committee. Sometimes, the office receptionist or administrative assistant was more helpful than the boss. If your list only includes the bigwigs, you do not understand how things really work.

This list may include:

- Destination management organizations (DMO) – chamber of commerce, convention and visitors bureau or state tourism agency;

- Local and state arts councils or agencies;

- Local economic development council; and

- Elected city and county officials, city and county managers and select department heads.

One final group of people should receive a framed poster. These are your elected state and federal officials – state representatives, members of the House of Representatives, state senators and U.S. senators. This is done for two important reasons:

1. Providing each has an office at the state capitol or in the local community, they host numerous community leaders and citizens stopping by or coming for meetings. The poster hanging on their wall indicates support of the event.

2. This will come in especially handy when the event submits a grant application from a state agency and elected officials are contacted to ask for support or background information.

Event Photographers/Videographers

Thank goodness this is the digital age and the days of processing film are long gone.

Have the Event Chairman, Sponsor Services Committee Chairman and Marketing Services Committee Chairman sit together and develop an initial photo assignment list based on their individual needs.

You'll most likely want to focus on three different areas: high-resolution results, low resolution/social media needs and video.

High Resolution Images for Print

These images are for long-term needs but can be converted to low-resolution files after the event if needed. The assignment or shoot list appears to take the photographer in multiple directions at the same time.

Shoot List:

- Will be part of a post-event, sponsor wrap-up booklet which will showcase key media coverage and images of each sponsor and its employees – volunteering, sporting sponsor shirts, accepting framed posters, participating in on-stage presentation and mingling in the Sponsor VIP Hospitality Tent with talent.

- Will be used to create gifts for the Event Chairman to give to each member of the Organizing Committee – capture members with crowds in the backgrounds, members interacting with fellow members and general volunteers.

- Will be used for historical purposes and possibly as a gift from the Event Chairman – a group photo of the Organizing Committee at the beginning of the last day. Gone are the opening day jitters, unexpected surprises and distractions. With a good night's rest, everyone should be refreshed and ready to go. Take plenty of shots to compensate for closed eyes. If a one-day event, consider taking the photo at the all-volunteer meeting prior to the event.

- Include close-ups of the crowd – standing, sitting, sampling, drinking, pouring, eating, dancing, watching the sky, etc.

- Include crowd photos shooting from various angles during the daytime, at sunset and after dark, for example, from the back of the venue through the crowd to the main stage and from the back of the stage through talent into the crowd.

- Include talent but be mindful that the photographer, as working media, has a media pass but no escort. The Stage Manager's rules apply to this photographer, too. For more detailed, see PUBLIC RELATIONS AND PUBLICITY – Media Instructions.

- Include photos of the event set-up – tents, port-o-lets, concessions, fencing and barricades, health inspections, etc.

- Include merchandise sales (avoiding cash handling photos), concessionaires, event workers, concessionaire menus, patrons purchasing merchandise and product shots like tee shirts and posters.

- Include shots of the sound and lighting crew in action, the stage crew, chefs preparing dishes, airplanes being inspected before flight, piano tuners, gas grills, trash pick-up, security gates, volunteers in the parking lots, etc.

- Include beauty shots – close-up of food, musical instruments, wine glasses, beer bottles or tappers – which may be used to transition from one shot to another in a video.

This photographer will also capture grip and grin photo ops at events like the poster unveiling, as well as photos to be sent with news releases, for example, hotel and airline representative news release announcing their sponsorships.

Ask the photographer to keep a reporter notebook handy to identify (left to right) individuals with correct spellings and company affiliations, if appropriate.

Low Resolution Images for the Web and Social Media

These images are needed for the short term and will be used to tease the event on social media. A Public Relations and Publicity Committee member can use a camera phone and almost like a shadow, they can follow the high-resolution photographer.

This same committee member should have loaded into their smartphone address book the contact information for each sponsor and concession social media support personnel. Upload the image to social media and then forward a copy to the appropriate sponsor counterpart to also upload to social media or make them aware of your post or tweet.

Videos

Before sending your videographer off and running, decide where you want to use the video footage. Your goal may be to add footage to your video and B-roll library or to add some atmosphere videos to your website, social media video sites or Facebook.

Footage for the sake of footage just means it will require considerable energy on someone's part to sift through the end results. Don't do it.

It's more efficient to write two 30-second spots with specific audio and video cues. The shot list is clear and set. By doing this, the videographer can spend quality time focusing on specific areas, netting better quality results versus shooting a lot of everything. Too much is just too much. This also allows them the ability to shoot at the time of day when lighting is optimum.

Negotiating Usage Rights – Photography and Video

The moment someone snaps a photo or shoots some video, they own it. It's copyright law. Exceptions to this rule are when someone "works for hire" and the company owns the work or copyright.

When volunteers take photos or videos for an event, there may not be a formal contract/agreement or paper trail. Your Public Relations and Publicity Committee Chairman should negotiate these rights in advance. Strive for the broadest rights possible. Ask for unlimited usage and full reproduction rights.

If at all possible, avoid negotiations where the event needs to return year after year to pay the photographer and/or videographer a fee to license usage for another time period for an additional sum of money. Once agreed upon, have the Public Relations and Publicity Committee Chairman initiate a brief contract/agreement clearly defining who owns what, how it can be used, how it can be credited and urge the photographer or videographer to add their information into the profile of each digital file. Give the photographer or videographer two copies of the contract/agreement – one to sign and return and one to keep.

As a general statement, it's best to ask that any still photography and video footage be treated as non-editorial. This allows the event to use it for editorial purposes as well as in advertising (non-editorial). In taking a non-editorial approach, ask the photographer and/or videographer to avoid featuring brand names – wine labels, beer labels, music equipment names – unless the event has the written approval in advance of the trademark, service mark or registered owner.

Many companies welcome the additional publicity; however, some desire control so their product is reflected in a favorable light. The perfect video clip or image may not be usable because brand names are prominently displayed in an image or footage and permission to use it cannot be granted. You can try after the fact but don't expect any guarantees.

If the event has secured unlimited usage and full reproduction rights of non-editorial photos and footage but would like to take it step further – because an image or footage has become your signature shot or clip – attempt one more round of negotiation for a fee or no fee. See if the copyright owner is willing to assign or transfer copyright of the work to the event. If this is the original author, offer to pay the assignment or transfer of copyright fee and prep the appropriate form (copyright owner's signature required) to have the image/clip officially recorded with the Library of

Congress. (Go to: http://www.copyright.gov.) If the event is the owner, process the same paperwork and submit with the appropriate fee.

While the Public Relations and Publicity Committee can control usage originally, many years and Organizing Committee members later, it will be difficult to guarantee usage rights will continue to be protected. When volunteers drive an event, usage right details have a tendency to get lost from year to year. Alternately, volunteers may not understand copyrights and the implications when used incorrectly. Below is an example of how copyright credits should be displayed with a photograph:

© 20XX, [Photographer Name], Provided Courtesy of [Event Name].

© = copyright. The year is the year the footage/image was taken. The photographer or videographer's name is provided as detailed on the negotiated contract/agreement. The event, as provider of the image, is then given credit for providing the image.

Here's an example of how quickly an event's copyright agreement can go off the rails. The event photographer gave the event his copyright-owned image to use. It was discovered in a local publication but credited to another photographer as the photographer. The image owner contacted the publication and asked the error be corrected next issue. Expecting an apology, the staff member instead said, "How do you think the other photographer will feel if his name is taken off the credit?" In the spirit of no good deed goes unpunished, take the extra step and ask your photographer to enter copyright ownership details in the profile of each digital file. For more details, see PUBLIC RELATIONS AND PUBLICITY – Toolkit – Image Library.

It is possible to copyright a collection or group of images with the Library of Congress. As such, all the images for a given year can be copyrighted by a photographer or the event at one time. In doing so, an entire collection can be assigned or transferred to the event by the author/photographer.

Email Marketing

If your Marketing Services Committee is interested in gathering names and email addresses to send news and updates, a simple email subscribe form should be set up on the event's website. This allows fans the ability to opt-in and agree to receive event information.

As a reminder, the federal CAN-SPAM Act prohibits mass emailing anyone without his or her consent. No valid reason exists to put your domain name at risk by being labeled as spam.

Numerous email-marketing services are available. When reviewing all the options available, take into consideration the event's total monthly costs based on the following:

- Is the event limited by the number of emails it can send?

- Is the event billed each month based on a not-to-exceed contact list count? Can it be increased over time? How much?

- Who owns the list once collected?

- Can the lists be downloaded or exported?

- Can the email HTML files be copied out?

- What type of reporting is available?

- Does the system automatically delete a bad email address after X attempts or emails sent?

- Is a contract required or can the event pay month-to-month?

What appears to be an inexpensive service can eventually become quite costly. Do you start with one service knowing it is currently cheap but move to another service later once the list grows? If yes, make a tickler on the event office calendar to note which year to review costs.

Advertising

If your event is new or fairly young, the advertising budget may be very small. While sponsor cash contributions may be the most welcome, never underestimate the importance of a contribution of cash and in-kind dollars especially when it comes as part of a newspaper or radio sponsorship. Each can provide invaluable exposure for the event.

Hold two newspaper ads to run post event:

1. A thank you to all of the sponsors, combining it with one last attempt to sell merchandise in an effort to decrease inventory and

add a few more dollars to the event coffers.

2. A Thanksgiving Day ad, assuming merchandise is available and popular, can encourage the purchase of event signature wear and memorabilia as holiday gifts.

Public Relations and Publicity

As the old saying goes, your most important job is in finding your replacement. This held true for a volunteer rising from Publicity Committee Chairman to Event Chairman. Unfortunately, the replacement individual's background was in publicity for the manufacturing industry. The Event Chairman wondered why the arts, entertainment and weekend reporters weren't responding to news releases as they'd done in the past. Apparently he used his own local media list instead of the event's list when news releases were distributed. The business and industry columnist upon receiving the releases was confused and threw them away.

In another example, a "Taste of" Organizing Committee member brought forth a co-worker who volunteered to handle the writing and distribution of the event's new releases. Her credentials and background indicated she should be quite capable. Because no arm-twisting was involved in securing this volunteer, it seemed odd that emails weren't being returned, she wasn't attending monthly meetings and things weren't being handled in a timely manner.

After some awkward conversation, the Publicity Committee Chairman agreed her plate was too full and resigned. Backed into the corner with no time to find a replacement, the Event Chairman pulled out the prior year's news releases, changed a few dates and updated the contact information to her new event title. She then asked another volunteer to distribute the releases to the list she previously used. Volunteer workers should lessen the role of the Event Chairman rather than create additional burdens.

Working alongside the Marketing Services Committee, the Public Relations and Publicity Committee now begins to plan. They play a two-prong role: to create a plan of action to promote the event and to be prepared to react to any and every scenario to keep the event in a positive light.

IT'S NOT PRETTY BUT SOMEONE'S GOT TO DO IT

Unofficial Moral Compass

Normally, a relationship will already exist between the Event Chairman and the Public Relations and Publicity Committee Chairman. This person will have accepted the public relations volunteer position knowing they have been given the latitude to bring uncomfortable topics to the table. Without that authority, it's difficult to do their job. They will bring sticky situations to the Event Chairman, such as illustrating why an innocent gesture creates a conflict of interest or explaining why a secondary tier sponsor's package has more value than a major sponsor who is paying big bucks. It won't just be dump and run; suggestions on how to resolve will also be made. Additionally, they will play devil's advocate and move any discussion six moves forward on the chessboard to see positive and negative implications.

Saying No

Your Public Relations and Publicity Committee Chairman should have a unique combination of talents and skills. They appear to be able to say no to anyone, including their own mother. After breaking bad news, people thank them for speaking with them. This person is full of insightful information regarding local laws, facts, ordinances, data and trivia and uses this information to save the offending party from doing something illegal or not allowed.

For instance, when a politician calls the same Event Chairman they helped secure a grant for the event to ask if they can hand out re-election fliers during the event, Mr. or Ms. Public Relations and Publicity Committee Chairman is the person to take that call. If someone manages to get into the event venue and is now selling glow-in-the-dark sticks, let them have a go at the vendor. Your local entertainment reporter, who was last seen illegally recording the talent, may need this person to tap him or her on the shoulder and remind them their own publication is a stickler about not having its copyrights violated.

Handling Uncomfortable Things

The Public Relations and Publicity Committee Chairman is the go-to guy or gal for any number of jobs many consider uncomfortable. They are the person who can slide up to a major sponsor just before an on-stage presentation and alert them and their staff to a potentially embarrassing situation and explain how it can be remedied. Afterward, they will slip into oblivion having diverted a potential crisis. It's all in a day's job and nothing seems to surprise this person.

They will also be out front reminding the Event Chairman to schedule a meeting each event day to address issues and concerns for the benefit and awareness of the entire Organizing Committee.

GETTING THE WORD OUT – TRADITIONALLY, AND VIA THE INTERNET AND SOCIAL MEDIA

Keeping The Public and Distribution Channels Informed

This has certainly changed since social media came on the scene. While this is one avenue to keep your information current, remember other, more traditional channels need to be kept informed, too.

These could also be called influencers or portals. If you can determine the majority of organizations that interested event-goers could contact, those are the ones the event needs to keep informed – any place that potentially could field consumer and media inquiries about the event or has a website which mentions, lists or showcases your event.

Not everyone automatically thinks about performing an online search for "fun event in anytime city in October" on websites like DuckDuckGo (a search engine that protects its user's privacy and doesn't profile its users and then feed ads accordingly). Not everyone will know the name or city. Case in point: a neighbor was telling us about her vacation in Pepsicola, Fla. (AKA Pensacola to others).

The Pareto Principle, named for Vilfredo Pareto, an Italian economist, also known as the "80/20 rule," applies. The Public Relations and Publicity Committee should be able to identify the influencers or portals used by 80 percent of your potential customers. Spend 20 percent of your energies keeping that information up-to-date or keeping them informed.

Before deciding to spend 80 percent of your time to find the other influencers and places the remaining 20 percent of your potential customers will use to learn more about your event, ask yourself this, "Could I contact a local college or university to see if it offers internships for communications, marketing or hospitality majors?" If the answer is yes, an intern may be a viable resource to help track down the remaining 20 percent.

Realize an internship needs to be a two-way street: a learning environment for an intern in exchange for slogging through time consuming tasks. For it to be truly beneficial to both parties, an intern needs to be managed, monitored, encouraged and given feedback. If you're thinking it's an opportunity to dump a time-intensive project and run to your next project deadline, an intern probably is not what you need.

To assist your influencers and portals, create and distribute to them a simple fact sheet that covers the event's basics. It's important to include the names and contact information for key members of the Organizing Committee. No sense in directing callers to the main event phone number where messages are left on an answering machine for days at a time. The shortest distance between two points puts the inquirer directly in front of the right person the first time.

When building a fact sheet, think about all the places people could call and why. For instance, when vendors and concessionaires know an event is held in a city park, they're likely to call the city or county's parks and recreation department wanting to know who to contact to be a vendor. Local bands wanting to perform may contact the same department or a past sponsor's public relations department. A large company targeting expansion in an area but having no local office, may be interested in learning more about sponsorship. It reaches out to the local chamber of commerce to see who is organizing the event. Media from outside the area may call City Hall to ask who the Event Chairman is for a news story. General consumer inquiries about the event most likely will contact the chamber of commerce or the convention and visitors bureau.

The basic fact sheet should also contain answers to who, what, where, when, why and how. List common questions and answers like:

- Can I bring a cooler?

- Where are handicap parking, seating and restrooms located?

- What food is being served?

- Who are the entertainers?

- Can I distribute fliers?

- Can I bring lawn chairs?

- What time does the sun set?

- Can I bring my dog?

Every member of the Organizing Committee should also be provided a copy of the fact sheet, and when a question comes up multiple times, it should be added to the Q&A section.

The Media

The ultimate goal is to get positive news coverage – an article, a TV story, a blog mention, etc. However, you can't discount the secondary value received when a news release is sent out to the media by a news distribution service, email or postal mail and links to your website are included in the resulting coverage. Each link gained from a quality source will positively impact your website's search engine optimization (SEO) and should help in improving your event's search rankings.

A local media list maintained in a spreadsheet should never be considered a waste of time. While generating such a list, make sure to include the email address for each contact. If no address is available and you'll need to submit information using a Contact Us form, make a note of that. If you plan to do a special event, such as a poster unveiling, it will be helpful to have the mailing address ready to send a formal invitation to the media.

A bit of a challenge exists nowadays when trying to determine the best way to write a news release. Do you follow a traditional news release format or do you use one with a shocking sensational headline to garner attention?

Ignore all the crazy off-the-wall suggestions. Pull out that old textbook that explains how to write a traditional news release. Read it and follow the tried and true. The news release audiences you are speaking to are real journalists. Speak to them in their language. If they are good at what they do, they can tell the difference between something that is news worthy and something that is filled with superlative nothingness.

Shoot straight with journalists and you will earn their respect and trust for not wasting their time.

Don't ever get too comfortable with a journalist because it is difficult to know which hat they are wearing – friendly business associate or reporter. Here's why – after months of not officially naming the next Event Chairman, the local reporter called and said, "Congratulations, Mrs. X, on being named the Event Chairman." Being polite, the person replied, "Thank you." The rumor was now confirmed by an authorized source. The story ran in the next day's newspaper.

Exclusivity and Scoops

If your community is home to two competing newspapers and one is a sponsor (expecting to get first dibs on the event's news), don't expect the non-sponsor newspaper to give the event much ink, especially if the event scoops news to the sponsor. It's best to give everyone fair and equal access to each news release at the same time. While there can be no guarantees, most newspapers will honor the release date.

Exclusivity situations can backfire. Without the threat of someone else covering it first, the urgency can fade or importance of coverage wane.

If a daily and/or a weekly serve your community, schedule releases to play to each. For instance, Thursday weeklies may have a Monday noon deadline while a daily works one-day prior. Distributing a release on a Monday morning can result in Thursday coverage by the weekly and Tuesday or Wednesday coverage by the daily.

News Releases

Much can be explained about news releases, and the topic is worthy of a book of its own. A news release in its simplest form has seven main parts.

1. Release date – This is when the release can be published. In many cases, these words will appear on the top portion of the page: "For Immediate Release" or "For Release on: Day of the Week, Month Date, 20XX." In some cases, a specific time is listed followed by an abbreviation of the time zone. Most legitimate media should honor this date and time.

2. Subject line – Keep it informative, factual, without subjective adjectives and to the point. Tease the reader to want more. Keep it to one line or two at most. The second line can serve as the sub-header. Use upper and lower case text. For more details, see PUBLIC RELATIONS AND PUBLICITY – News Release Topics.

3. The dateline features the city and state (location) of the news story and the date of the release or the date the release is intended to be made public and reinforces item #1 above. This information appears in the first portion of the opening paragraph.

4. The body of the news release is much like an inverted pyramid. In the opening paragraph, explain in an overview or summary – who, what, where, when, why and how about the news release topic. Like the headline, this copy needs to be engaging enough to make the reader want more. Additional paragraphs should support the subject line and opening paragraph. The copy is double-spaced for ease in reading and editing.

5. The closing paragraph is a summary statement about the organization presenting the news. Realize when space is an issue, copy is normally cut from the bottom up.

6. Media industry language signals when a release continues to a new page or when it ends. If a release has more than one page, insert " -more- " centered at the bottom of the page. On the top of the next (continued) page in the upper left corner, the first line displays "Add One" or "2-2-2." A single spaced second line with an abbreviated version of the subject line follows this. All releases end with " # # # " centered at the bottom of the page or the last page of the release.

7. The contact information is contained at the top if being mailed or emailed to local media and at the bottom when sent via a news distribution service. When possible, provide a name, title, phone number and email address. For more details, see PUBLIC RELATIONS AND PUBLICITY – News Distribution Services.

Note: the quote marks shown above are for purposes of this example only.

News releases are printed on an event's letterhead or digital letterhead template but can be flowed into the body of an email, too. If sent by email, please feature a short summary teaser paragraph above the release. At the very bottom, include a list of social media platforms the event maintains with a link to each.

News Release Topics

Any number of news releases will be written and sent to the media – referring to traditional print media, radio and TV stations, as well as bloggers. This information will also be distributed to the event's social media handler and added to the various social media platforms in their respective formats.

Your news releases, once approved and distributed, should also be provided to the person overseeing the event's social media. NEVER let the event's social media contact scoop your official announcements. It's bad form.

Below is a list of possible news release topics:

Mark Your Calendar for [Month Date or Date Range], 20XX for the Xth Annual* [Event Name]

Bob Jones Named Honorary Chairman of the Xth Annual* [Event Name]

Note: First-time events are not annual. They only become annual in the second year, unless an event is held every other year and then the event is held biennially. First-time events are often described as inaugural events.

[Name] to Headline the Xth Annual* [Event Name]

[Name] Brought Back by Popular Demand

Best Selling Author [Name] to Speak at the Xth Annual* [Event Name]

Author of Book Title Announced as Keynote Speaker at the Xth Annual* [Event Name]

Award-Winning Chef [Name] to Demonstrate How to XXXXX

Craft Beer Competition to Feature X, Y and Z

Award-Winning Winemakers to be Showcased at Xth Annual* [Event Name]

Bonded Wineries in XYZ Region Invited to Enter Wine Competition

BBQ Champs Return to Compete for Title

Design Contest Announced for Xth Annual* [Event Name] Poster

[Name], [Name] and [Name] to Judge Wines at the Xth Annual* [Event Name]

Downtown Kick-Off Party Slated for [Day of the Week, Month Date]

[Name] to Headline [Day of the Week] Night at the Xth Annual* [Event Name]

Complete Line-up Announced for the Xth Annual* [Event Name]

Music Lovers Mark Your Calendar for the Xth Annual* [Event Name]

Xth Annual* [Event Name] Poster Unveiled

[Event Name] Tickets Now On Sale

Discount Tickets Now on Sale Until [Day of the Week, Month Day]

Tickets for the Xth Annual* [Event Name] Now on Sale Online

Call for Volunteers for Xth Annual* [Event Name]

Xth Annual* [Event Name] Is Free Thanks to Sponsors

Children's Activities Added to [Event Name] Line-Up

Proceeds from the Xth Annual* [Event Name] to Benefit Scholarships

[Event Name] Sizzles with Saucy and Spicy Food

[Event Name] Mixes Great Food with [Style of Music]

After-Hours Jam Sessions Announced

Scholarship Winners Announced

Related Events to Round Out Xth Annual* [Event Name]

Wine Competition Medalists Announced for Xth Annual* [Event Name]

Diners & Judges to Select Winners

Brewery Tours Added to Craft Beer Competition Schedule

Parking Readily Available for the Xth Annual* [Event Name]

Note: Attach a map with the number of spaces noted for each parking lot, deck or garage.

Host Hotel Packages Now Available

A Perfect Combination – [Destination's Assets] with [Event Name]

Beer Festival Announces Musical Acts

Applications Now Available for Food Vendors and Exhibitors

Cooking Contest to Showcase Local Products

You can announce each sponsor as it is contracted and include it in your news release closing paragraph; however, the news will likely only be "picked up" (AKA printed or used) by the event and in the sponsor's in-house publications or blogs.

News Distribution Services

I like news distribution services for a number of reasons. It is a very time efficient, cost effective mechanism when an event wants to communicate with a large number of media outlets. These services allow the user to target distribution to specific geographic areas, categories of interest and types of media (print, radio, television, bloggers, etc.). Many recipients of the release automatically post it online providing a link to the event's website which can aid in its ranking on search engines.

It's important the Public Relations and Publicity Committee Chairman set realistic expectations for the type of news coverage the event may receive. If the Event Chairman and Organizing Committee are expecting immediate guaranteed results, those are called ads.

If the event is new, short of budget, building a reputation and primarily wants to draw a local or regional audience, it may make more sense for your Public Relations and Publicity Committee Chairman to forgo a news distribution service and, instead, using an existing media list they already maintain. Update the list to meet the event's needs, then work professional or personal contacts – phone, email or drop off news releases.

A number of news distribution services are available. PR Newswire (Go to: http://www.prnewswire.com) is one, as well as PR Web (Go to: http://www.prweb.com) and e releases (Go to: http://www.erelcases.com).

Most news distribution services have distribution categories across the country when what you may really want and need is a specific media distribution category such as jazz radio stations but only within your local area or region. Why pay the extra money to reach national distribution when you only want to reach a handful? In those cases, you may select the "local" news service distribution category, but then postal mail (or email, if you have an existing relationship) a single news release to your genre-specific radio stations. Why pay for full category distribution when you only want to reach one or two media outlets in that category?

For privacy sake, if your release will be distributed by a news service and be posted on the Internet, you may want to use the main phone number knowing someone will answer in a timely manner or create a phone number specifically for news releases. The same goes for email addresses for news release distribution: create a media-release-only email address that forwards to Public Relations and Publicity Committee Chairman's regular event account.

A news release standard format is explained in PUBLIC RELATIONS AND PUBLICITY – News Releases.

News Release Distribution by Mail

Even if these media outlets are duplicates from what is on the news service, take the time to postal mail each release to your relevant local newspapers, magazines, and radio and TV stations unless an online submission form is available. Postal mail versions will serve to reinforce your event and provide the news desk or reporters something that won't disappear in their email in-basket after the day is gone. Paper releases are sometimes like gum on a shoe. It may stick around a little longer, giving reporters time to add the event to their calendar (three days after it was received) or giving them time to add your event's Public Relations and Publicity Committee Chairman information to their contact list.

News Release Distribution by Email

Once a reporter knows you, you may then ask if it is OK to send releases by email or as email attachments. This improves deliverability and fear from being labeled spam.

Submission Forms

Many, and I'd almost lean towards most, daily and weekly newspapers have online submission forms today. By requiring information be submitted in this manner, the content it receives is in an apples to apples format versus requiring staff to sift through piles of information.

In advance of sending out your event's news, spend some time pulling together the links to submission forms for local media. In some cases you can cut and paste your entire news release into the form. Some may have character counters so note that on the front end when compiling the list of links. Keep those limitations in mind when writing the release. Add a note at the end indicating additional materials are available upon request and list specifics.

Community Calendars

Many libraries, magazines and radio and TV stations also offer community calendars. It will be much the same drill with calendar submissions. In some cases the listing form will include nothing more than the name of the event, dates, venue/location and the event's website address. The volume of requests to promote events in magazines and on radio and TV is sizable. Self-submissions allow the media to provide a community service while minimizing staff time.

Bloggers

This is a category unique unto itself and is composed of a group of people who are digitally and electronically minded. In many cases, each has a particular subject matter they write about or follows. Some may be in your own backyard but may be difficult to connect with unless contact information is on the blog. Many bloggers have a presence on Twitter which may provide a way to reach. For more details, see PUBLIC RELATIONS AND PUBLICITY – Social Media.

If no contact information is listed, reach out to someone featured in the blog. The logic is a bit odd, but you may be able to back into contact details, at least on the local level, by touching base with someone previously featured in the blog.

If a blogger covers topics that are a match for your event, cultivate them. Spend some time discovering what type of news they cover and their approach. Typically, bloggers speak a different language from that of a traditional journalist. A blog can have a much more casual energy. It is often tied to the blogger's personal interests, experiences or point of view. Spend some time getting to know their work. Determine how large or small and influential the blogger is. Then, if appropriate to your event, take a very targeted approach. Otherwise, move on to the next blogger.

Developing a blogger relationship is similar to dating. Engage them – comment on a story, applaud a particular blog, etc. Do not send a news release without asking "would it be OK to send one?" Don't find a blog that was written a while ago and ask to include your event. Once a blog is written, unless a blatant error, don't ask it be updated. Focus on a future story.

Work with your local convention and visitors bureau's public relations staff to see if they can help you reach out to bloggers. They may be able to open up a door or two for the event. In some cases, these destination management organizations (DMOs) – chamber of commerce, convention and visitors bureau or state tourism agency – may be interested in bringing bloggers to the area with your event as the focal point. A special event is a great activity to build an itinerary around.

Social Media

Social media is a commitment. Before the event creates numerous social media accounts, spend a bit of time thinking about all of the social media platforms and which ones are a match for your event's demographics. Once decided, the Public Relations and Publicity Committee should establish objectives, strategies and policies so the event has a framework within which to operate. Then carefully decide what the account name needs to be, backed by the perfect description, images and artwork.

More than once, I've heard someone say, "I'll just have one of the young kids handle it because they do posts and tweets all the time." WRONG. Having a presence on social media needs to be a very strategic effort that is approved and calendared. If not strategically planned, it's highly possible someone on the Organizing Committee would leave an important meeting and start tapping away the name of the featured chef or headliner. Much like publicity, it has to come across as a smooth, orderly, authorized flow of communication and by someone with a clear understanding of the event.

Create a presence on state and local tourism websites, on chamber of commerce and economic development websites as well as LinkedIn® (a business page), Facebook, Twitter, Instagram and Pinterest® if your demographic is a match. If you add content to Wikipedia® (no search engine optimization (SEO) value), their terms of use require you to disclose your affiliation with the event. If you are being paid, this can create a potential conflict of interest or bias.

Maintain a spreadsheet of all organizational website listings and a link to those pages plus a list of user IDs and passwords of each, the date updated and by whom and indicate who your contact person is with the organization in a secure location. This will save an immense amount of time when data, images and logos need to be updated – and they will.

It's important to know and understand your social media audience and how the information contained in each is used. Communicate to each site with an appropriate message. Above all, do not sell. Tell a story.

When adding or updating information online, realize many social media websites ask for an address. Have the Public Relations and Publicity Committee Chairman determine in advance if the event will list the physical address of the venue or of the office if one exists. This address most likely will be mapped and appear on, as an example, the event's Facebook page. If at all possible, also list your event's mailing address where possible. More than once, I've seen a post office box listed as the address which is not helpful to someone seeking directions to an event.

Social Media Objectives, Strategies and Helpful Hints

When assigning a member of the Public Relations and Publicity Committee the task of social media, it's important to develop a brief document that defines expectations and reinforces the standards adhered to by the Organizing Committee. Below is an example.

Objectives:

- To consistently promote the event brand/image to social media users, for example, Facebook and Twitter, among a host of others.

- To use social media to connect and engage in dialogue with those who already have experienced the event and to create a connection with potential event-goers.

- To utilize social media to communicate with market segments that do and do not use traditional media.

- To develop a mechanism/standard to provide feedback to patrons and potential customers.

- To share the gained perspective (market intelligence) with the Event Chairman and the Public Relations and Publicity Committee Chairman in order to develop new strategies or make adjustments.

- To increase brand awareness and social capital but not necessarily revenue.

Strategies:

- To communicate in a casual, common sense manner that espouses the values of the event.

- To communicate using standard language as well as shortcut or common texting abbreviations but still using proper grammar and spelling.

- To establish links to organizations/others having relationships with the event, for example, sponsors.

- To feature relevant images and videos that support the event's values or the values of its demographics.

- To quickly update friends, groups, members, fans and those who like the event about event activities.

- To utilize social media to potentially reach target customers during pre- and post-event hours, for example, traffic conditions.

- To address concerns and opportunities as they arise.

- To cross-promote social media platforms on marketing materials and other communication tools.

Helpful Hints: Legal, Security, Professionalism, Courtesy and Timeliness

- Understand the fundamentals of trademarks, copyrighted materials, model and property releases and use appropriately when posting on social media. For example, do not take images or logos from other websites or other locations without written permission (in advance) of the owner. Establish standards for documenting "permissions."

- Recognize that any data contained on Facebook becomes the property of Facebook.

- Recognize that any and all comments are public and should not include terms or thoughts that can be misinterpreted or taken the wrong way (if several interpretations).

- Understand the event's logos and images are trademarked and copyrighted, respectively, and should bear those designations, or credit or courtesy lines.

- Provide notice in advance that the event will be taking photographs and videotaping during the event. This can be done by posting a notice on your website, advising volunteers at the all-volunteer meeting, placing a sign at each entrance and posting signs in conspicuous places at the venue. Document these by taking photos of each notice every day. This provides you the proof when people say they didn't know their photo was being taken or a video was being made, and didn't give you permission to do so.

- Respect the privacy of others. Some event goers may be attending with their boyfriend or girlfriend and not their spouse. Be careful with your own personal information as well as that of your event. Not all information in your knowledge base should to be shared.

- Take care when it comes to potential security issues and use credible sources. Do not embed HTML coding into your social media pages unless provided by an approved/authorized person and do not click on links/attachments from those that are unfamiliar.

- Avoid posting negative comments of your fellow volunteers, volunteer supervisor, festival chairman, concessions, current and former sponsors, etc.

- Recognize links to other websites serve as endorsements, for example, those running for office, promoting a business or products or services.

- Post to social media within the time frame approved by your supervisor. Timely posts are more valuable.

- Respond to immediate patrons' needs rather than responding to social media needs (do not text in the presence of others unless approved to do so).

- Respond, but do not react, unless you have thoroughly thought through the response which may include discussion with a supervisor.

The Toolkit

Below are a number of handy items to include in your publicity toolkit.

Make It Easy

Have you ever had someone send you a request asking if you want to update your profile but then fails to send you the current profile?

Always, always, always make it easy for the end users. Give them everything they need in one place. Play it forward 12 steps. Eliminate the need for them to have to stop what they are doing, find the glue and Popsicle sticks and put them together and then wait for them to dry. In all likelihood, in most if not all cases, people are busy and easily interrupted by his or her boss, emails, phone calls, deadlines, fellow employees, spouses, etc. Make it easy for them to help you promote your event. Give them everything the first time.

And yes, you're probably busy too, but thinking things through to the next 12 steps and giving them information for all 12 steps will also reduce the number of inquiries you receive and the time to chase them down after the fact. Work smart, not harder. In the end, this effort will net you the most timely exposure and appreciation for those with whom you work.

Fact Sheet or Backgrounder

This is a great all-round resource that can be easily adapted to any event theme type. The document, typically printed on event letterhead or digital letterhead template, is an overview of key information: who, what, where, when, why and how. As a bonus, it can be used for multiple purposes.

WHO

The Event Chairman, Organizing Committee, the host organization, the presenting organization and/or the event sponsors.

WHAT

The Xth Annual [Event Name].

WHERE

[Venue/Location], [Physical Address, City, State and Zip Code] (even if no mail delivery). If in a park, list the park name. Some may include GPS coordinates or generic description, for example, waterfront, etc.

WHEN

The days of the week and the date range. If some formula, indicate it, for example, the third weekend of a given month.

WHY

The history behind the event, a short summary of how the event evolved, what year it was started and if the event was created to serve a purpose, for example, to highlight the importance of seedless watermelon to the local economy and to showcase a given area's unique agricultural product.

HOW

It's a yearlong planning process with an all-volunteer organizing team composed of 25 members and an event volunteer force of 400 individuals from the community. It would not be possible without the support of the following major and contributing sponsors: [insert list here].

General inquiry information

This includes the event's website address, office mailing address and phone number with area code. If it is only a voice mail recorder, indicate the frequency someone will respond in the outgoing message.

Why the event is unique

It is the only free festival of its type in the state or Southwest; first of its type in the U.S.

Attendance and Free/Admission

If the first year, eliminate attendance. Listing anticipated attendance and missing the mark set the event up to be questioned on other matters. Make sure the attendance numbers can be substantiated at the event level even if not actually shared with the media or general public. For more details, see PUBLIC RELATIONS AND PUBLICITY – Attendance Counts.

Contact information

Media point person – Public Relations and Publicity Committee
Chairman – with full contact information
Event Chairman – with full contact information

Contact person for specific information

This is a laundry list of all key people involved and who is responsible for what area; it is not the full list of the Organizing Committee. The list below is shown in alphabetical order.

> *Entertainment* – (talent – headliners, artists, speakers, musicians, pilots, performers, winemakers, authors, chefs, entertainers, brewmasters, etc.) – When the event's schedule of entertainment has not yet been released, indicate if or when this decision will be finalized.
>
> Entertainment Committee Chairman – Name, phone number (indicate hours available) or event email address.
>
> *Concessions*
>
> Concession Committee Chairman – Name, phone number (indicate hours available) or event email address.
>
> *Media*
>
> Public Relations and Publicity Committee Chairman – Name, phone number (indicate hours available) or event email address.
>
> *Merchandise*
>
> Merchandise Committee Chairman – Name, phone number (indicate hours available) or event email address.

Sponsors/Underwriters/In-Kind Contributions

Sponsor Services Committee Chairman – Name, phone number (indicate hours available) or event email address.

Venue/Location

Site Services Committee Chairman – Name, phone number (indicate hours available) or event email address.

Volunteers

Volunteer Services Committee Chairman – Name, phone number (indicate hours available) or event email address.

Overview Statement

This may be a lift from the event's standard closing paragraph of each news release or one of the word listings. For more details, see PUBLIC RELATIONS AND PUBLICITY – The Toolkit – 15, 25, 50 and 100 Word Listings.

Fact Sheet or Backgrounder - Version 2

The original fact sheet or backgrounder can be revised to include more detailed information on each committee. This is helpful in keeping key contacts updated. For more details, see PUBLIC RELATIONS AND PUBLICITY – Keeping The Public and Distribution Channels Informed.

Under "Contact person for specific information" now add parameters which will further help those who respond to inquiries about the event. For instance:

Entertainment – (talent – headliners, artists, speakers, musicians, pilots, performers, winemakers, authors, chefs, entertainers, brewmasters, etc.) – Define the specific parameters as to what the event desires for talent, for example, only bestselling authors, veteran entertainers, winemakers from a specific region, only craft brewers, chefs' creations showcasing local foods and products, etc. Otherwise, the event will receive phone calls, emails and packages promoting services not a match for the event.

Even when the event outlines its needs, for example, only

live acoustic entertainment or only chefs with experience in local organic meals, people won't read. You will have bands with significant electrical needs, DJs and non-organic BBQ pitmasters asking for a place on the schedule.

It's important to work with people who follow instructions and people who do a little research versus those cold calling every event in the state. Talent interested in appearing at the event will most likely inundate the Entertainment Committee.

Concessions – Define the specific parameters as to what is needed to be considered for a future event: deadline for applications, key decision dates, if a food-only event, if merchandise can be sold, preferred beverage products, if limited only to local vendors, etc. Vendors interested in selling their products at the event will solicit the Concession Committee Chairman.

Merchandise – Indicate if products are available from previous years, prices and how to order by mail or online. Indicate when the current year's merchandise will be available for sale. Define the specific parameters as to what is needed to be considered for a future event, for example, must be a local business, how to be added to the bid list, etc.

Volunteers – Indicate how interested volunteers can sign up to help the event.

A Chronological List of Activities

To keep tabs on all of the events and activities and to make sure none are unintentionally scheduled at the same time, maintain a detailed running list of all activities. If it's important that the Event Chairman make an appearance at each event, double check that this is possible based on the event's hours, its location, requisite attire and travel time. Post an abbreviated version of the list on the event's website for everyone to see.

The detailed list should indicate if the event is public or private, if free or requiring paid admission, which Organizing Committee Chairman is the point of contact, who is sponsoring or underwriting the event, the venue/location and the address and specific start and end times.

If it is a related event under the event umbrella but not organized by the event, also include contact information. For instance, if the featured chef on a dinner cruise is the person who will be recognized on stage on a particular day of the event, make sure the dinner cruise and the presentation aren't scheduled simultaneously. If a local musician is performing at a children's workshop and the event, make sure enough travel time is built in between appearances.

Guests, such as travel agents participating in a FAM trip or those hosted by the local economic development agency, should be added to the agenda so security knows to expect them and will let their motorcoach through for unloading and loading. For more details, see RELATED EVENTS AND ACTIVITIES – Economic Development – The Travel Industry.

Event Chairman and Organizing Committee Bios

It's important to maintain a list of all members of the Organizing Committee, their event responsibilities and a short blurb detailing work background, prior event experience and other volunteer experiences. This can be maintained as a single document and each member should be given equal depth in content. Do not include contact information here, because all inquiries need to flow through the Public Relations and Publicity Committee Chairman. This is done so the Public Relations and Publicity Committee can prep fellow Organizing Committee members in advance of a reporter's scheduled call or interview for all possible questions the media could ask.

The Event Chairman's bio will most likely be longer than that of Organizing Committee members, assuming he or she has held other work or volunteer leadership positions during their career. The Event Chairman should have a studio photo (color which can be converted to black and white) readily available to respond to inquiries. For more details, see PUBLIC RELATIONS AND PUBLICITY – The Toolkit – Image Library.

15, 25, 50 and 100 Word Listings

Word listings are odd things. They can sit in the Public Relations and Publicity Committee's files for years and not be used and then one day, the need presents itself. Having them prepped and ready to go will save time from having to pull them together quickly.

They are a great tool to use when updating tourism websites and calendar listings. Make sure to keep a running list, a spreadsheet with publication or name or web address, date updated, copy posted, contact person if known and contact info – phone and email. This will make it easier when the event expands from two days to three. If a user ID and password are required to add content, add those to your records, making sure they are strong passwords related to the event and not someone's personal information.

The Public Relations and Publicity Committee Chairman should be asked if they have a specific user ID and password that should be used for all event needs.

If the Public Relations and Publicity Committee Chairman asks one of its team members to scour the Internet for places the event's listing can be added, do not send an email to the Contact Us form and only write, "We would appreciate our [Event Name] being added to your listings." To improve the chances of the listing actually being added, do the homework. Provide everything that website needs down to a detailed description and images. If you can't determine this easily, ask. Include this sentence, as part of the request, "Please advise what specific information is needed, for example, number of characters or words in the description and size of image, and we will be pleased to provide. Thank you."

Public Service Announcements (PSAs) – How They Work

This section focuses on television and radio PSAs and not print since those can be effectively reached using news releases. An important thing to remember is that if the event is a nonprofit and publicizing a free event or service or putting out a call for volunteers, it is probably eligible to receive public service announcements from a local TV or radio station. For-profits are not eligible for PSAs. While many seek airtime, having a listing on the station's website event calendar may be a viable alternative and is great exposure, too. For more details, see PUBLIC RELATIONS AND PUBLICITY – Submission Forms and Community Calendars.

Note: Send out a PSA on special news release stationery or event letterhead if distributed by postal mail. When sending by email, use a digital news release or letterhead stationery template. In any case, include contact information for the Public Relations and Publicity Committee Chairman.

To minimize the touch-time of limited staffers, some stations require that online forms be submitted. This is tedious, yes, but it is one of the reasons the word listings were created. Don't go through the effort to record the actual PSA but, instead, maintain an inventory of PSA scripts with fill-in the blanks where entertainers' names can be inserted from year to year.

- Do your research to make sure you have followed the station's required submission format.

- Run through the list of excluded events – typically ones with a limited audience.

- Some stations allow PSAs for events charging admissions as long as the price doesn't exceed $X.

- Check to see how far in advance the PSA needs to be sent.

- Check to see if a standard press release, brochure or program is as effective.

- If you have a PSA in the can (produced), you can share this information, but many stations prefer to work from their scripts as it will minimize the chance of it becoming a commercial instead of a PSA.

- Make sure whatever is submitted includes contact information for the media as well as the general public.

- Double check that the event's media contact is readily available immediately after a PSA is distributed and not on vacation or too busy to respond to inquiries. This person should have a distribution list "attached" to each PSA sent out so they know who potentially could be contacting them.

- Remember FCC regulations encourage public radio stations to avoid promoting fundraisers for others, because public radio stations hold their own fund drives to cover operating costs.

- Stations do not have the manpower to follow-up and advise if or when the event's PSA aired. If you truly are a listener or viewer of a station, you'll know if it aired.

TV stations are required as part of their licensing with the Federal Communications Commission (FCC) to serve the public interest of the community through a number of weekly local news programs and important issues of community interest. Stations are required to file reports. (Go to: https://stations.fcc.gov). These documents are available for public viewing and provide a glimpse of the topics covered and time allotted.

Do not expect a PSA to run during prime time. These are fillers for unsold ad space and can appear at any hour.

A Gift and A Request

You may want to try this as a way to entice the station to give your event a bit more attention:

> *Please find enclosed a copy of the Xth Annual [Event Name] poster [or tee shirt], a schedule of events and a Public Service Announcement.*

> *If you need assistance with an [Event Name] promotion or interview, please contact the Public Relations and Publicity Committee Chairman [First and Last Name] at phone number and email address.*

B-Roll or Stock/File Footage

Like word listings, the Public Relations and Publicity Committee should have B-roll sitting on the shelf in order to quickly respond to requests. The term B-roll is used generically to describe stock, background and digital video or file footage. This is miscellaneous event footage that can be used for a variety of purposes by the media to transition into and out of a commercial or news story or to provide supplemental footage. If at all possible, use high definition quality footage, since this can cover the very worst to best needs. It should be without audio because the end user will most likely insert audio – voice over and/or add music over the footage.

When an event has B-roll on file, it can be made available to third parties such as news media, destination management organizations (DMOs) – chamber of commerce, convention and visitors bureau or state tourism agency, to assist them in producing a news story, feature or video blog. Additionally, the footage can be incorporated into the event's promotional videos and commercials and displayed on social media video sites.

When creating B-roll, try to not exceed 5-10 minutes. Isn't the average attention span nine minutes? Break the footage into segments to save the end user time.

Examples of possible event footage:

- Crowd shots – Still and panning at ground level, a shot from the stage out into the audience, a shot from the back of the venue showing the stage in the distance with featured headliner during the day and evening.

- Entertainment – A speaker, chef preparing food, wine being poured, wine judging, beer competition, author with a book in hand, people dining at a table, planes performing aerobatics, a musician performing, a group of musicians singing, etc.

- Concessions – Close-ups of people eating food, people walking down an aisle with food vendors on either side.

- Committee members in the event uniform in action and regular volunteers in service, for example, security at gates, stage crew during a set change, etc.

- Sale of merchandise with a transaction in process and close-ups of merchandise (avoiding cash handling shots).

- Close-up of people sitting in chairs or on blankets or walking at the event; people interacting with a chef cooking food, sampling wine, tasting beer, listening to an author speak; people tapping their toes or dancing.

To be able to respond to a last minute request for B-roll, upload the files on a password protected website. This will save the Public Relations and Publicity Committee Chairman from re-arranging his or her already busy day job to respond. All they need to do is provide a web link and the passwords. Always ask when the story will air and then make arrangements to have the segment recorded. Remember to ask if the event can send, for instance, the chef an mp4 file of the demonstration afterward.

Image Library

If the Event Chairman wants to know how savvy the Public Relations and Publicity Committee Chairman and committee members are about copyright law, ask this question, "If I need a photo or a logo in a hurry, can I just take it off of a company's website?" If they say, "Sure, no problem," these are not the volunteers you want serving in this capacity. They are a liability to the event, and they do not understand copyright law.

Here's an easy way to explain it:

Just because you leave your car keys on the top of your desk does not mean someone can take them and then go drive your car. Website elements are the same. No one should take artwork or photos from a website without the express written permission of the owner. Taking anything without permission and using it is stealing.

The person who snapped the photo automatically owns the photograph. The person who drew the artwork is the author and owns the copyrights to the artwork. Images and artwork placed on websites are secured with unlimited rights or limited usage rights from its owner or author.

The fee paid to the photographer or artist varies depending on the contract negotiations/agreement between the creator and the buyer. Unless a photographer or artist transferred in writing the ownership rights, they continue to own their creations. This person is the only one who can elect to give away all, none or some of the usage rights and for a select period of time, an unlimited period of time and for a fee or for free.

With an image library, especially in a volunteer environment where turnover occurs, each item in the library needs to have a detailed paper trail – image owner, rights granted, photo credit required – and with, if for editorial use only or non-editorial (can be used in advertising). Having a form signed by each copyright owner detailing those rights is even better.

Often an image library can be placed on an unpublished page of the event's website. To assure that the Public Relations and Publicity Committee controls who is using the materials, set this area up to require a user ID and password.

Some Festival Chairmen want all of the event photos in an image library. However, many Marketing Services Committee Chairmen prefer to keep signature or promotional images as well as select logos stored away in a top-secret area that can only be used by the event itself.

It is not necessary to put the largest file size of the image in the online library. Normally nothing beyond 7 inches at the widest edge at 300 dpi is needed for most uses. A reputable publication will have the staff with technical skills to resize it to meet its needs. Include this line of copy on the image library webpage: "Larger files are available upon request." Legitimate media will understand. When responding by email to any request for images, if appropriate include the sentence again along with the user ID and password to access the files.

Before any image goes online, consider using photo-imaging software to add metadata info into each digital image. While the file automatically captures the camera's settings and the date it was taken, take the extra time to:

1. Name the image. This may be different than the name used as the image label or caption beneath the thumbnail image in the online library.

2. Include details about the copyright owner or author, even if the image rights have been transferred to the event. The name of the owner or author may be the event, a person or the photographer or artist's company name.

3. List who currently owns the copyright.

4. Detail the usage rights.

5. Include a description of the image and/or the names of the people (left to right) in the image.

6. List key search words.

7. Include the event name, mailing address, the Public Relations and Publicity Committee Chairman's generic event email address and the event's phone number.

You may wonder why it is so important to go through this effort for each image. Improperly credited works or copyright materials used without permission can lead to copyright infringement lawsuits. Copyright lawyers can seek and receive awards for the plaintiff for statutory damages ranging from $750 to $30,000 and as high as $150,000 if willfully committed, plus reasonable attorney's fees.

Some quick facts about copyright law:

- Using a work where no copyright © notice is displayed, still requires permission. Otherwise, it is copyright infringement.

- Using a work without permission but giving credit is copyright infringement.

- Using a portion, part or piece of the work and not the entire copyrighted work is copyright infringement.

- Using a work, whether by a nonprofit or by a for-profit requires permission. Otherwise, it is copyright infringement.

- Using a copyrighted work and then modifying it is copyright infringement.

- Using a work assumed to be in the public domain may be copyright infringement among other infringements.

- Using a work posted on the Internet thinking it is public domain is copyright infringement.

- Using a work with the promise of securing permission later is copyright infringement.

- Always ask the copyright owner in advance for written permission to use their work.

Public Access TV

Some cities have public access cable channels as part of the cable company's franchise agreement with local government. These channels air government meetings, city or county generated programming, documentaries, public service announcements and programming from outside services. Check with your local government to determine if it is possible to promote the event on a public access channel or if the Event Chairman can be interviewed as part of a public access show. Some cities post aired programs on social media video sites, so the promotional value of an appearance continues for quite some time.

Circle the Date on the Calendar

Numerous organizations and websites offer listing opportunities. Many are calendars, some are by topic – jazz, blues, wine, craft beer, festivals, food, film, air shows, etc.

Before you begin the process of signing up or filling out submission forms, make sure the websites are being updated routinely. Two years from now, it may be impossible to get bad data removed. When possible, promote your event as the third weekend of [month] versus the actual date. This will add some timelessness to your listing; otherwise in nine months, you'll be updating it all over again.

The 15, 25, 50 and 100 word listings will come in handy for this project. For more details, see PUBLIC RELATIONS AND PUBLICITY – The Toolkit – 15, 25, 50 and 100 Word Listings.

For those listings allowing the event to include an image, designate one image as the event's signature image. Use it in all your promotional materials in order to keep a consistent image or to "build a brand" as those who work with packaged goods like to say.

In tiny print on the right-hand margin of the photo, display the appropriate text sideways: © 20XX, [Photographer Name], Provided Courtesy of [Event Name]. The text can be added using photo-imaging software.

SEEKING CREDIBILITY

Honors and Awards

Many opportunities for recognition simply need for submission forms to be completed and turned in. For many years now, the Southeast Tourism Society based in Atlanta has named the Top 20 Events each quarter. (Go to: http://southeasttourism.org.) The short submission form is extremely basic. Much of the information in the form should be contained in the event's fact sheet or backgrounder.

Check with your local destination management organizations (DMOs) – chamber of commerce, convention and visitors bureau or state tourism agency – to see if they are aware of other similar programs. Requirements for submission may include any of the following: the event cannot be a first-time event, may need to meet minimum attendance figures, quarterly or annual deadlines, photography, etc.

The presenting organization such as Southeast Tourism Society will typically send out a news release to announce the winners. The end result is the event may gain exposure in places it would not otherwise garner coverage. As a side benefit, the event will gain search engine optimization (SEO) from a link from the award-giving organization and any media coverage obtained. The event can also promote this honor or award at every opportunity – in sponsorship packages, stage announcements during the event, at the sponsor breakfast, in fact sheets and backgrounders for the media and various public and distribution channels.

ATTENDANCE, PROFITS AND INSTRUCTING THE MEDIA

Attendance Counts

How are attendance counts determined?

If your event charges for tickets, this is one of the easiest ways to track attendance. Add the ticket check-ins from your online advance ticket sales and the on-site ticket sales to obtain total attendance. Note this may include complimentary tickets for sponsors and VIPs and, therefore, is not a true indicator of ticket sales revenue.

Don't forget to add in all the volunteers, vendors and exhibitors who most likely are not counted through normal channels. You may end up with a duplicate count for those who volunteer and then return off-shift and pay.

When a reporter comes asking how many people attended the event, direct them to law enforcement. It will keep you at arm's length. In many cases the local police department or sheriff's office will not provide an estimate unless provided a count by the event organizers. Ask your local law enforcement agency in advance what its policy is. Please consider the total attendance count the event would like to use and show a count for each day. Make sure the figures add up. Be realistic.

One way to determine attendance at a free event is to determine total acreage of your venue and then count a sub-section of land with people (daytime count and evening count). Multiply that for the overall park or venue, subtracting non-viewing areas, such as lakes, ponds, bushes and sculptures to get an accurate estimate. Then, much like a restaurant turns tables, the event will need to know how often the allocated space turns over. For instance, do people who come in the afternoon stay to the very end? Does your event's programming change such that a local children's jazz band performing in the afternoon will draw mom, dad, the grandparents and neighbors who exit immediately after the performance? Does the mid-afternoon easy listening performer have a fan club that comes out in droves and stays for an act or two? Is the big name act such a draw that patrons come in the afternoon to spread out blankets to save their space? By evening, more patrons arrive with their beach chairs and the venue is packed.

Another way to track attendance for a free event is to require a ticket. Many online ticketing services allow free online tickets be issued. Reporting features can provide invaluable data.

Here's an interesting and, some might say, unorthodox way to count. The one man who knows more than anyone else is the guy who pumps out the port-o-lets each day. Years of experience have taught the vendor to weigh in on the counts. Before he does, don't be surprised if he asks what types of beverages were for sale and if coolers could be brought to the venue.

Inquiries During the Event

For more details, see THE BIG EVENT – Taking Care of Business Especially During the Event.

How Much Profit

Decide in advance if the event plans to share this information with the media. Some event organizers will not share it beyond the Organizing Committee. Here's why:

1. This is the barometer many will use to determine if the event was successful. An event may miss the mark on the total profit but still have a profit.

2. A balance sheet only takes into account income/revenue and expenses. It does not list if an event had an excellent turnout, received fabulous mentions in the news and accolades from the talent, or had excellent or inclement weather. It only shows the impact of these things.

3. If an event appears to make too much money, a sponsor may question why the event needs the amount of support it asks of a sponsor.

4. If patrons perceive an event's ticket price and fees are rather high and profits are also high, they may question why the ticket price is so expensive. An audience rebellion on social media may result in fewer people attending the following year.

5. Patrons can be as loyal as the next event if they perceive it to be a better value. Perception in many cases is reality.

6. In-kind contributions can also be affected. Why should we donate XYZ when the event has all this money?

7. If the event does not have a benefactor for its profits and the following year the Organizing Committee is given expensive shirts and the letterhead features metallic gold embossing, patrons and sponsors will begin to wonder if the event has lost its way.

8. If the event has earmarked how profits will be spent, it makes it easier to share profitability. However, the "message" needs to be repeatedly tied to the profits and the benefactor. Giving the monies away, as an example, in the form of scholarships and educational programs helps soften the impact.

9. Announcing the event is in the hole or in the red may make it a cause for concern for sponsors. Were funds mismanaged? Does my company want to be part of a sinking ship?

Media Instructions

An oxymoron you might think! You WANT the media to attend your event. You've most likely spent months cultivating them, and now you'll need to set some parameters for them to operate within while attending the event. Can the media ever be truly contained?

Here are some suggestions:

•   Ask the media to check in at an information booth where they will be given proper credentials for the event. If they are from a credible news outlet, they most likely will be able to present their company's media pass or a business card.

- They must wear the event's media pass while working at the event. The Organizing Committee and volunteers should have been directed to steer clear of the media (except the Public Relations and Publicity Committee) and to report to a supervisor if media is present. This is done so no one involved with the event can be overheard discussing something that could become a news story or someone self-anoints him or herself a spokesman.

   The media may want a comment from an event-goer. Those can be found out in the crowd. An event volunteer should not be quoted unless under the supervision or direction of the Public Relations and Publicity Committee Chairman. Quotable volunteers should be vetted and quizzed in advance.

- From the check-in area, an escort, hopefully with some expertise in working with the media, will take the media to a predefined location. It may be a staging area or an area not accessible to the general public. Someone should communicate the media is on its way if enough walking distance exists between the two locations.

- Upon entering the controlled area, the escort should immediately contact the person responsible for the area, such as the Stage Manager or their assistant, providing they are not in the midst of a set change, changeover in talent or huddled preparing for the next set change. It is within their domain that the media is being granted access. A Stage Manager is extremely protective of their equipment and the talent. His or her goal is to create an optimum experience for everyone involved.

- At an air show, this point person may be the Air Show Boss or the aviation authority's public relations (PR) person.

- The escort should not allow the media to have contact with any talent, or wander off, until being introduced and given any last minute instructions from the individual controlling this area.

- The Stage Manager can set a time frame by which the media needs to complete its assignment and leave the restricted area.

- Set the parameters and provide a diagram of where the media are allowed, all with an escort within distance of the media's shadow. This area is the only place where the media can speak to the talent, take photos and/or video.

- Under no circumstances allow close-ups or filming outside the designated area. A flash or hot lights are distracting to talent when performing and draws attention to the media and not to the talent.

- Even if granted access and within the defined areas, when the media is asked to move, the escort should make sure this happens promptly.

- After the allocated time frame is reached or the assignment is completed, the media will need to immediately leave the area. In some cases, they may want to hang out to talk to the talent afterwards. Sorry, no hangers-on. Much happens between acts – movement of equipment, talent coming and going from the stage and staging area. There may be an on-air personality on stage making or waiting to make announcements. Sponsors may be in the wings preparing for an upcoming stage presentation. Adding one more person to the mix is unnecessary and poses additional liability for the event.

- Media working for credible publications should have contacted the talent in advance of the event to arrange interviews and then publish the story to tease the event. Some reporters or writers who are also fans of the talent may want to briefly stop by, meet the talent in person and provide a copy of the finished article or story. In, out and done.

- Any media otherwise wanting to do an interview on the spot needed to have prearranged one through the Public Relations and Publicity Committee Chairman.

- Because of the volume of activity in the staging area, interviews should be conducted elsewhere if permitted after the talent has performed.

WORKING ALL THE ANGLES

Media Days & Photo Ops

A media day is typically held before an event is open to the public. This provides the media access to areas otherwise off limits during the event, to event organizers not readily available once the event kicks off and, sometimes, to talent. As an example, an air show pilot may have a scheduled practice with an open seat. The local TV station's videographer may want to join them to grab some aerial footage. A reporter may want to write a story from the pilot's perspective. Those opportunities don't exist during the actual event.

What's going to get more attention – a news story or a photo on the front page? Video and photos of an event set-up are a great way to tease readers about an upcoming event. If you're putting on an air show, invite a reporter, writer or photographer to experience the event from a different angle.

Speech Writing

Not every Event Chairman has the time to pull together their thoughts and write a speech for a sponsor event. Some prefer just a few handwritten notes and can ad lib without sweaty palm syndrome. Some fear they will accidentally forget to include something important or offend someone by excluding them and ask others to review the speech or notes just to double check.

The Public Relations and Publicity Committee Chairman may be called upon to review or write a speech. As such, it's important to listen carefully to what words the Event Chairman uses – particular expressions, how they say them and their mannerisms. Good speech writers can hear the voice of the intended speaker in their head and write to capture that spirit. You can easily tell the difference when someone is naturally nervous addressing a crowd and when the speech writer is unfamiliar with the speaker's phraseology and style. The end result of the latter is disjointed and out-of-sync.

While everyone would like to have as much time as possible to draft a speech, unfortunately, it can come when least expected and with short notice. Good speech writing includes incomplete sentences and cues like – long pause, short pause, applause, and " ... now back to you, Jim." Always double space a speech for ease in reading and bold, underline, all caps and italicize should the speaker want to just use the highlighted words as touch and go markers.

Proclamation from the City

If you've attended local government meetings or watched them on television, you may have seen a proclamation be given to someone for a heroic act, to an organization to honor its work, or to recognize a day, week or month. Ever wonder how that happens? In most cases, someone brought the idea to the attention of the mayor's office. What most people don't realize is the requesting party actually wrote the proclamation – the whereas this and whereas that. Please reach out to City Hall well in advance to schedule.

The event's Public Relations and Publicity Committee Chairman may have already written a few of these in their career. If not, City Hall can most likely provide a few examples which can serve as a basis for your event's proclamation: "[Month Date to Date] Officially Named [Event Name] Weekend."

The actual presentation can occur during a regular government meeting or at the event. Televised meetings are often run multiple times each month, providing additional exposure to the event.

Special Recognition

Within your community there may be an individual worthy of a lifetime achievement award – someone who has contributed to the advancement of the theme of your event. They do so without reward simply because they enjoy it. The event should not honor the individual for the sake of publicity, but instead, because the individual is worthy and deserves recognition.

IT'S NOT WHAT YOU SAY; IT'S WHAT IT LOOKS LIKE

Events are held in the public's trust – monies given to an organization are to be spent wisely. Here are examples of things not to do:

- If you've asked for and received tax dollars or dollars from a nonprofit organization through a grants process, it most likely requires a post-event audit. Make sure to find out what a certified audit costs in advance, and budget to have an audit conducted. One nonprofit pays $3,000 annually for this service from a certified public accounting firm; anything less than certified really isn't an audit. These would be scheduled to occur before tax returns are filed the year following the event or when required by the granting agency or nonprofit. For more details, see MONEY MATTERS – Audits.

- If your event was canceled and a cancellation policy was in place allowing for refunds, make sure every ticket is refunded. Bad press, especially on social media, can spiral out of control quickly.

- How the Organizing Committee carries and outfits itself says much. Do team members drive around the event in golf carts like they belong to an exclusive country club or do they walk the event? Is each given four complimentary high-end signature polo shirts and hats to wear during the event? Has a member of the event Organizing Committee solicited an area hotel for hotel rooms for each member of the team – to be used during the event – regardless of how close each person lives to the event? Are these or are they not in-kind contributions?

- Does the event maintain a membership at a local club and hold meetings at the club, or does it use a community room at a library or a local business?

- Does the event bring a large contingent of team members, all expenses paid, to festival and event conferences?

- Has one of your musicians said or written how much they appreciated performing at the event because the amount the Talent/Programming Coordinator offered to pay was much higher than their normal fee?

- Does the event spend a significant amount of money giving Organizing Committee members awards and trophies?

- Does the event pay to have each Organizing Committee member's poster framed or ask for a discount for committee members who are paying for framing out of their own pocket?

Sometimes, it's not what it is; it's what it looks like. The Public Relations and Publicity Committee Chairman needs to be given permission to have frank conversations whenever leadership or Organizing Committee members create situations that can harm the event's reputation.

The Main Event

Back in the 1950s, limousines provided transportation service from the city of Colorado Springs up to Pikes Peak. At more than 14,000-feet above sea level, Pikes Peak is the highest peak on the front range of the Rocky Mountains. The winding road to the summit offers breathtaking views and plenty of hairpin curves. A group of young women hired the service. At one of the few pullouts on the steep climb, the driver pulled off and everyone got out of the car. As he raised the hood, he saw smoke coming out of the engine and yelled out to the women who had congregated elsewhere to look at the scenery. After a minute he stuck his head around the hood of the car only to find his passengers laying a distance from the car, face down with their hands over their heads. The driver had yelled, "Get some dirt." They thought he had said, "Hit the dirt."

Communication is key. Therefore, it's important that absolutely everything revolving around your main event be clearly communicated and feedback received acknowledging what was actually said and heard.

FESTIVALS AND EVENTS OF ALL SHAPES, KINDS AND SIZES

If you're a first-time event, or one looking to revisit it's purpose, think long and hard about the type of event theme and the audience you want to attract. Will it be strictly a community event? Do you want to attract residents as well as locals? Answers to these questions affect a lot of the planning decisions. For more details, see GETTING

STARTED – Selecting the Event's Mission and Theme.

When Music is the Main Event

For the purposes of this publication, a music and food festival serve as the base layer simply because they are the key components of so many festivals. The actual event theme may vary, and those unique needs are highlighted in this section.

When Food, Wine and Beer are the Main Event

Events such as these typically occur on a single day or over a weekend. They are held within a city park, on downtown streets or at a local convention center, among many other venues. They provide the opportunity for event-goers to learn more about craft beer, local vineyards, wineries, organic foods and hometown products as well as area chefs and restaurants. Some events include arts and crafts vendors and consumer product vendors – home improvement projects, like gutters, gardens, windows, security systems, etc.

Before you go much further in planning your event, decide where you want to set the bar or standard. Does the Organizing Committee want to show the event is serious about food by not allowing carnival food-style vendors? Does it want to convey this beer and wine event is a quality event and limits booth space to only select food, beer and wine types? The income from home improvement project vendors may be good, but it may also impact the reputation of the event. In some cases, those vendors are more appropriate for a home show.

Because food, beer and wine events are the focal point, the event's layout is extremely important. It affects the flow of traffic and should allow guests a logical pattern of movement. How often have you zigged and zagged down aisles in a park, only to find that you have to repeat one to get back to your entry point? Would the Organizing Committee like to have similar vendors grouped together or have them be interspersed between food vendors, demonstration areas, a Sponsors VIP Hospitality Tent and entertainment stage areas? If a concessionaire makes food that creates smoke, that may not be a good thing if located next to a wine booth where guests swirl their glass to capture the aroma of a particular varietal of grape before taking their first sip. With every decision, play it forward at least six steps.

A food, beer or wine event may be free; however, vendors may charge for their tastings or samples. Some of these types of events may charge an admission fee which includes a commemorative beer stein or wine glass and up to X beers or wine pours. Paper tickets may be bought online in advance or purchased at the door and then can be scanned with each beer or pour or be exchanged each time.

Interested in more beer or wine pours? Additional quantities may also be available for purchase online or at the gate. For the convenience of patrons, cases or six packs of beer or bottles of wines may be purchased and then ferried to the beer or wine pick up station near the event's exit. Patrons do not need to be tied down with packages, and it allows guests to easily retrieve items before leaving or shipping when the law allows. For more details, see MONEY MATTERS – Concession Tickets.

When holding multiple day food, beer and wine events, consider packaging nearby accommodations with event tickets. A hotel within walking distance has considerable benefits when alcohol is served. Perhaps incorporate transportation service into the ticket price. Make it easy for patrons by selling an all-inclusive ticket with unlimited or up to X glasses of wine or beer or spirits and gratuities, a parking fee or complimentary parking. For more details, see SPONSORS – A Hotel Sponsorship Package – Official Host Hotel.

If celebrity chefs are also authors, package an event ticket with an autographed copy of their most recent book or a signature product. It may be just as easy to offer the book as an add-on purchase to the ticket.

Food

With a food event, it's not unusual to find a demonstration tent or raised stage with a chef preparing a meal from regionally sourced products donated by local purveyors – free range chicken, organic fruits and vegetables and ice cream made from milk from local cows. To complement the meal, it's paired with wine from the region. A newspaper food critic, a food blogger, local radio or TV station on-air personality or a noted chef from outside the area can host the demonstrations. Their role is to introduce the demonstration chef, explain today's menu and ingredients, mention the local purveyors and ask questions about cooking techniques.

Patrons are seated under or outside the demonstration tent or in front of the stage area. From the entire audience, a dozen are so are selected to taste the finished results because that's a manageable amount of food a chef can prepare during a demonstration. How to decide who the taste testers are? Place an X on the back of a handout, put a dot on the underside of a chair or let your host get creative ... all those who have a birthday this month raise your hand, etc.

In many cases, local chefs freely give up their time for the exposure and the ability to pass out freebies such as recipe cards of the prepared dishes, ad specialty items and incentives or an invitation to visit their restaurant to have a more complete experience.

For many, cuisine is best if shared in a communal environment, whether it be with family and friends or an opportunity to meet new people. Food events can be just as rewarding for chefs, too, who may rarely get out of their own kitchens. These types of events can provide the fire to fuel their creativity, an opportunity to visit and cook with old friends and to share recipes, ingredients, techniques, etc.

If possible, the Organizing Committee should set up to video the demonstration showing the host and the chef. Also place a video camera overhead to capture the meal preparation from another angle. Extend the life of the event by posting the kitchen demonstration including overhead clips on the event's website; provide a digital copy to the chef, too. If a large enough crowd usually attends the demonstration, place a large screen on either side of the tent with one displaying the wide angle and the other the close-up.

Food events can cover a variety of topics:

- Local and organic ingredients – fruit, vegetables, spices, cheese, meats, seafood, chocolate, wines and craft beers.

- Celebrity chefs each preparing a different course.

- Unusual cooking techniques and equipment.

- Stepping outside a chef's comfort zone with an "I've always wanted to do that" meal.

- A different chef each night featuring their respective specialties while other chefs take on a supporting role.

- Chef preparing the meal and then taking the microphone to discuss the meal, ingredients, etc.

- Chef joining each table throughout the evening for one-on-one conversations and questions.

- A chef and winemaker explaining the course and the wine pairing.

- Adapting outdoor meal preparations otherwise prepared indoors.

- Multiple small plate courses.

- Family-style service.

- VIP chef's table with an over-the-top menu and chef joining them for dinner.

- Rare or unusual products not found on menus today.

- A chef's competition.

- Dine around with prix fixe menu.

Wine

A wine demonstration can explain how to make wine at home. The presenters (who may happen to also be festival concessionaires) may share the process from "bright wine idea" to the first of many wine batches, or from fermentation to racking the wine and leaving the sediment behind, or from airlocks to bottling the finished product to changing up the ingredients. Wine demonstrations should have a master of ceremonies or a host with an understanding of the winemaking process who can offer up timely questions to the featured speakers (to answers they already know). The announcer can also keep the program on schedule or the crowds in check if necessary.

In some cases, the presenting winemakers have gone from concept to full-fledged wine operations. If this is the case, they may offer freebies – bottles of wine – to be given away throughout the entire event in exchange for publicity. Be careful to not offend those wine vendors who have paid to be there who may believe they should also be given a fair and equal chance for exposure.

When a dual focused event, a wine and a food demonstrator may pair a meal together at the chef's off-site but nearby restaurant with dinner and wines by a particular winery. The Organizing Committee may offer to sell tickets for this related event in combination with festival tickets.

Wine can be enjoyed by a sip, the bottle or a barrel. This is evidenced by the numerous wine and food events paired over a series of days.

Patrons have the ability to select from a menu of events and activities, such as:

- VIP events with exclusive pours of top local or regional wines.

- Educational seminars with a wide range of subjects: 1) learn who led the charge and applied to designate your area its namesake appellation, a geographic grape growing region; 2) grape varietals and winemaking; 3) how to become a sommelier and/or be designated a Master Sommelier or Master of Wine; 4) challenges for winemakers; 5) moving from a boutique winemaker to mass producer; 6) good neighbors: helping those who grow grapes but have no processing equipment; 7) why all the fuss about a particular varietal; 8) reviving a varietal; 9) tending to the grape; 10) winemaker panels – forecast for the future; 11) wine sommelier panels – what makes a good wine; 12) wine critics or wine publication panels; 13) domestic wines – new wines, new wineries, new vineyards; 14) international wines – new wines, new wineries, new vineyards; 15) what to consider when pairing wine with food; 16) cider – a trend or a rebirth?; 17) reds vs. whites – and the winner is … ; and 18) family run vs. a corporation.

- Field trips: 1) local sources to complement the wine – a visit to the farm or dairy with participants sampling wine and cheese; 2) local seafood and the challenges facing the industry with overfishing, water quality, etc. and participants sampling farm-raised seafood; and 3) tours of local wineries and tastings, plus businesses benefiting from the wine industry.

- Old foods reborn.

- Blind tastings.

- The new vintage or the unveiling.

- Competition of the appellations.

- Gourmet market – selling local and organic products.

Beer

Beer demonstrations can be similar to wine demonstrations with presenters taking patrons from the early days of making small batches of beer in the basement or garage. Learn the story behind different ingredients, the pain points in moving from kegs of beer to bottling and distribution, and community relationship and bragging rights like being named the official beer of XYZ. In many cases that designation is not happenstance but a carefully negotiated contract.

As before an inquisitive host can plant questions when needed, such as, "Where locally can your products be purchased?" Patrons can be awarded growlers or six packs, private tasting parties and invitations to tour the brewery.

Hurray for all those who took to making beer as a hobby and transcended to a mega brewery. With every brewpub's success story, two more guys sit in their basement or garage tinkering with their latest batch of beer. Sharing it with their friends, their dream starts to take shape.

Multiple day beer festivals can include the following:

- VIP packages with VIP events with brewmasters – testing kitchens, dining experiences with beer pairings, etc.

- Educational seminars with a wide range of topics: 1) seasonal flavors and ingredients; 2) home brewing; 3) how to become a brewmaster; 4) challenges for brewmasters; 5) moving from a garage to brewpub to mass producer; 6) defining a brewpub, microbrewery, tavern, etc.; 7) stylized – American, Belgium, English, German and Irish-styles of beer; 8) old recipes; 9) why food is such an important element of the beer experience; 10) brewmaster panels – forecast for the future; 11) beer bloggers – what makes a good beer and why; 12) the impact of craft beer on the economy and on big beer corporations; 13) beer corporations – if you can't beat craft beer, join them; 14) local and U.S. craft beers – new beers, new breweries; 15) international craft beers – new beers, new breweries; 16) what to consider when pairing beer with food; 17) taste the difference – ales (IPA, brown, pale porter and stout) and lagers (pale, pilsner and bocks); and 18) color charting beer.

- Field trips: 1) visiting local farmers to see where ingredients are sourced; 2) tours of local breweries and tastings, plus businesses benefiting from the beer industry.

- Blind tastings.

- The newest small batch.

When An Air Show is the Main Event

While the health department controls food, beer and wine event activities, air shows are overseen by another government agency, the Federal Aviation Authority (FAA). Health department staff may also make an appearance here if food is involved. For this reason, the vast majority of air shows are held at airports or at military bases/stations where aviation is key to their operation – Navy, Air Force and Coast Guard. In some cases these types of events are wrapped into an open house and serve to promote: the airport or base/station as a good community neighbor; to create awareness about the military and aviation; to encourage joining the military or learning how to fly; and/or to stimulate interest in a career in the military or aviation – airframe and power plant, aeronautical engineering, professional and amateur pilots, aeronautical administration, etc.

Air show demonstrations occur in the air, as well as on the ground. The Air Boss is the air show's version of a Stage Manager. As traffic controller, they direct takeoffs and landings of in-air performers as well as ground operations and ground personnel.

Air show schedules typically promote in advance what time select performances will occur – aerobatic teams, military flight demonstrations (U.S. Navy Blue Angels or the U.S. Air Force Thunderbirds), wing walkers, vintage flying formation teams, helicopter and glider pilots, and comedy aviators among others.

Static ground exhibits are on display on airport ramps or aprons and provide patrons the opportunity to get a close-up view of military and civilian aircraft, war birds, restored vintage airplanes and military equipment from local National Guard Reserve units when not deployed. Some events offer patrons fee-for-service rides in helicopters, balloons and nostalgia rides during the off hours of the show.

Just like food, beer and wine demonstrations, a special seating area is set up for the in-air portion of the show. In many cases, find a VIP seating area out front (for a fee), bleacher seats, or plenty of open space to stand and gaze skyward.

All events have times when visitation peaks. This is confirmed by the volume of in-bound traffic and demand for parking spaces within close proximity of the event. Patrons typically expect this and plan accordingly. Traveling in off-peak hours can minimize congestion and delays and net ample parking.

Understand the difference in what your event offers. Demonstrations supplemental to the event and not the focal point of an event, as is the case with many food, beer and wine events, affects traffic and parking differently than an air show. Traffic congestion will build around the overall event. With an air show, the in-air demonstrations are the featured activity – the focal point. While guests will trail in throughout the event, traffic congestion will be peak one to two hours before the start of the "entertainment." Many airports and military bases may be limited by one-way in and one-way out. This can cause further delays.

It's important to note photo identification may also be required to attend an air show at a military base. This can also slow traffic.

It is possible to hold an air show at a location other than an airport or military base. However, for the in-air demonstrations to occur, an airport should be within close proximity. In some cases, the "show" occurs over uninhabited airspace, such as an open field or open body of water with no commercial or recreational activities. If this is the situation, the Air Boss will need extra feet on the ground at the event site to communicate throughout the show.

When a Book Festival is the Main Event

Book festivals thrive in places where the local libraries, colleges and universities, literary societies and regional authors are supportive of such an event. Successful festivals are composed of a variety of activities – workshops, presentations, panel discussions, meet the author lunches or cocktail receptions, book readings with author commentary, and book sales and book signings. Some events include performances of works and author demonstrations – from cooking to crafts. A children's program serves to encourage a lifetime love of reading.

With book festivals, scheduling is key to assure similar genre book presentations or authors are not stacked on top of each other during the same track. Of the many interesting festival choices, the Organizing

Committee should try to minimize forcing patrons to make difficult decisions when two or more are on their must-do list. In some cases, it may be possible for identical presentations to be scheduled during two or more tracks on the same or separate days. The cost of another room night may be fairly inexpensive in order to have a popular second-tier author or speaker appear twice. This of course would most likely not be the event's bestselling author whose limited time would only permit a single appearance.

Book stores, museums, churches, local libraries, colleges and universities can all serve as venues along with tents in a nearby street and/or city park. Tents work well for entertainment, say cookbook and craft authors and their respective demonstrations, as well as family and children's activities because they allow for a no fuss, no muss environment.

Unlike food, beer and wine events and air shows, book festival patrons may need transportation to move from venue to venue. The more distance between venues the more time the Organizing Committee will need to spend on logistics to assure enough travel time is factored into the equation and that convenient parking and access is available between each. Each of the events will have their own draw and a need for ample parking. Traffic congestion could be spread out over a number of mini-hubs rather than one central location.

While some patrons may want to experience a vast majority of the sessions, others may be more selective in what events they desire to attend. Consider housing the events within close proximity of each other, creating a walkable solution.

Often a book event will need to house their talent – be it authors, publisher reps, book editors, etc. Work with a local hotel, convenient to the event, to serve as the official host hotel. Usually as part of the room trade – complimentary or reduced rate rooms – the hotel will bear the "official host hotel" designation and patrons wanting accommodations will be directed to the hotel. It may also provide book lovers a story to tell: "Guess who I rode down the elevator with?" For more details, see SPONSORS – A Hotel Sponsorship Package – Official Host Hotel.

Consider packaging event tickets with an autographed copy of an author's most recent book. Unsigned copies could also be purchased with the ticket and held at will call for pick-up and an in-person signing opportunity.

Book events can cover a variety of topics:

- Books for children with or without performances.

- Children's authors.

- Writing techniques.

- Publishing house panels.

- Self-publishing services.

- Great literary characters or books.

- The book review.

- Book genres.

- The future of hard and soft cover books vs. online books.

- Nurturing student writings.

- The poet.

- Regional authors shine in national spotlight.

- The long and the short of stories.

- What's cooking with cookbooks.

- For the love of reading – funding literacy programs.

- Summer reading programs.

- Starting a book club.

- New York Times best seller's list – where are they now?

- Bio-sphere ... the world of biographies.

- The market place – selling books, tapes and reading devices.

When a Film Festival is the Main Event

Ah, the film festival ... but before we get started, "Who wants some popcorn, GOOBERS®, RAISINETS® or Milk Duds ® chocolate?"

Film genres – action, adventure, classics, comedy, crime, drama, fantasy, history, horror, romance, sci-fi, thriller and westerns – are as varied as film festivals themselves – documentaries, shorts, feature length, animations, foreign films, etc.

Film festivals, an odd name considering digital files have replaced film, are a movie marathon. Find a synergy around film festivals fed by movie lovers: those desiring a career in the industry – some quite talented and others not; those who are veterans in the industry; film students; the local, regional or state film commission office; local production companies; and those involved with a film shot on location in the local area, among many others. Some seek fortune and fame; others try to avoid the paparazzi.

It's not unusual for a film festival to have ties with a local college or university film program and in many cases is a natural fit. This provides students a venue to perhaps showcase their works and/or to better understand the value of these types of events.

A number of film festivals also offer year-round programming to maintain a presence in their hometown. In some instances, they serve to educate the community and local industry; lobby for government incentives for location shoots; pair films with unusual cultural organizations for showings; organize movies in the park on the side of a building; cultivate relationships with film schools, colleges and universities; hold events and fundraisers such as meet the actor and/or director; present film screenings by local up-and-comers; and promote careers in the movie industry.

When a film festival desires to hold a reception or a dinner to honor a member of the industry and also needs to house distinguished guests and out of town speakers, approach a local hotel to see if they may be interested in becoming the official host hotel. In doing so, the hotel will lock in a meal function (revenue) and the potential to house patrons coming in for the event (more revenue). The number of room nights blocked for the event's talent at a reduced rate or given complimentary may be small in proportion to other full or discounted room rates to patrons. Knowing the who's who of the event are also staying at the hotel may be an added incentive for festival patrons to book here. You never know who you might run into in the restaurant or the bar. For more details, see SPONSORS – A Hotel Sponsorship Package – Official Host Hotel.

Unlike food, beer and wine events and air shows, film festival patrons will need transportation to move around town to attend the various screenings. Rather than one central location, activities are scattered, resulting in less traffic congestion. Each venue should have ample and convenient parking. If the event is lucky enough to be housed in one general area, it may be possible for patrons to park once and then walk to each venue or take public transportation.

Passes and Lanyards

Many film festivals sell tickets and/or passes online. They then ask ticket or pass holders to present them in exchange for a lanyard. Lanyards are the clear plastic sleeve about the size of a 3" x 5" card where the ticket or pass holder's ticket is inserted. Lanyards come with a string or ribbon, allowing them to be hung around a patron's neck. The ticket or pass is clearly labeled or color-coded as to the type of access given or programming purchased. In many cases, a barcode or QR code is also displayed and can easily be scanned. This scan validates the purchase for a given event and helps the event track attendance. For more details, see MONEY MATTERS – Tickets, Please!

Film festivals level the playing field, allowing fans and filmmakers the chance to rub elbows with those in the movie industry. Special events can include:

- Panel discussions.

- Premieres.

- Foreign films.

- Screenings followed by question and answer sessions (Q&As).

- Private parties with actors, filmmakers, etc.

- Pitch parties.

- Achievement awards for legendary members of the industry.

- Cartoons for the whole family.

- Conversations with ...

- Film critic panels.

- Receptions.

- Concerts.

- Round table – ask the experts.

TALENT – FROM WISH LISTS TO REALITY

Researching All the Options

As you begin to explore all possible talent – headliners, artists, speakers, musicians, pilots, performers, winemakers, authors, chefs, entertainers, brewmasters, etc. – available to be featured at your event, consider up-and-comers and veterans. They will be much more affordable than the stars of today. The true genius though lies in discovering the up-and-comers before they make it big. Veterans may have a following, just not a recent hit, book, award or publicity campaign. Both types should give your event quality entertainment. There will be plenty of names on your wish list with prices beyond your reach. Save these. Some day they may be affordable to your event.

Chicken or Egg

How can you lock in the talent when the event doesn't have contracts from sponsors underwriting the event? Simply send the proposed talent a letter of intent and advise what is required before the event can commit fully.

To avoid a financial fiasco, require your Entertainment Committee's Talent/Programming Coordinator to understand and practice "until the budget is approved and signed sponsorship agreements are received, no talent contract can be negotiated to the extent a contract is requested or sent."

It All Comes Down to Money

If the sky were the limit, wouldn't every festival or event feature A-list talent? Unfortunately, that's not possible, especially in an event's first year or when the nest egg was used the year before to cover lost revenue due to rain.

A great approach is to feature local talent early each day before the crowds start to build. The type of local talent will vary depending on where the event's talent bar is set. A first-time event may bring out area youngsters who are studying a particular genre of music, or tumble, tap or dance. Schools welcome the chance for their students to perform in front of an audience and gain crowd experience. A more established event may feature local or regional talent, not students, and build up to a headline name.

Experience it for Yourself and Reference Checks

The Entertainment Committee should, just as the Concession Committee does with potential concessionaires, spend some time researching the talent they are interested in contracting. If at all possible, budget to see a live performance to observe first hand the individual(s) at work. Often, it may not be convenient or in your back yard. In some cases it may take several years from the time someone is shopped until the time they land on the event's calendar.

Video and audio performance "demos" often have quite a bit of studio work done to create the final version and bears little resemblance to the live version. While it's great to obtain a video, a live performance provides a more realistic sense of someone's work and stage presence.

A reference check with another event organizer will give you a much different perspective than an artist or manager when they've got their sales hat on and are trying to secure a booking. That event organizer can provide you more accurate details: was talent on time, friendly, demanding, nothing like management indicated, arrogant, self-deprecating, kind, courteous, professional, difficult, short-tempered, an absolute pleasure, obnoxious, intoxicated or rude?

THE BOOKING PROCESS

Making Talent Decisions

One of the best ways to budget for talent is to build three matrices:
1) projected talent costs; 2) projected room night stays and 3) projected
airfare costs. Realize if one talent level price or room night stay goes up,
another will need to come down. To make this work, bottom line expenses
shouldn't increase. Below are examples of how this works:

TALENT

Talent	Calculate an average rate within each category
Level A (Headliner)	4 nights @ $15,000 = $60,000
Level B (Opening Act)	4 nights @ $8,000 = $32,000
Level C (Late Afternoon)	4 days @ $5,000 = $20,000
Level D (National/State Recognition)	4 days @ $2,500 = $10,000
Level E (Regional/Local Exposure)	4 days @ $1,000 = $ 4,000
	$126,000

HOTEL ROOM NIGHT STAYS*

Level A (Headliner)
        4 nights x 5 people in a group = 20 x 2 (nights each) = 40
Level B (Opening Act)
        4 nights x 4 people in a group = 16 x 2 (nights each) = 32
Level C (Late Afternoon)
        4 nights x 4 people in a group = 16 x 2 (nights each) = 32
Level D (National/State Recognition)
        4 nights x 4 people in a group = 16 x 2 (nights each) = 32
Level E (Regional/Local Exposure)
        NONE   136 room nights

*Verify this number of room nights matches the sponsor hotel's allocation as per the contract.

AIRFARES
Level A – Airfare between X and Y
    4 different flights with 5 people per = 20 x $400 airfares = $8000
Level B – Airfare between W and Y
    4 different flights with 4 people per = 16 x $260 airfares = $4,160
Level C – Airfare between Z and Y
    4 different flights with 8 people per = 32 x $120 airfares = $3,840

42 airfares = $16,000

Negotiating the Contracts

Some talent, agents and managers love to haggle over price. Others prefer to say, "This is my price; take it or leave it." It's more professional to dicker over price when the event can immediately sign a contract and send a check. Avoid arguing over a price and then dragging your feet on signing the contract and sending a deposit.

When the event's budget has a bottom line number it can pay, it may be easier to say, "This is all the event has budgeted for this time slot. I realize it is below the normal rate. Before you answer, I'd like to offer to you a list of talent who have performed at the event. If you would like to contact them and ask about their experience, it might give a better indication as to how we take care of those who are part of our programming. If we are unable to book you or your client, we understand. The Entertainment Committee will keep the talent, agent or manager's name and contact information on file should the situation change."

When negotiating, always ask what type of deposit is needed and when it is needed. It lets the talent, agent or manager know you understand this is a business.

There's a delicate balance in timing between negotiating with the event's talent and having the event's sponsor agreements signed and in hand. For this reason, a letter of intent can be created and will save on numerous phone calls. Indicate the event's interest in booking the talent but make it contingent upon the sponsorship dollars being received by a specific date.

Contracts, Addenda and Green M&Ms®

Not all contract terms and conditions should be accepted as written. Realize it's acceptable to make changes to a contract but, before doing so, discuss your concerns with the sender to see why the language is included. Many contracts are designed as one size fits all. If you know the event can't meet the terms of the contract, don't sign a contract that will be in breach.

The entire purpose of a contract is to clearly define expectations for both parties. It doesn't need to be complicated, but it needs to be in writing and signed by both parties. The event may want to work with a local lawyer to create a basic contract, as well as an addendum. An addendum is a document the event can attach or make part of a standard contract that addresses unusual elements that do not fit neatly into the contract.

Remember though, if you are the sender, you should be the last party to sign. In the event the recipient makes changes, the Entertainment Committee Chairman, and perhaps legal, need to review the revisions and accept or further negotiate the terms. When acceptable, present the contract to the Event Chairman asking them to sign the contract and initial the changes.

Major talent or their management firms have contracts and most likely will initiate the contract process. Individuals may be less likely to have one in their files and will be amendable to the event sending its standard contract once the fee and details are negotiated. Avoid delays by offering to initiate the contract process.

While some Festival Chairmen are comfortable in organizing events with their peers, it's always best to have a paper trail of sorts beyond emails and handshakes. Assume the worst could happen and a bus does hit someone; in that way someone knows what was agreed upon.

Expect just about anything and everything when it comes to special requests in talent contracts – vegan dishes, green M&Ms®, herbal tea, etc.

The Paper Trail – Contracts

For the purpose of checks and balances – and making sure all correspondence is timely received – require all correspondence, especially contracts, be directed to the event's mailing address. Remind volunteers to have mail sent to the event's mailing address versus re-routing contracts to their home or company address. It wouldn't be the first time a volunteer forgot to hand deliver an important piece of mail.

It will help if all contractors (talent, concessionaires, port-o-lets, etc.) are given the respective Committee Chairman's and the Event Chairman's contact information. Back it up with an explanation: the Entertainment Committee Chairman and the Event Chairman approve all the contracts and, on occasion, legal will be reviewing them as well. This lays the groundwork when a contract is amended and is different from what was initially negotiated. Talent and vendors do talk to others in their respective industries; so when communicating, don't send conflicting messages.

Talent may not always understand that the volunteer Talent/ Programming Coordinator can't say no to them and will promise anything because they are star struck. Such is the case when one event's entertainer sent a letter post event to the event mailing address thanking the event for paying them more than their normal fee.

Fully Executed Contracts

Once all parties have agreed to the terms and conditions of the contract and both parties have signed and initialed all changes, a copy of the fully executed copy should be returned to talent. The Entertainment Committee should retain a copy with the original sent to the Treasurer. Remember to provide key paperwork, along with the equipment requirement addendum, to the Stage Manager because they need to be able to comply with its terms.

Deposits and Payments

Deposits can usually be handled in the form of a check if paid in plenty of time for the talent, agent or manager to make sure the check is good. When agents or management firms are sent the check, they can cash it and take their commission. When a talent group performs, many ask the final payment be paid in cash. This allows the lead talent to pay each group member immediately. This is even more helpful when the members are from different parts of the country.

As part of the contract's addendum, each member of the group is required to be listed along with their social security number and mailing address. Should the amount paid meet Internal Revenue Service requirements, a completed 1099-MISC form will need to be sent to individual talent members before the end of January the following year. For more details, see MONEY MATTERS – 1099s.

If your event is held on a weekend, the Entertainment Committee Chairman will need to make arrangements with the Treasurer in advance to have ample cash on hand to pay the various talent groups. Depending on the size of the event and caliber of talent, the amounts may vary. Bundle each day's payments together and perhaps break them into afternoon and evening payments. Finding a place to securely store these funds over a weekend may require a bit of investigation. Consider a business open 24/7, say a hotel with safety deposit boxes. Avoid being predictable when picking up the funds and in the route traveling to the location.

Two Organizing Committee members should always be present when the funds are picked up, transported and disbursed to minimize the potential for embezzlement or being accused of it. From a safety standpoint, it's always better to have one person handling the transaction and another watching people and surroundings.

The Treasurer should also provide a receipt book so each payment can be signed as received. While treating business as business, realize the receipt book may be the only autograph the Entertainment Committee Chairman may get, unless this person takes the opportunity to get a separate autograph for him or herself!

The Traffic Coordinator

It's best if one person, such as the Entertainment Committee Chairman, maintains the master list of all event talent, noting if confirmed or pending. Distribute updates on a regular basis to the Entertainment Committee. Distribute a confirmed list to the Organizing Committee. To eliminate outdated information from surfacing, change the file name to the revision date and also update the date within the document. This works well as one wide spreadsheet with all important talent information.

COORDINATING TRAVEL & HOSPITALITY

Arrivals, Departures, Accommodations, Equipment and Special Requests

Smartphones and apps have certainly made it easier to track flights, road traffic, accidents and construction and give door-to-door directions. They also make it much easier for the Entertainment Committee's Transportation Committee to coordinate airport pick-ups and transfers to and from the hotel and venue.

The tricky part is when someone arrives with more luggage than planned, and the size vehicle scheduled for the airport pick up can't hold everything. When talent is coming from different points and one is late or no shows, the Transportation Committee needs to move into action quickly to get the arriving passengers to the hotel and checked in so they can transport the next act to the venue in advance of their performance time. At the same time, an Entertainment Committee member can contact the airline representative or travel agent to see if they can track down the late passenger so an alternate pick up can be coordinated.

Sure enough, someone connected to the Organizing Committee or talent will ask if they can stay at the host hotel or if they can stay there one-night longer. A "no complimentary hotel rooms" announcement by the Event Chairman early on and reinforced by the Entertainment Committee Chairman will make this much easier. Ask the hotel, provided space is available, if it can offer a special rate for those asking for freebies.

There can be challenges with your Talent/Programming Coordinator if they want everyone to like them and don't know how to say no to anyone. Don't be surprised if the Talent/Programming Coordinator goes straight to the host hotel's front desk to see if rooms are available and orders a room for talent without authorization. The Entertainment Committee Chairman should anticipate this happening and ask to speak with the hotel's Front Office Manager each day of the event to reinforce that all requests for additional room nights go through them.

Talent that normally does not perform or work together, but are brought together by the Talent/Programming Coordinator, can place an undue burden on the Organizing Committee, especially when conflicts are not shared in advance. At the last minute, the Talent/Programming Coordinator asks the hotel staff if the group can practice or go over their group activity in a spare meeting space. Efforts are now needed to make sure everyone knows when and where they need to practice or meet, including the talent who is in route from the airport. The Talent/Programming Coordinator has no clue the Transportation Committee is busy texting each other to make last minute changes to their hectic schedule to get talent to the hotel versus adhering to the planned itinerary.

Booking Air Transportation

If you do not have an airline sponsorship arrangement, check to see if a local travel agency would provide in-kind service in making the arrangements with the event picking up the cost of the tickets and other fees (baggage, taxes, etc.). Travel agents know the ins and outs of the travel industry and should be able to quickly make arrangements including seat assignments, most direct routes and good connections. They may be able to find a special U or Y coach seat rate versus a Q coach seat rate. If talent is traveling with an upright bass or oversized luggage, they'll know what to do.

Local Transportation

Depending on the type of event, your talent may drive into town or they may fly.

For drive-in talent who may not be familiar with local roads, special traffic routes and road closures during the event and who are staying at the host hotel, ask them to use the Entertainment Committee's Transportation Committee's vehicles to get to and from the venue. Nothing is worse than talent getting lost or caught in traffic and failing to report to the Stage Manager.

Logistics will require the Transportation Committee Chairman be prepared for fly and drive scenarios. Those who drive into town will need their credentials and parking passes in advance as well as directions to the hotel and perhaps the venue if not using the committee's services.

The Transportation Committee, as the first point of contact for talent, will most likely be the ones asked for additional credentials or parking passes. Having the contract require the name of each member of the group established a baseline as to how many credentials and parking passes were actually needed.

Even though your event qualifies as work (and most people don't take their spouse, significant other, friends and other families to work), that's exactly what can happen at an event. Have the Transportation Committee anticipate the request for more credentials and be prepared to drag their feet before contacting the Site Services Committee's Security Committee Chairman who may allow the hangers-on access. Whoever doles out the credentials or passes, clearly explain where they can and cannot be during the changeover or performance.

The one great thing, if the event provides local transportation service, is your Transportation Committee usually can keep tabs on all the talent.

Welcome to Our Fair City

While the event's talent may not spend much time in their rooms, it's the gesture that counts. At a minimum, create a welcome letter and include a token gift representative of the destination. It may be nothing more than a local visitor guide.

FROM PRE-SHOW TO POST-SHOW

Sound Checks

Ask everyone wanting a sound check to come several hours before the event starts on the day of the performance in order to give them plenty of time to discuss their needs with the sound and lighting crew. The bigger the name, the more likely they will want a sound check. Hopefully, your Stage Manager has connected talent, agent or manager with the event's sound and lighting personnel in advance and shared their background, equipment list, talents and skill level.

On the backside of this, realize sound and lighting crews are pulling long hours and would prefer to stay at the venue once they arrive. Sound checks an hour or so beforehand make more sense than asking the techs to come in early and then require them to hang out until the start of the first act.

The Green Room

There are green rooms and then there are green rooms. The dividing line between the two is how much privacy your talent requires, some of which is predicated by their celebrity status. Many are quite content to hang out under the Talent Hospitality Tent and visit with others in their group or other talent on the line-up.

For the headline acts, it is sometimes necessary to bring in a VIP green room, for example, a recreational vehicle (RV). These can easily be rented or loaned. If rented, a security deposit for cleaning and damages can be part of the arrangements. Loaned vehicles will require the event bring it back in better-than-loaned condition, especially if the event will want to borrow it again.

Many RVs have curtains, which can be closed, adding to the privacy. They also have air conditioning and heating units, dressing areas, plus refrigerators and televisions. It's best to post someone outside the RV to minimize someone entering without permission and to assist talent on the retractable steps.

The challenge is when talent decides to smoke in the unit or drops ashes that burn the carpet or the upholstery. Remember to post no smoking signs throughout the RV to limit potential liability.

The No Show

Never see this as a challenge as much as an opportunity. No shows can be the result of too little time allowed between airline connections, illness or a death in the family. These type of events can result in a better than planned scenario. Quite often fellow talent will come together in support of the no show or in spite of the no show and offer themselves up as substitutes to fill the time slot. The sum of the parts may greatly exceed the whole.

After the event has ended, pull out the contract and determine who owes whom what. Minimize time and energy in dealing with the matter. It's water under the bridge.

The Performance

Happy talent will sing the event's praises and become an evangelist for the event. If their experience was positive, ask if they will provide the event a testimonial for promotional purposes. Ask your Entertainment Committee's Transportation Committee to make this happen. They are in a unique position to have developed a rapport with talent and may be able to get a number of the event's commemorative posters signed on the way to the airport.

Local Musicians Union

Some musicians unions are active; others are not. Be prepared to recognize and welcome your local musicians union president if at the event.

Surprises and the Unexpected

Every entertainer has a pre-performance routine. Some pace in quiet reflection. Some frantically run up to the last minute getting things lined up or warmed up. Some have to be pulled from conversations and reminded that it's time to go onstage.

A Stage Manager has seen it all over the years. Some talent (performers) need a little sip of courage, while others bring their own stash. What was that smell wafting through the air? Others are so focused on what's next that they forget about the present. A Stage Manager will usually take one last look to make sure talent is put together and presentable.

Entertainers have usually experienced a bigger world while out touring the countryside. They may not be familiar with the event's regional culture or religious beliefs. Don't be shocked by what you see. The lifestyle of your talent may not be that of your own or your patrons. They have been contracted to perform. Focus your concern on their ability to perform and entertain.

Autographs and Old Friends

If you're a fan of big-time stock car racing, you know many of the drivers readily and freely sign autographs. From the drivers of the cars down to the shop workers, they all know who made them what they are – the fans. They will sign autographs as long as they need to do so and as long as it doesn't interfere with a race.

Other talent may take the same or a different approach. Some talent managers come on fairly strong and can lead the Entertainment Committee to believe their client will not be signing autographs under any condition. Surprisingly, these are the ones most likely to kick off the high heels and stand barefooted at the back fence talking to fans and signing autographs. Younger entertainers may not have as much of a following and be less in demand. Older musicians, with fewer albums in recent years, are more likely to have friends hang over the same fence asking anyone they can catch to pass a note to their old friend Charlie who will make his way to visit – once recognizing them as legitimate friends he hasn't seen in years versus just being a fan. Introverted authors may be less likely to mingle with the crowd and more likely to sign autographs as long as a table is in between.

AND A LITTLE THING CALLED LICENSES AND COPYRIGHTS

Copyrights and Licensing Agreements

If you aren't familiar with the laws governing copyrights, you'll be in for an education when it comes to the use of music at your event or festival. Unless a member of the Organizing Committee has prior experience, many new events with music are unaware of Broadcast Music, Inc.® (BMI) and the American Society of Composers, Authors and Publishers (ASCAP). While an event should take pro-active steps to contact both, many new events are so focused on the basics they fail to do so.

Broadcast Music, Inc.® (Go to: http://www.bmi.com) is a global leader in music rights management, serving as an advocate for the value of music.

BMI represents the public performance rights in more than 10.5 million musical works created and owned by more than 700,000 songwriters, composers and music publishers.

As a user of copyrighted material it is festival organizer's responsibility to get the appropriate license. Basically, if anyone involved with the performance, whether as a performer, promoter or organizer, is paid, a music license must be obtained. The need to obtain permission to authorize the public performance of music is not contingent upon the profitability of the presenter's organization. "Charitable" use of music is exempt only under very narrow exceptions.

BMI negotiates music license agreements and distributes the fees it generates as royalties to its affiliated writers and publishers when their songs are performed in public. This company is dedicated to protecting and promoting all creative resources so the rich musical culture continues to define those it serves artistically and, in turn, economically. BMI has, throughout its history, returned all revenues generated, less operating expenses, to the musical creators and copyright owners it represents. For every dollar collected, approximately 87 cents is currently distributed as royalties to BMI's songwriters, composers and music publishers.

Licensing fees are based on several factors including type of venue, attraction (concerts, variety shows, pageants, etc. ...), seating capacity, gross ticket sales for paid events and whether or not it is a benefit or charitable event. For first-time promoters, it is best to contact BMI to see what license is best for you as there are different licenses for concert venues, festivals/special events, and promoters/presenters.

The American Society of Composers, Authors and Publishers (ASCAP) (Go to: http://www.ascap.com) is a professional membership organization of songwriters, composers and music publishers of every genre of music. ASCAP's mission is to license and promote the music of its members and foreign affiliates, to obtain fair compensation for the public performance of their works and to distribute the royalties it collects based upon those performances. According to its website, ASCAP members write the world's best-loved music and ASCAP has pioneered the efficient licensing of that music to hundreds of thousands of enterprises who use it to add value to their business – from bars, restaurants and retail; to radio, TV and cable; to Internet, mobile services and more. The ASCAP license offers an efficient solution for businesses to legally perform ASCAP music while respecting the right of songwriters and composers to be paid fairly. With 540,000 members representing more than 10 million copyrighted works, ASCAP is the worldwide leader in performance royalties, service and advocacy for songwriters and composers, and is the only American performing rights organization (PRO) owned and governed by its writer and publisher members.

The annual rate charged depends on the type of business. Generally, rates are based on the manner in which music is performed (live, recorded or audio only or audio/visual) and the size of the establishment or potential audience for the music. For example, rates for restaurants, nightclubs, bars and similar establishments depend on whether the music is live or recorded, whether it's audio only or audio visual, the number of nights per week music is offered, whether admission is charged and several other factors.

Concert rates are based on the ticket revenue and seating capacity of the facility. College and university rates are based upon the number of full time students; retail store rates depend on the number of speakers and square footage. Hotel rates are based on a percentage of entertainment expenses for live music and an additional charge if recorded music is used.

Because ASCAP has more than a hundred different licenses and rate schedules, one will likely fit your event. ASCAP operates under the principle that similarly situated users should be treated similarly. This assures fairness and consistency in its licensing. For example, rates for restaurants of the same size with the same use of music are the same regardless of whether the restaurant is in Oshkosh or New York City.

Volunteers

Over the years, I've observed many Event Chairmen surround themselves with extremely competent volunteers and together they create an event bigger than the sum of all the parts.

Unfortunately, this is not how it always works. In one case, the Event Chairman of a brand new music festival made arrangements about the venue and parking in a vacuum without consulting the volunteer responsible for this area. She arbitrarily did this for other areas as well. As expected, she had control over many important aspects of the festival but rarely communicated the details. To no one's surprise, the event ran into numerous problems.

Because the Event Chairman had most of the answers, the Organizing Committee Chairmen initially came to her with the various challenges each encountered during the event. By the end of the first day, all the team members tried to handle any issue themselves in order to avoid the Event Chairman, who either ran hot – short-tempered – or cold – was nowhere to be found. Many of the volunteers loved the event's mission and offered to return the next year, providing the Event Chairman was no longer involved.

If you believe the task of finding Organizing Committee members is challenging, the fun has just begun. A critical position for a smooth-running event is a Volunteer Services Committee Chairman. While this committee chairman may appear to have little to report until weeks before the event, they will have been busy behind the scenes, networking and developing a base of support. An army of volunteers will show up on cue to provide help to those who have been working year-round to present the event.

KEEPER OF THE MASTER LIST

In addition to the event volunteers, ask the Volunteer Services Committee Chairman to maintain a master list of all Organizing Committee members. Make sure to include contact information and distribute it among fellow committee members. It's an easy task and logically falls within this area.

DETERMINING YOUR VOLUNTEER NEEDS AND WANTS

Where does an event find volunteers if it's a first-time event? If lucky, the event's year-round Volunteer Services Committee Chairman for your festival or event is someone who does this for a living. As such, they most likely will be plugged into a professional organization of volunteer coordinators. Yes, these groups do exist. With a single email to their peers, they can send out a call for help. However, it is possible for the Volunteer Services Committee Chairman to be in another line of work, be well known in the community and be able to assemble a large group of volunteers from their network of contacts.

Before your Volunteer Services Committee Chairman can ask for help though, they will need a clear understanding of all the event's needs. They will want to meet with every Committee Chairman and determine that area's requirements, how many people are desired for each task and what hours they believe need to be staffed.

This person will throw all of this information into one big pot and come back with a plan – job descriptions, shifts, counts – and ask fellow committee members to review and comment. Don't be surprised if they show more volunteers are needed than requested or has included a job description for a floater. A good Volunteer Services Committee Chairman knows a certain percentage of volunteers will be no-shows and adjusts accordingly.

Armed with a full list of needs versus a generic cry for help, they are now ready to communicate with their peers. Most likely your Volunteer Services Committee Chairman will seek out those whose demographics match your event's needs. Why solicit a 75-year old senior who volunteers mid-day at the hospital when the event will be held after dark and the music genre might not be to their liking? Yet, there may be important tasks pre-event for this person to accomplish.

Job Descriptions

The event's volunteer job descriptions do not need to be detailed but should clearly explain the task at hand. List if a certain skill set is desired or required. Indicate if sitting, standing, lifting, moving, loud sounds, working outside or carrying objects is needed. Some volunteers have physical restrictions.

The primary goal is to give potential volunteers an overview of what each volunteer job entails. Here's a sampling of volunteer jobs:

Sponsor Services – Volunteers serve in the Sponsor VIP Hospitality Tent. Duties include:

- Greet sponsors and VIPs and answer questions about the event.

- Refresh food and drinks.

- Gatekeep – allowing only those with appropriate credentials to enter this area.

Main Event – Volunteers serve at the event in the Talent Hospitality Tent/Green Room. Duties include:

- Greet talent and answer questions about the event.

- Refresh food and drinks.

- Gatekeep – allowing only those with appropriate credentials to enter this area.

Volunteers – Volunteers serve in a variety of capacities at the event. Duties include:

- Check in volunteers.

- Check on volunteers in their assigned positions.

- Offer refreshments to working volunteers.

- Provide information to the general public; serve as lost and found and first aid station.

Center Stage – Volunteers serve on stage and back stage areas. Technical skill sets and experience are desired. May be required to commit to work the entire event. Duties include:

- Take and follow direction from the Stage Manager.

- Provide secondary support to the sound and lighting vendors.

- Load in and load out equipment; lifting is involved.

- Gatekeep – allowing only those with appropriate credentials to enter this area.

Merchandise – Volunteers serve in the merchandise booth. This is a retail environment. Volunteers must work well under pressure; this area can become hectic during breaks or intermission. Standing is involved. Duties include:

- Greet patrons and answer questions about the event.

- Assist in retail sales of event merchandise.

- Cash handling.

- Package sold items for customer.

Site – Volunteers serve in locations in and around the park. Duties include:

- Arrive before and after the event to assist in getting the infrastructure set-up – fencing and barricades, tables, chairs, etc.; lifting is involved.

- Assist in transferring trash from venue to the dumpster and picking up miscellaneous trash at the venue.

Parking – Volunteers serve in locations in and around the venue including parking lots and at key ingress/egress locations. Work environment varies from asphalt to grass to concrete. Walking and standing are involved. Duties include:

- Greet patrons and answer questions about the event.

- Serve as first on-site event contact.

- Direct sponsors, VIPs and those with handicapped parking stickers to appropriate parking areas.

- Gatekeep – allowing only those with appropriate credentials to enter this area. May come in contact with people not willing to conform or follow rules; contact event supervisor.

Concessions – Volunteers serve in concession booths. Duties include:

- Provide supplemental support to concessionaires.

- Assist in processing customer orders.

Beverage Stands/Trailers – Volunteers serve in the event's beverage stands/ trailers. This is a retail environment. Volunteers must work well under pressure; this area can become hectic during breaks or intermission. Standing is involved. Beverage experience a plus. Duties include:

- Greet patrons and answer questions about the event.

- Prepare and serve drinks.

- Cash handling.

Ice – Volunteers travel between the icehouse, the concessions and the beverage stands/trailers. Heavy lifting is involved. Duties include:

- Deliver ice to concessionaires and beverage stands/trailers stored in the icehouse.

- Prepare and deliver receipts.

- Track deliveries.

Security – Volunteers serve in locations in and around the venue at key ingress/egress locations. Work environment varies from asphalt to grass to concrete. Walking and standing is involved. Duties include:

- Greet patrons and answer questions about the event.

- May come in contact with people not willing to conform or follow rules; contact event supervisor.

- Serve as an extra pair of eyes and ears for law enforcement.

- Document/photograph questionable activity.

Marketing, Public Relations and Publicity, On-Site Ticket Sales, Transportation and Treasurer – Normally these are handpicked – no volunteers needed.

SHIFTING INTO HIGH GEAR

Volunteer Shifts

When setting up the length of time for each shift and the actual start and end time for each shift, consider travel, traffic and parking because it will impact your volunteers' ability to reach the venue. When should crowds start to build? Should the volunteers' shift start just before then, allowing them easier access to parking? If the shift ends after the event is over, will these volunteers be able to safely return to their vehicles? Will they need an escort? How long is too long for a shift? Will volunteers be attending the event before or after their shift?

As part of the on-site orientation at check-in, provide each volunteer with a copy of the event's schedule and a map showing where key amenities and services are located. This should include important items, for example, first aid or emergency medical personnel, restrooms, the closest automatic teller machine (ATM), etc.

Sign Me Up

In the past, these would have been paper sign-up sheets. Nowadays, much of this can be done online with a simple registration form. Once submitted, the volunteer receives their confirmation detailing their volunteer job and shifts desired to work.

The Volunteer Services Committee Chairman can pull a report, assign and re-assign jobs. During the all-volunteer meeting, a list of shift assignments should be distributed. Afterward, any additional changes can be made to the master schedule and posted online on an unpublished page. Volunteers can be sent an email providing access to this otherwise inaccessible page.

For more details, see THE FINAL COUNTDOWN – All-Volunteer Meeting.

Sponsor Volunteers

The Volunteer Services Committee Chairman should work closely with the Sponsor Services Committee Chairman who will provide the entrée to the event's sponsors. While not all sponsors will be interested in having their employees volunteer, many companies have employee groups that provide service to the community.

Early on, ask your sponsor contact if they believe company personnel would be interested in volunteering and, if so, ask for an estimated number of volunteers. The Volunteer Services Committee will also want to know how the company typically communicates with its employees, for example, meetings, newsletters, emails, etc.

Each sponsor's point person should be personally contacted by the Volunteer Services Committee Chairman and sent a paper sign-up form or be given access to an online volunteer registration form. Ask that the company share it with the employee volunteer group or workforce. The sign-up form should provide volunteers the ability to indicate if they work for one of the sponsors. It is key that sponsor volunteers be matched during the first round of shift assignments.

The Volunteer Services Committee Chairman will also pave the way for the Marketing Services Committee Chairman who will seek to determine if the sponsor would like to purchase additional event tee shirts beyond whatever quantity is included in the sponsorship package. Of course, these can be imprinted with the sponsor's logo if desired.

SURVIVING THE EVENT

All-Volunteer Meeting

For more details, see THE FINAL COUNTDOWN – All-Volunteer Meeting.

Volunteers and Committee Members: How to Survive the Event

Whether your event is one day, a long weekend or a full week, it's likely many of the volunteers will be doing something out of the ordinary. Be prepared for one's body to talk back.

Here are some tips:

1. Volunteers should wear comfortable, close-toed shoes. Avoid wearing new shoes. Try building up one's legs, feet, etc., a few weeks before the event. For instance, if you'll be standing for

eight-hour shifts outdoors, find a situation that requires four hours of standing. Slowly ease into it. Your event experience should be much better as a result.

2. Wear comfortable clothes and layer. Be prepared for warmer and cooler weather. See if you'll be able to store your layers at the event as you add and subtract.

3. Eat regularly and within your normal routine. Eating foods outside your normal diet may cause you to react, meaning more sugar will bring your blood sugar levels to greater highs and lows. If you're not used to spicy food, you may be spending more time standing in line at the port-o-lets.

4. Drink lots of water and stay hydrated, especially if standing in the sun without benefit of shade.

5. If you don't normally drink caffeine, avoid it; stick to water. As you lie awake at 2 a.m., realize it could be the soda (soft drinks or pop) you drank earlier in the evening.

6. Give yourself a break from standing or sitting too long at the festival. Walk around if you've been seated for an extended period of time.

7. Wear a hat if you'll be outside in the sun. Make sure to cover the tops of your ears as well as your neck. Apply additional layers of sunscreen, if needed, throughout the day.

8. Consider whether you will need insect repellent.

9. Wear a fanny pack. OK, someone may make fun of you, but it's a great place to store things too big or too uncomfortable to put in your pockets.

The Final Countdown

Its extremely rewarding to stand at the sidelines of an all-volunteer meeting and watch the transformation take place. It begins with each Organizing Committee standing in a designated area with its committee members. Then with what seems like the waving of a magic wand, all those assembled grass-roots volunteers are asked to join their assigned committee. In that moment, the enthusiasm and energy moves to an exciting new level.

"For so long we were such an insular group," a food and wine festival Event Chairman shared. "Now joined by that next outer ring of festival volunteers, the various members of the Organizing Committee recognized the event was so much bigger. After months and months of planning, the event had reached the point of no return. It was now operating on its own momentum."

HAVE WE FORGOTTEN ANYTHING?

It is important for the Organizing Committee to meet a week before the event. Work through a checklist to make sure all the last minute details are covered and that nothing has slipped through the cracks.

At this final run through, the Event Chairman should lay the groundwork for what will happen during and after the event closes. Define the expectations so the Organizing Committee can begin to pull things together.

Last Minute Details

- Are there any checks that need to be prepared for deliveries during the event set up?

- Has the Treasurer purchased a receipt book for the ice that will be sold during the event to the concessionaires?

- Are there any changes to flight arrangements for the event's talent? If yes, has the Entertainment Committee's Transportation Committee been advised? Does it impact the hotel arrival or departure dates?

- Have arrangements been made for money drops during the event? Have police escorts been arranged?

- Will the Transportation Committee be asking the talent to sign this year's poster when taking them to the hotel or airport? Have they made arrangements to get a supply of posters? Are they being stored so they won't be damaged?

- Has someone on the stage crew been assigned to get local artists to sign the posters, too, or will the Transportation Committee handle this?

- Is someone bringing a hair dryer to dry out the piano strings if it rains? Who has the squeegee for the floor?

- Can we pay the piano tuner on the last day? Have they been given a VIP parking pass?

- Does everyone in the Sponsor VIP Hospitality Tent know you don't chill red wine?

- Are there VIPs that will need special attention? Any ruffled feathers need to be smoothed over?

- Will the mayor and elected officials be in attendance?

- Has the Event Chairman and Public Relations and Publicity Committee Chairman arranged to talk with law enforcement about crowd counts?

- Has the Treasurer determined where the bundled cash payments for the talent will be kept over the weekend?

- Where are the fire extinguishers, the fire alarms and the main breaker box for electricity?

- What's protocol for an emergency? I repeat, what's protocol for an emergency? Is there a defibrillator box at the venue?

- If a criminal act is taking place, what pertinent information needs to be locked into memory?

- Who is allowed back stage? What's the difference between each set of security credentials or passes?

- Do we expect any problems with the media?

- Does the committee have any unexpected expenses (approved, of course) the Treasurer needs to be made aware?

- Anyone throwing their weight around claiming to be worthy of access? Is this the same character that did this the last two years?

- Who always calls at the last minute asking for a VIP parking pass? Can this be anticipated and handled in advance?

- Is there a list of all Past Chairmen who should be recognized? Were they invited to attend the event? Given VIP parking passes?

- Are any entertainers expecting local friends to visit? Has security been informed?

- Remember to smile everyone, people will be watching you. Smile even if you are dealing with a problem.

- Remind the Organizing Committee that everyone is expected to meet for 30 minutes at the end of each day to review any issues, surprises or problems and discuss how each was solved or will be resolved.

All-Volunteer Meeting

About a week to 10 days before the event, the Volunteer Services Committee Chairman should schedule a mid-week, one-hour meeting in the early evening at the event venue/location for all volunteers. This is where the next wave of volunteers will be added to the event.

Key elements of the meeting are:

1. A welcome by the Event Chairman who, among other things, says thank you.

2. An introduction of the Organizing Committee.

3. Remarks by the Volunteer Services Committee Chairman who repeatedly says thank you and addresses the following: a) where volunteers can park; b) what time volunteers should arrive; c) where the information booth, also the volunteer check-in booth, will be located; d) suggested attire; e) what to do if you volunteer for more than one shift; f) how to access closed areas if you've been assigned those areas; g) who to call if they are unable to work or can't work more shifts; h) if the venue is compliant with the Americans with Disability Act (ADA) and the location of handicap parking, ramps, restrooms and special viewing areas for wheel chair patrons; i) key locations – restrooms, concessions, first aid, emergency personnel, police, merchandise booth, automatic teller machines (ATMs), lost and found including how lost children announcements are made; j) review rules concerning pets, alcohol and distribution of fliers, as well as what to do with outside vendors selling things at the venue that are not on the approved concessionaires list; k) map of the park; l) schedule of talent; and m) what to do if asked a question by the general public or the media.

4. Allow time for questions and answers.

5. Each member of the Organizing Committee needing volunteers is directed to a specific location and the assigned volunteers are asked to join them and get a more detailed explanation of their duties, plus a big thank you for volunteering!

Center Stage

Months ago, each member of the Organizing Committee was given the responsibility and authority for their respective area. The event is now on autopilot and literally nothing will stop the festival because the event has its own momentum. While each area is important, the spotlight shines on center stage or on any number of stages or on the event theme itself.

EVERYTHING PIVOTS FROM HERE

Once your event begins, the Event Chairman will turn the reigns over to the Stage Manager. Everything pivots around center stage or the focal point of the event. It doesn't matter if it's music, a wine tasting, an air show, food festival, film fest, book festival or a craft beer event. By no means does this indicate other areas are less important; it only means from this point forward, anything that happens will be driven by your event theme and your event's Stage Manager. They will control:

- When the equipment is set up and acts can go on to perform, demonstrations can be done, planes depart, etc.

- When the on-air personality makes announcements.

- When talent needs to make their way from the green room to the stage, and when talent needs to wrap up their performance.

- When talent should relinquish the stage. The Stage Manager will have advised the lead talent of the signal they will give five minutes before the talent's set or segment will end. Immediately after this, a member of the stage crew will announce to the Concession Committee Chairman, the Beverage Stands Coordinator and the Merchandise Committee Chairman that the talent is wrapping up and in less than five minutes intermission will start and crowds will be coming.

- When to make emergency announcements.

- When to pull the talent off the stage, out of the air or out from under the tents or from the theaters because of threatening or inclement weather. Most likely the Event Chairman and Public Relations and Publicity Committee Chairman will be consulted before this occurs.

- When it's safe to return to the stage, air, tents and theaters.

- Where an on-air personality, talent, sponsors and the media can stand or sit.

The focus is center stage and the person now running the event is the Stage Manager.

Stage Manager and Stage Crew

Imagine living within a confined area throughout an entire event. Back stage or the staging area regardless of the event is a notoriously small area. There never seems to be enough room for all the equipment plus everyone clamoring to be there – close to the talent.

What makes someone want to give up a full weekend to be a Stage Manager or serve on a stage crew? In many cases, these people have a connection with the event – loves people and organizing; loves music; performs music; likes being in the kitchen; reads voraciously; can recite famous lines from movies; collects wine; is a home brewer; or is a licensed pilot or retired military. They have some connection, some affinity to the event. Because of this relationship, they understand the lingo, be it chords on a guitar, how drum kits are set up, the proper knife to use to cut up steak versus veggies, how a gas top stove works, the proper temperature to store meat, how to use digital video equipment, how a movie is made, FAA regulations, how to serve red wine properly or how to tap a keg of beer. Simply, they understand what the event's talent is doing and, therefore, they don't need to be educated about this type of an event. They get it. They just want to be a part of it.

Avoid team members with egos and seek those who are patient, even tempered and open to taking direction. Be alert for useless groupies or stalkers, disguised as volunteers, as their focus will be elsewhere.

A good Stage Manager knows what standing on your feet for any number of hours can do to a body. The motherly types will have plenty of portable chairs, plus a cooler packed with water to keep her team hydrated. To keep the crew's blood sugar in check and everyone well fed, the Stage Manager will recommend or provide food to sustain them when there are few breaks. This helps keep the crew's rhythm steady and tempers even during long days outside or even indoors.

This is a tight group of people who normally volunteer to serve from start to finish. Throughout the event, they orchestrate every set change.

Just as the airline rep has touched base with talent to make flight arrangements or the Entertainment Committee's Transportation Committee Chairman has reached out to those driving to the event, the Stage Manager will have made contact with talent to discuss equipment needs. In some cases, these are clearly spelled out in the contract and addendum; in other cases, the Stage Manager communicates to explain the types of equipment being rented by the event for talent to use.

The Stage Manager will arrive at the event with their binder filled with a stage diagram and drawing for each talent group indicating where equipment will be placed. Backing up each of these is the key paperwork, such as the equipment list, just in case of questions.

When the lead talent arrives for each group, they will come searching for the Stage Manager. They know the Stage Manager is the orchestra leader. Jointly, they will review music and sound equipment placement, as well as lighting to make sure everything is correct. If not, adjustments will be made. The Stage Manager will walk through how the set change occurs and where the talent group needs to be before, during and after the performance. The Stage Manager will have one person on the stage crew who will make sure talent knows where to find food and where water will be placed once talent is on stage.

At least 15 minutes before one act is scheduled to end, the Stage Manager and stage crew will huddle together to walk through the diagram for the next act. He or she will delegate various responsibilities as to who moves what, when and where. When each act ends, the stage crew "strikes" the set and each carefully choreographed piece of equipment will be taken off the stage in an exact order and moved to a specific place. Particular care will be taken with the talent's personal equipment if the stage crew is even allowed to touch it.

As swiftly as one group exits the stage, the next act's equipment is put in place, adjusted and tests are initiated to make sure everything is functioning properly.

SETTING THE STAGE

Sound and Lighting

Some talent requires their sound and lighting technicians run "the boards" (equipment). It's best if this is planned well in advance, because some sound and lighting companies won't let outsiders touch their "babies." In these cases, it's important for the Stage Manager to convey the level of expertise of the sound and lighting vendor to talent.

The Stage Manager should ask talent to have their tech guys talk or meet with the event's sound and lighting technicians to walk through talent's needs. This should usually occur before the event or at the very latest before the start of the day of the performance. Talent's personnel may be able to share the boards with the event's techs; or, if they happen to know each other from years in the industry, your vendor may use this as the opportunity to take off their headset and get off the scaffolding for this act.

In many cases, talent desires to be showcased in the best light (and sound). A local AV company, which talent's tech staff may encounter while on the road, probably doesn't have the same level of experience as a seasoned sound guy.

A sound and lighting contract may include the following:

Technical

- Accommodations from the day the sound and lighting equipment is loaded in until the time it is loaded out. (Depending on where your sound and lighting vendors are located, they may not overnight after load out; they may head home.)

- Electrical service requirements and specifications.

- On-site electrician at load in for tie-in and at load out for disconnecting.

- Labor or stage crew to assist with load in or load out.

- Parking space within close proximity to the main stage.

- Forklift to assist in moving equipment on load in, load out and during the event if a major storm.

- Food (specific list) to be delivered to techs during the event.

Standard Equipment List

- Onstage monitor system to include: console, wedge and side monitors, drive, microphones, etc.

- Sound system equipment list to include: console, outboard, drive, snakes, power distribution, etc.

- Lighting to include lifts, trusses, racks, canisters, a gobo, controllers, dimmers, follow spots, follow spot operators, etc.

- Specialized Back-line Equipment List

- Audio amplification used behind talent – Unique needs requested by the event as part of the bid.

The event may be required to provide adequate security to protect the equipment from theft and damage. For more details, see SITE – Security – Hired Flashlights.

Sound and Lighting Bids

If the Stage Manager desires to receive bids for apples, oranges, bananas and pears, just ask sound and lighting companies to send a bid. These are much more difficult to compare, so it's best for the event to create a bid request or request for proposal (RFP) dictating the event's needs. Allow ample space for bidders to insert pricing.

Equipment

After each talent contract is fully executed, key paperwork including the equipment requirement addendum should be provided to the Stage Manager to review required equipment. In some cases, it is more cost effective for the event to rent equipment than for talent to bring their own. Talent may be fine not subjecting their equipment to airline wear and tear and/or worrying about safety and security when left in a hotel room.

By renting commonly used equipment, it can save on airfares and baggage fees, reduce the event's liability for damaged talent equipment and eliminate the need for vans or trailers to transfer equipment to and from the airport, venue and hotel.

Some equipment is fairly common, like a grand piano, drum kit, stove and sink, refrigerator truck, AV equipment, tents, tables and chairs, etc. and readily available. From a time standpoint, renting it may make more sense as the stage crew can then eliminate the need to set up and tear down before and after each act.

As the paperwork and equipment requirement addenda come in, the Stage Manager should also liaison with the sound and lighting equipment company to make sure it can meet all of talent's needs. This is especially important for musical events. Some talent have very particular needs; others list specific equipment as preferred. Your local supplier may only have an XYZ when an ABC is requested; but it will work.

Communication is key and a good Stage Manager should be firm in explaining what is available in your region and sell how it can work just as well. Nothing is worse than talent showing up and expecting what is in the contact, only to then learn the equipment is not as agreed. If talent is focused on being wronged, their performance may be less than stellar.

If the event involves food, beer or wine, most likely your local health department's regulations will control how things work. It is the Stage Manager's job to have meet with health officials early in the process to walk through the list of special equipment needs and then convey to the talent what is feasible based on local laws. Don't have your chef show up with a charcoal grill to find out only gas grills are permitted. The same thing holds for grease traps and sinks. Spend time early on communicating with your talent.

A forklift is a critical piece of rental equipment. It will be used to install the scaffolding for the sound and lighting equipment tower. The sound and lighting crew will also use it to place speakers on the scaffolding and the Site Services Committee's Beverage Stands Coordinator will use it to move the beverage trailers into grassy areas versus having the beverage dealer's truck potentially damage the turf.

SOME IMPORTANT STAGING DETAILS

Access

The back stage area should be limited to only essential personnel, especially if this area is small. Each person will have an appropriate credential or pass to gain access. Many of these faces will be on site throughout the event, so they will be familiar ones.

Sound and Lighting Staff – Rarely will you see them linger. They normally have a specific purpose for being in a given location.

Piano Tuner or Technician – They have been hired to perform this service. This may be a daily visit if the piano is left out in the elements for any part of the day or may come following rain. Weather conditions greatly affect pianos.

Stage Crew – This is their home for the event. When they aren't working, they may have the opportunity to enjoy the event, just with a different vantage point than most.

Organizing Committee – In many cases, the Event Chairman and various Committee Chairmen are only stopping by to take a break from their own responsibilities, to say hello or are searching for a fellow Committee Chairman. If this is one area with indoor plumbing, that may also be the draw.

Talent – The girlfriends, spouses, friends and hangers-on can see them from outside the fence, or if advance notice was provided, may be able to access the Talent Hospitality Tent/Green Room.

Electrician – If this is a city venue, this may be a city electrician. In many cases, they will be more visible during the event set-up rather than during the event, unless an emergency.

Lack of Access

Don't be surprised if longtime friends of talent show up and hang at the back fence waiting to say hello. It's usually best to have them write a legible note and then have the Stage Manager pass it to talent when walking off the stage. In that way, these folks won't see them shrug their shoulders when reading the note and saying, "I don't recognize this name."

Some managers may also come with talent, some planned and some unexpected. Some are gems and others require more maintenance than the talent while others paint their client in a completely different light than the Organizing Committee will experience.

The Toolkit

Just like other committees, the Stage Manager will have a toolkit on site. These are suggested items for a musical event and items may also apply to other event theme types:

- Duct tape (and a lot of it) – You never know when you might need to quickly wrap heavy-duty plastic sheeting around large speakers and secure it before a rain storm hits with 30 miles per hour wind gusts.

- A toolbox with basic tools – Hammer, regular and needle nose pliers, wrenches, screwdrivers, socket sets, etc.

- WD-40® and a degreasing product.

- Clothespins – Great for keeping sheet music in place if the winds kick up.

- Coolers for beverages – Large ones to ice up plenty of water to keep the stage crew hydrated before, during and after the event.

- A regular cooler – Use this to store food, but in an emergency the ice may come in handy if someone is injured.

- Tall beverage cups – It saves on lots of half empty bottles of water – and a marker to write the owner's name on the cup.

- Napkins or paper towels.

- Nuts, such as peanuts – To recharge the stage crew's batteries quickly. While there should be enough time to eat between acts, inclement weather can knock things off schedule quickly.

- Clean rags – It wouldn't be the first time talent knocked over his drink during a performance or rainwater had formed a puddle and needed to be removed near a microphone or key access point.

- Towels – For talent and equipment – to wipe away sweat or perspiration.

- A 27" stool – Some talent like to sit while a colleague is performing.

- Plexiglas – 10 total 11" x 17" sheets are a great way to protect music sheets when it's rainy or windy.

- A chair and a stool – These will be used by the keyboardist (not the piano player).

- Standard office supplies – Pen, paper, tape, pencils, etc.

- First aid kit.

- Paper telephone book.

- Phone number of the venue and address posted above the public or house phone (in case of an emergency).

- Phone message pad and pen on a string near the public or house phone. How loud is the ringer?

- Wi-Fi availability, access and passwords.

- Phone re-charging station.

- Trash can and liners.

- Ashtray or cigarette or cigar butt bucket.

- Catered food for the sound and lighting technical crew as per the contract. Depending on the event's needs, it may be possible for the vendor to use fewer roadies (sound and lighting support crew) if the Stage Manager promises to keep them well fed and watered and to have members of the stage crew spell them for bathroom breaks and serve as follow spot operators.

More than once, an event has made them promises it did not keep, so they may be leery of anything but bringing their team's food and water. Even though sound and lighting crews put in long hours during an event, there needs to be a strong bond of trust to allow anyone else to touch their equipment.

Now a Word from Our Sponsor

How many of us have attended a festival where it took forever to transition from one act to another? What are you going to do? Get up and leave after you have bought your ticket and are now at the venue? You're a captive audience. While quick set changes are to be applauded, realize the time between acts is also a valuable time for an event and concessions to generate revenue.

If your event has a reputation for quick set changes, everyone rushes the concessions, merchandise and port-o-lets at once, creating lines. However, if your event has a moderate transition time between acts, a patron who might otherwise not have jumped up to buy food or drink may instead be enticed by someone else's purchase.

Timing is everything. Provide your vendors a chance to sell their products but don't allow the break or intermission to linger too long. Sometimes it can't be helped. A bad connection between a microphone and monitor may take a bit of time to isolate. Your sound and lighting company, most likely, would prefer everything to run on schedule. A delay now means it will prolong the end of a long day.

Merchandise

C an lightning strike twice in the same place? "The answer is yes, but you can't count on a brilliant festival artwork design to be followed by another one year after year," advised the Event Chairman of a food festival. "Case in point is our tee-shirt design. One year it was stellar and demand exceeded inventory.

We anticipated and budgeted for the same impactful design the next year. However, the Merchandise Committee Chairman couldn't figure out why it was taking so long for last year's creative genius to present concepts. Seems the artist was a one hit wonder. The one late-to-the-game concept the artist presented fell flat. The committee had little choice but to produce a minimum number of tee shirts with the new design and to ramp up for sales of the stellar design."

The Merchandise Committee drives revenues, as well as serves as an important tool in promoting the event. Its function is interwoven among all the other committees – Sponsor Services, Treasurer, Marketing Services, Public Relations and Publicity, Volunteers, Stage Manager, Site Services and Concessions.

MAKE IT OR BREAK IT WITH THE RIGHT DESIGN

Signature Merchandise

One of the best ways to generate event revenue is to sell signature items bearing the event's name, logo or design.

The big variable here, in addition to the weather during the event, is the popularity of each year's artwork or design. The merchandise area requires a mix of creativity, inventory, retail experience, promotion and sales, plus shipping and delivery. Setting a to-do calendar and staying on task are key, especially if it takes several efforts for the artist to land on a winning design.

The Merchandise Committee Chairman usually has seen multiple concepts and worked closely with the graphic designer or artist to fine tune one or two concepts for the poster or tee shirt. These are not something they will bring to the table without the support of the Merchandise Committee. Only then will the concepts be presented to the Event Chairman for final selection or approval. A good testing ground for the design's acceptance is the Organizing Committee's overall response or reaction.

Designs from some years are more popular than others and inventory will sell out more quickly. Understanding consumer buying habits is tricky. Even in a bad year, die-hard fans will typically keep their collection going and continue to make an annual purchase. The event should, and your patrons will, demand more than a mediocre design. Everyone involved will want a "need it, gotta have it" concept, so it will generate revenue, meet budget projections and keep the event's fans smiling.

Placing a merchandise order involves more than just the perfect artwork. Are the tee shirts the right fabric and color? How many need to be ordered and in what sizes? If the temperatures vary from day to evening, should sweatshirts also be sold? What about hats, mugs, and on and on? If this is the event's first year, start with a very narrow selection in order to not tie up a lot of money in a large variety of inventory.

Consider it from this perspective. If a patron has X amount of dollars to spend, would they prefer to have a vast array of inventory or a very narrow selection to choose from? Will your patrons buy more items or only spend to their limit? Will they buy lower priced items rather than higher priced ones? As with selecting talent, a magical matrix also exists in determining the merchandise product mix.

Because members of the Organizing Committee will put in countless hours to create the event, the Event Chairman may ask the Merchandise Committee Chairman to budget for complimentary items for the Organizing Committee. These can include a limited number of the commemorative posters, clothing to be worn during the event such as tee shirts or polo shirts, hats, or other merchandise. Team members may also be given the option to purchase additional quantities at a discounted price for a limited period of time.

This Year's Design or Theme

It's not unusual for an event to switch up its design or theme each year. This is a big plus when selling merchandise because it gives buyers a reason to have the latest tee shirt. While some attendees will know the event by the headliner artist or food served or wine featured, others will remember it for the poster design.

If you are interested in holding a design contest to select a new theme, reach out to your local arts council or arts agency to see if they are interested and what level of support they can offer. Typically, they have a database of artists, graphic designers or creative types in your community and can send out a call for entries. Having submissions delivered to the arts council or arts agency's office is a significant time saver. Contest rules should clearly indicate that there might not be a winner selected from the entries and that all copyrights must be transferred in writing to the event immediately after the contest winner is named.

However, the Event Chairman and Marketing Services Committee Chairman need to have a Plan B just in case no submissions are workable. Encourage at least a three–person panel of judges to review all the entries – perhaps an event representative, a local printer, arts organization staff or board member and a local artist.

Event organizers need to allow as much time as possible to put out the call for entries and to let the arts community know they are serious by offering an honorarium to the winner. In addition, the winner should be recognized throughout the event, invited to pull the curtain during the official poster unveiling, recognized in the poster unveiling news release, plus be introduced to the audience during the event.

Build additional time into the production schedule just in case none of the entries are a match for the event. While Plan B sits in the drawer, the hope is that it won't need to be used. Breathe a sigh of relief when the winner is picked. For more details, see MERCHANDISE – The Production Schedule.

Once the winner is selected, send thank-you letters to all contestants offering the event's appreciation and encourage them to submit again in the future, if warranted. Also, remember to add the arts agency to your roster of community VIPs and send all key personnel an extra big thank you for their support in this project.

CREATING A TO-DO LIST AND A TIMETABLE

The Production Schedule

If this is the event's first year, put together a list of tasks and then schedule each to be completed by a specific date, giving the Merchandise Committee plenty of lead time. Base this on merchandise only being sold on site at the event and not online.

The schedule will need to be modified if materials will also be sold online. This is especially true when a new signature design is unveiled. Roughly one (1) month to three (3) months in advance of the event, merchandise could go on sale online. Ticket sales and merchandise usually go on sale at the same time.

ARTWORK	In Advance of Event
Solicit artwork design	
If in the form of a competition with the local arts council or agency, allow this amount of lead time.	10-11 months
Entries Received	8 months
Judging	7 months, 3 weeks
If using the creative services of one of your sponsors like the local daily newspaper with a graphic designer or artist on staff, this amount of lead time should be needed.	6 months, 2 weeks
Final decision	5 months, 2 weeks

TEE SHIRTS/SWEATSHIRTS	In Advance of Event
Bids for tee shirts and sweatshirts sent/let	5 months, 2 weeks
Bids for tee shirts and sweatshirts due	5 months
Tee shirt and sweatshirts vendor selected	4 months, 3 weeks
Tee shirt and sweatshirt sample order placed	4 months
Tee shirt and sweatshirt artwork due	3 months, 3 weeks
Provide "top secret" artwork to tee shirt and sweatshirt vendor	3 months, 3 weeks
Tee shirt samples available for sponsor breakfast	3 months
Send letter to sponsors with order form and sample tee shirts	2 months, 3 weeks
Distribute order form to Organizing Committee for event tee shirts	2 months, 3 weeks
Order form returned from sponsors and Organizing Committee	2 months
Tee shirt order placed for sponsors	1 month, 3 weeks
All tee shirts and sweatshirts ordered	1 month
Sponsor and Organizing Committee tee shirts delivered	3 weeks
All remaining tee shirts and sweatshirts inventoried and tagged/labeled	3 weeks
Presales begin	

POSTER	In Advance of Event
Bids for posters sent/let	5 months, 2 weeks
Bids for posters due	5 months
Poster design due	5 months
Copy for poster due (to include sponsor logos, names Organizing Committee members and talent)	4 months, 2 weeks
Poster final proof reviewed and approved	4 months
Provide "top secret" artwork to poster printer	3 months, 3 weeks
Poster delivered from printer	3 months, 2 weeks
Posters to frame vendor for sponsor breakfast poster unveiling and sponsor gifts	3 months, 2 weeks
Framed posters picked up from frame vendor	3 months
Presales begin	

Merchandise Bids

When determining the poster size, consider the possibility of using a standard picture frame size. It will make it much easier for the Merchandise Committee responsible for framing posters for the event's sponsors as well as those who purchase the posters.

The bid letter for tee shirts, sweatshirts and the poster should be sent to secure a quote on each project. Once the graphic designer has finalized the artwork, the selected bidder may be asked to refresh its quote to the exact specifications (specs) since details are now known.

A big difference can exist when it comes to paper stock for the poster. A thicker, textured or smooth, dull stock may convey a poster that is more a piece of art; a thinner, glossier stock may come across as an inexpensive movie promotion piece. Perhaps a more collectible paper stock could be used for sponsors and resale purposes.

Alternately, promotional posters may be a reduced version of the real thing. These could then be printed on a shiny, less expensive stock; and if the quantity (run size) is smaller, it may be more affordable to have these digitally printed. Anticipate promo posters will disappear before and after the event.

The list of information to be included on the poster will be generated by at least four different areas: Event Chairman (a list of Organizing Committee members and places of employment), Sponsor Services (a list of sponsors by category with spelling, punctuation and capitalization based upon the information on the Sponsor Checklist, along with digital logo files), Entertainment (schedule of talent by day and date with name of act as detailed in the contract); and Merchandise Committee (name of artist, photographer and/or graphic designer).

The Event Chairman and the Merchandise Committee Chairman should both be involved in proofing the poster's final copy to assure no one is missed and spellings are correct. Have someone who has not been involved in the process, perhaps the Marketing Services Committee Chairman or the Public Relations and Publicity Committee Chairman, review the final proof (for consistency) from the graphic designer/artist before the job goes to the shirt vendor or the printer.

While the term final proof is used by the graphic designer or artist, it's actually a misnomer; two more rounds of proofing occur: a matchprint color proof prepared by the printer to assure the digital files provided by the graphic designer or artist "match" before the project is put on the press; and the final proof comes during the press check when the job is on the press. Don't be surprised if a glaring error pops up that no one saw before. The cost to make the correction and see a new proof is negligible in order for the poster to be accurate.

If your Merchandise Committee Chairman has a strong printing background, let them handle the press check.

Let's take a step back and review what's involved in bidding a tee shirt and a poster. If you have no idea where to send the bids, investigate other events held around town and their shirts. How is the artwork printed on the shirt? Examine the fabric of the shirt. Realize the price points on the shirts for those particular events may be higher or lower, but it's a starting point.

The Merchandise Committee's initial goal should be to gather names of tee shirt vendors and references. While checking off items on the event's wish list – in addition to pricing, fabric and style options – determine if these are local businesses or a franchise. Is the owner on site while the shirts are being printed or do they delegate and disappear?

Find out from your references which of these businesses and/or suppliers stand behind their products if there is a defect in product or workmanship. Is the company reliable? Does it adhere to a schedule? Is it easy to work with? Does it deliver? Do they know if the vendor could print more shirts on short notice or overnight if your event had an extremely popular design?

NOW ON SALE

Inventory

After the initial tee shirt and sweatshirt order is delivered to the event's off-site location, the Merchandise Committee should gather to begin preparing the items for sale. For smaller events, a great way to reconcile sold items with cash in the register is to tag each item with a two-part perforated label. Once sold, the bottom tear-off goes in the register and the top label remains affixed to the product. This is a little time intensive on the front end, but it can provide a very basic system for tracking inventory against sales.

An alternative for larger festivals is to tag each item with a barcoded label with each barcode representing product (tee shirt or sweatshirt), size and color. Cash registers with barcode scanners are relatively inexpensive. Consult with local store owners in your community who use barcode scanners to get feedback.

Also, read online reviews to see if reliable. While the event may not use the register year-round, it will get heavy use for a short period of time and needs to be reliable. Double check whether the event's equipment storage facility is a good match for the register – temperature controlled with good airflow, avoiding too hot or cold conditions because it may affect the electronics and working parts.

One person should take responsibility for the entire inventory. Initially, the Merchandise Committee Chairman may sign for the orders as they are being delivered; but once counted, tagged, bagged and re-boxed, the Inventory Control Coordinator should assume responsibility for all the materials. That would include overseeing or loading them into the temporary inventory storage facility, (possibly a walk-in rent-a-trailer) and then transporting to the event venue.

The Inventory Control Coordinator will be the one person responsible for stocking and replenishing the merchandise booth for the event and throughout the event. The replenishing should occur at intervals and be done at a dozen at a time. This assumes Merchandise Committee members would have placed tee shirts and sweatshirts in the same size and color in a clear plastic bag with 12 in each and then sealed the bag with a heat sealer.

All inventory should be tracked, including:

- Items for sponsors.

- Complimentary items the Event Chairman authorized be distributed to the Organizing Committee such as clothing to be worn during the event. Team members may also be given the option to purchase additional items at a discounted price for a limited period of time.

- Gifts for talent as well as copies of the commemorative poster or other merchandise talent is being asked to sign

- Items that will be used for promotional purposes, for example, given to the media, other organizations, elected officials, etc.

- Items that are damaged and/or held to be returned for credit.

- Items which will be destroyed after the event (this is best done as a two-person decision and both sign their names next to those for fear they will be accused of stealing in later years).

Business is business, so it's important to have sponsors and committee members sign for their items when received.

Presales

Sales in advance of the event can include merchandise sold online, merchandise sold at off-site locations by third parties and merchandise sold at sanctioned related events by the Merchandise Committee. While it may appear to be a good idea to sell merchandise at off-site locations, a number of things are involved and can be quite time intensive for the revenue returned, not to mention the risk of lost or damaged merchandise. With merchandise as well as tickets being available online, it is difficult to justify off-site sales. For more details, see MONEY MATTERS – Selling Merchandise Online.

On-Site Inventory Control

As each bag is removed from inventory storage before and during the event, the Inventory Control Coordinator should track the product, size and color.

Special care should be taken when placing the inventory trailer at the event site. It should be located within a fenced in or secure area with vehicles blocking the hitch. Add a lock to the hitch for an additional layer of security. The Inventory Control Coordinator should be the only person authorized to enter and exit the locked trailer so inventory counts fall on one person, thus avoiding the he-said, she-said later.

The Inventory Control Coordinator should be the one who has the only key to access the trailer. As a back up, the Treasurer or Event Chairman should have one too but not use it without the Inventory Control Coordinator being present. Things can get hectic during an event, and it wouldn't be the first time keys were accidentally locked inside. Keep a can of WD-40® handy should the lock become temperamental.

Each day, after the close of sales, the Inventory Control Coordinator will re-inventory the trailer stock and update the Treasurer. This will be compared against merchandise "on the shelf" and booth sales.

Merchandise Booth

With a good design, an event's merchandise booth can generate a fair amount of revenue for a festival.

The booth is a miniature storefront and can often be placed amid food concessions providing the neighboring vendor's products do not create smoke or grease. Some storefronts are a single booth width, while larger events can take up more spaces or locations.

Consider using wire grids/slatgrid displays on the walls and overhead to showcase the tee shirts and sweatshirts in various sizes. Decorate the booth, too, as if the space were a full-time retail store. Lightweight poster frames can be used to hang this year's poster as well as those from the past. The booth should be well lit and have ample space to accommodate members of the Merchandise Committee and other volunteers moving about, especially during hectic intermissions.

The price should be clearly marked on each product and visible from a distance. A full menu of items, similar to a food concession, should showcase all available merchandise and pricing.

Join with other concessionaires in hanging a banner above the front of the event's merchandise booth to the same standards and specs. It should be visible from a distance so patrons in the crowd can find the booth among many.

Like the beverage stands/trailers, the Treasurer will need to set up procedures regarding money handling for the merchandise booth. For more details, see MONEY MATTERS – Money Handling Procedures and Toolkit – Cash Handling Supplies.

DO'S AND DONT'S

Limited Edition Merchandise

If the event is going to offer limited edition merchandise, order enough items, for example, posters, from the start. By limiting the number available for purchase over the event's lifetime, the event automatically enhances the value of the product.

An important thing to remember is that if an item is signed and numbered, there should be no more available after the last one is sold. Producing more could negate the terms of the author's original agreement especially if reproduction rights were limited to a specific quantity.

Imagine the graphic artist's surprise when he learned the most popular festival poster which he designed free of charge and featured his name was reproduced without his permission. He was not asked to be at the press check to make sure the end product was to his standard. The event had no idea the graphic artist owned the copyright to the poster as the event had failed to ask the author to transfer the rights. As such, the event had no right to contact the printer and order more. The printer failed, too, because it was the graphic artist who brought the project to them in the first place.

Holiday Sales

Some events promote signature wear and event posters as holiday gifts to the community between Thanksgiving and Christmas. Organizing Committee members too caught up in running the event may be offered their discounted rate again. For more details, see MARKETING – Advertising.

Site

Events control their own destinies by the type of entertainment they book. Be prepared for the arrival of diehard fans. One such festival believing its venue was perfect and parking adequate, failed to check the types of crowds one group drew. In addition to not assigning volunteer parking lot attendants to maximize available space, the festival didn't meet with transportation officials to determine the traffic limitations of nearby roads. The end result was backups, congestion, requests for refunds, clogged phone lines, irate festival goers, not-so-nice social media posts and bad press which followed them to the next event. The event has ceased to exist.

A year's worth of planning begins to unfold a few days before the event begins. It's amazing to watch the venue be transformed and a short time later be taken down, folded back up and put in storage for another year.

IT ALL COMES TOGETHER IN THE END

From Zero to Set Up

If your event is held within a town, city or county, or city or county facility – like a park – a special event permit may be required. It's not unusual for a pre-event meeting to be required with all affected government departments, for example, streets, sanitation, parks and recreation, power, police, etc. This one gathering makes it easier to review the event once, versus sending numerous emails and chasing phone calls and messages. This meeting aids in addressing questions perhaps otherwise not anticipated.

For instance, if an unauthorized vendor enters the park and starts selling neon necklaces, who will ask them to leave? If a candidate for elected office shows up and begins handing out campaign literature, which committee will handle this? If one isn't on the approved concessionaire list given to the police department or the candidate does not have a permit or is authorized by the event to distribute fliers, law enforcement can ask both of them to leave.

As your event begins to set up, a particular order needs to be followed as the largest items usually go in first, or the items needing to be located in the center of the venue are installed, moving outward. Conversely, some start at the perimeter. If closing off the outer edges first, make sure to maintain access to the venue. The most important thing is to have a plan. This will reduce items being moved or installed, removed and reinstalled.

The venue usually has considerable activity on set-up day. Ask your Volunteer Services Committee Chairman to provide a handful of security volunteers to sit back and be its eyes and ears. Have them watch for people appearing to be part of set-up but who aren't. This is especially helpful when everyone at the venue is busy working and focused on getting things up and running.

The Site Map

If you're lucky, the city, county or venue will have (artwork of) a site map, or perhaps the Marketing Services Committee can generate one. The map will have multiple applications. For the Site Services Committee, the map can show vendors where to place port-o-lets, concession tents, beverage stands/trailers, Sponsor VIP and Talent Hospitality tents, as well as the placement of trash cans, fencing and barricades. For the Volunteer Services Committee, it can be used to show volunteers where they will be stationed.

The Entertainment Committee will use it to indicate what needs to be roped off, where to park equipment trucks once unloaded and placement of sound and lighting towers, equipment and large screen TVs. The Sponsor Services Committee will send it to sponsors to show them the location of VIP parking, VIP seats and the Sponsor VIP Hospitality Tent.

The Public Relations and Publicity Committee may send a digital version of it out with news releases or ask the local media to include the artwork showing where the event entrances are located. The Concession Committee Chairman and Beverage Stands Coordinator will send it to vendors showing the location of each vendor and where to enter the event site for set up. Share a copy with local law enforcement officers before the event as well as overnight security if hired.

Insurance

Festival and event insurance is a specialized type of insurance. Depending on your kind of event, the coverage needed will vary. When events are held at a city or county parks, the government agency's risk management department may dictate the minimum amount of liability insurance required, for instance, $1,000,000 in liability may be required for any event with 50 or more people.

The insurance policy application will most likely require:

- The event's name and mailing address.

- Dates of the event, including set up and tear down.

- A description of the event including how many years the event has been in existence.

- Venue locations if the event is held at one or more sites.

- Location if held indoors or outside or both.

- The number previously in attendance each day and the average for the entire event, plus the total estimated count for the upcoming event for all days.

- Information on whether alcohol will be sold at the event and if so by whom – the event organizer, concessionaires or vendors, nonprofits, a combination of the above or the venue itself.

- Accommodation details if offered at the event, such as camping (think greater risks due to campfires and darkness).

- A breakdown of the types of concessions or vendors – merchandise, food and beverages and/or rides.

- Security if provided at the event. If yes, describe if contracted, volunteer, local law enforcement, etc.

- Anticipated gross revenue.

- Anticipated total expenses.

- Any past claims or losses, providing details.

- The amount of general liability limits per incident desired (again, check if the venue or a government agency requires a minimum amount).

Check if liquor liability insurance is required. The event may not sell liquor but, if coolers are permitted, this can become a gray area unless signage prohibiting alcohol is clearly displayed. If rental equipment is used, the event may want to consider property coverage. Other types of insurance to consider are weather, non-appearance, volunteer accident and event cancellation.

Co-Insurance

Often the venue requires the event organizer to list it as a co-insured on the event insurance policy. This is normal and is done in order to protect the venue. In today's litigious society, anyone suing is likely to sue everyone involved.

RUNNING DOWN THE CHECKLIST

Sprucing Up the Landscape

When booking the venue, remember to ask when routine and annual maintenance is performed. This will provide ample time for the venue to reschedule activities to before or after your event. For instance, trim back bushes in advance of the event in order to minimize the chance someone could hide behind them and attack one of your patrons.

Rain makes everything grow. Watch for low hanging branches, plants, shrubs and bushes or those that have the potential to grow before the event kicks off. Providing as much notice as possible to maintenance staff will be appreciated because they most likely will be tagged to help with lots of last minute things.

Be aware: shaking the bushes sometimes brings out wildlife that lives at your venue year-round.

Spraying for Bugs

Not familiar with pesky outdoor insects and what time of year they are active? A handful of people can assist. Check with the staff at your local County Extension Center affiliated with a major state university. They are well versed in agriculture, horticulture and insects. If none are available and your event is in a public park, check with the maintenance staff. They can advise if the park is sprayed for mosquitoes or other insects – like no-see-ums, sand fleas, etc. Ask if scheduled spraying can be done before your event.

If it has been particularly rainy in the six months before the event, stay in touch with the venue to make sure no areas allow for standing water where mosquitoes can breed.

Light Bulbs OK? Check.

It may not seem like a big deal, but a burned out light bulb can stick out like a sore thumb during the event. Ask maintenance to let you know where a supply of extra bulbs and a ladder can be found in the off chance you need to change one during your event. Visit the venue after dark before your event to see if any bulbs need attention. Dark areas create potential liability issues. Why set up the event for a problem?

Lawn Mowed? Check.

While it may not seem like a big deal, the height of the grass between your parking lot and an indoor venue makes a difference as does the grass height at an outdoor event, say in a county park. Work closely with the maintenance staff to make sure the grass is mowed before the event. Take recent weather conditions and forecasts into consideration. Grass type and height affect walking. Too high and people can trip, creating potential liability issues. Too short and grass can die quickly during the heat of summer and under heavy foot traffic.

Many grounds keepers fertilize, aerate the soil and sow seed in the fall. Spring seeding sometimes involves extra watering to aid rooting. Communicate well in advance to see if these are planned prior to your event because these activities will impact the physical site. Unexpected roping off a seeded area may reduce the size of planned parking or seating areas. More cars and people in less space are not ideal. It can affect your guests' experience, number of social media posts and potential ticket and merchandise revenue.

Parking – Availability

If your Site Services Committee Chairman is working closely with the city or other government agencies, they may be able to secure a list of available parking lots, decks and garages and number of spaces in each. If an artwork file is available, please provide this information to the Public Relations and Publicity Committee Chairman who can prep and distribute a news release about parking. If a mobile app or website is available, advise how to access or provide a link. Include parking fees and payment options – credit card, coins, etc., if applicable. The Marketing Services Committee should also be sent a copy of a parking map or a link to include on the event's website.

Fencing and Barricades

While it's not the prettiest thing around, fencing – be it orange plastic mesh or chain link – and barricades are to keep some people out and others in. In some cases, it's used to contain the event for the sole purpose of ticket sales.

Fencing and barricades at an entrance gate may need to be much more sturdy than fencing behind a concession area unless, of course, this area involves lots of cash handling and the event wants to make sure absolutely no one can gain access. When considering fencing around the concessions, think the worse case. What happens if a grease fire occurs? Will this type of fence hinder the ability to escape? Or would an orange plastic mesh fence work instead? The fire marshal and the local health department may need to be consulted.

In the Sponsor VIP Hospitality Tent and Talent Hospitality Tent/Green Room, fencing may be decorative white plastic picket fence. This type serves as a low level barrier for entry or to re-direct traffic flow.

MAKING SURE YOUR EVENT IS SAFE AND SECURE

Local Law Enforcement

Regardless of whether a pre-event meeting (for many city and county government venues) is required when pulling a special event permit, it's always wise to reach out to your local law enforcement and the officer assigned to the event. Help them help you!

Sometimes an event and its traffic will fall under the jurisdiction of adjoining law enforcement agencies; communicate to all. There may need to be some coordination among two or more agencies to make sure event patrons are receiving consistent messages regarding road closures, parking availability or closed lots, the status of an accident or routing vehicles to closed areas. It can happen and has happened and it will happen again.

Correspondence sent to local law enforcement should include the following:

1. Event Chairman's name and how they can be contacted during the event, plus the next in command which may be a Vice Chairman or the Site Services Committee Chairman. This allows the officer in charge to go straight to the top if an issue arises. Also, it can quickly deride someone who claims to be in charge when they have no affiliation with the event whatsoever. This is one of the cases where law enforcement wants the closest distance between a question and an answer to be the right answer from the right person.

2. Describe the uniform being worn by the Organizing Committee. An officer may have a concern during the event and may reach out to the first person wearing the Organizing Committee uniform. The Event Chairman should have defined when and how they should be contacted in the event of an emergency or critical need. Perhaps law enforcement is asked to contact the Site Services Committee's Security Committee Chairman to handle an issue and to make the decision whether the Event Chairman should be involved.

3. Detail where the Event Chairman and second-in-command should be located throughout the event.

4. Provide the name of your daytime or nighttime security vendor. Share the hours it will be on site and who it will turn over the "keys" to at the end of its shift.

5. Provide a sample of each type of security credential or pass and the restrictions or restricted areas each can access. Advise who is responsible for this area and what efforts were made to minimize the chances of credentials and passes being reproduced.

6. Indicate how many and where volunteer security posts will be located on the site map.

7. Provide a sample of the VIP parking passes and the access each provides. Indicate who should have received these. If the Entertainment Committee's Transportation Committee will be making frequent trips, let law enforcement know what route they plan to take.

8. Provide a list of the authorized concessionaires or vendors and the products each will be selling. Include a copy of the Rules, Regulations and Concession Agreement. Advise who is responsible for this area.

9. Provide the name of the port-o-let vendor because it will be coming in the off hours.

10. Provide the name of the tent vendor and indicate the total number of tents to be installed.

11. Detail what access or routes emergency medical services will have available. Explain how first aid will be provided and where.

12. Provide a map of the park with key elements noted. This will help the police see possible traffic patterns used by your patrons, identify restricted areas and anticipate locations or routes for criminal activities and where criminals could hide.

Anticipate law enforcement offering suggestions for safety and security to you and the Organizing Committee. These are normally helpful hints. For example, when discussing volunteers working in parking lots, orange vests may be recommended to make them more visible.

Security

Volunteers

Every volunteer position requires specific skill sets. The Site Services Committee's Security Committee is no different. These volunteers will be solicited by and checked-in through the Volunteer Services Committee. They should be polite, cordial, have the ability to approach people in a diplomatic manner when the need arises and be smart enough to know when to call in law enforcement to take over.

They need to be familiar with statutes, ordinances or rules governing the venue and not attempt to instill their personal belief system. Because they will be out in the crowd, they'll be better able to observe situations a uniformed officer may not – alcohol, pets, illegal drugs, underage children drinking, a fight, domestic violence, children being approached or watched by strangers, robbery, theft, etc.

They will also need to act if an unauthorized vendor is selling wares or if a local politician is handing out re-election fliers.

Hired Flashlights

For most events, even those that are single day events, nighttime security will be needed. This is one of those needs that require paid personnel. If your event is like many events on a shoestring budget, paying for overnight security can be a luxury as well as a necessity.

In interviewing security companies, ask how frequently its personnel make routine walk-throughs. If it responds, "Every hour or half-hour," that's the wrong answer. The frequency is not the issue; it's that it's done at the same time. Predictable behavior is exactly what thieves want. Find out what methods are used so its staff members do not doze off.

Ask about its procedures: 1) if they see someone suspicious, 2) if they catch someone stealing and 3) any number of what-if scenarios. If all answers are "call the police," then is there a better, less costly way to handle overnight security?

Question what limits of the law do its security officers have compared to a police officer? What happens if an incident occurs, and it eventually ends up in court? If the guard is called as a witness, will the event need to pay for additional time and/or expenses?

Ask about the types of background checks and drug testing done before hiring. Find out in general what type of work experience these individuals have. Are they retired or off-duty police? Are they licensed to fire a gun and do they carry one?

While this may seem petty, ask how fast its staff can run. I'm sure we've all seen the not-so-fit security guard who lumbers in at the appointed hour as the crowds are filing out. If someone suspicious was seen across the park, would the guard most likely stroll across the park and work up a sweat or could they sprint across the park?

Find out what the firm uses to communicate – cell phones, radio-to-base or phone/radio combinations. In the event of an overnight incident, do they contact the event? What happens if it is a significant incident? What are the steps to notify who and when?

Lastly, ask what type of report the Site Services Committee Chairman will receive after the incident as well as at the conclusion of the event.

Event organizers, do your part, too. Ask the Sponsor Services Committee's Sponsor VIP Hospitality Coordinator to keep a pot of coffee brewing overnight or to have high-octane drinks available with some healthy food or doughnuts to keep security personnel wide-eyed until the morning shift takes over.

Always raise all the concession tent walls and keep all the lights on overnight to deter unwanted visitors. While ordering the tent(s), ask if you can "borrow" some extra light bulbs should a few go out during the event.

Sound and lighting personnel like to chat with the overnight security people and provide their contact information. They want and need to know if something happens – lightning hits the sound tower, high winds blow in, tornado warning, etc. After some long hours, the techs can sleep through almost anything – except a wild and crazy ring tone on their phones.

If the stage area is one that can be locked down and the Stage Manager has assumed full responsibility for all items under their domain, you can bet they won't easily turn over the keys between the time the lights go off and the start of the next day. For any locked down areas, confirm who will have the key during the off hours and how they can be reached.

The Site Services Committee Chairman needs to provide a list of those servicing the venue in the early morning hours such as sanitation, port-o-let vendors, etc. You usually can't stop them from entering if the venue is a public facility, but the metal detector guys may make an appearance, too.

Credentials and Passes

These can be as simple or as complicated as you'd like. Most of all they need to be something that cannot be reproduced easily. In general, credentials and passes fall into two categories – all access or limited access to specific areas.

The event most likely has a select number of entry points (assuming other ingress/egress points have been fenced or access is blocked). Each of these entrances should be a location a security volunteer is assigned to check for credentials and passes. Use the site map, created or obtained by the Site Services Committee Chairman or others, to clearly identify and label each point of entry and which credentials and passes travel through each. Many of those receiving passes will be directed to a specific entrance.

Organizing Committee – Unlimited access. Consider adding a reverse side which includes the phone numbers to all key contacts for the event.

Sponsor Services – VIPs and Sponsors should be limited to the Sponsor VIP Hospitality Tent area and perhaps a VIP seating area. These passes can be marked for a specific day or date they are valid. It allows more even distribution of guests throughout the event. Realize not every VIP will show up on the correct day. Roll with it.

Center Stage – 1) Sound and lighting technicians, stage crew, talent, transportation (airport to hotel and back). These credentials provide access to the Talent Hospitality Tent/Green Room, back stage and the main stage. Consider including the specific (contracted) day for talent on the pass but realize it could give access to them throughout the event. Often drivers are attempting to locate talent in order to do a return run, so providing them access allows them to more quickly track down talent. 2) Entertainer – Others – These provide access only to the Talent Hospitality Tent/Green Room. These normally are the husbands, wives, boyfriends, girlfriends and significant others of working talent.

Media – Media credentials provide access with an escort to the Talent Hospitality Tent/Green Room, back stage and the main stage. All other areas are unescorted. The purpose of the credentials or media pass is so members of the Organizing Committee and volunteers can recognize working media.

Concessions, Merchandise Booth, Beverage Stands/Trailers and Ice – All concessionaire personnel and volunteers should be limited to their specific areas. Food concessionaires or vendors may desire to have wristbands because they can be worn throughout the festival. The temperature in some kitchens becomes so hot vendors will change clothes multiple times and there goes the security credential or pass. Passes on chains can pose safety concerns for those preparing food.

Treasurer – Those working with the Treasurer – money handlers above the cashier level – should receive security clearance a level above of the concessions, merchandise booth, beverage stands/ trailers and ice delivery person – perhaps a deeper color or with four stars or the word "priority" on their security credential or pass.

There will always be someone who wants additional security passes than those allocated. In those cases, it's usually for hangers-on and abuse normally follows. Unfortunately, the requesting party once securing the passes rarely explains to the end pass holder the limitations of use. Hard feelings occur when security personnel and volunteers enforce access. For this reason, it's usually best to ask the person wanting "more" to come along with the person desiring the pass and request a security pass each and every time.

I've actually observed a member of an Entertainment Committee who interfaced with talent and negotiated the fees to request 20 additional passes. It seems he desired to impress the talent, spouses and significant others he was trying to cultivate for personal gratification. He implied to them that he ran the entire event, which he did not. While it's a waste of time for the Site Services Committee's Security Committee Chairman to dole the passes out one at a time, it can do one thing. It can require the individual needing the pass to introduce the person needing access. It's a little harder to claim to be in charge when having to go through this exercise.

Parking Passes

Parking passes and security passes work hand in hand. The holder is directed to a specific parking area, asked to present their day-coded VIP parking pass and then enters the venue via a specific gate.

The Organizing Committee should be given parking passes since they arrive early and leave late. Should someone need to leave the event site during the day, they need quick in and out access. Like the Organizing Committee, the sound and lighting techs normally arrive early and leave late, sometimes in large trucks. VIP parking just makes their long day easier. The Treasurer's team of money handlers, like the Organizing Committee, will arrive early and leave late and should have access to close-in parking.

For obvious reasons, VIPs and Sponsors should have close-in parking. In some cases, they may just be coming to do an on-stage presentation and then leaving for another engagement. If a sponsor shows up with the wrong day-coded VIP parking pass, wave them through. The day coding should be designed to balance out the use of parking spaces and VIP seating.

If parking spaces are at a premium and GPS directions inaccurate due to the event's road closures, it's best if the Entertainment Committee's Transportation Committee is the only way talent can get to the event. Transportation Committee vehicles rarely sit for any length of time, so the committee's parking passes allow quick, close-up access for passenger drop off and pick up. For more details, see THE MAIN EVENT – Local Transportation.

Each concessionaire or vendor should be given parking access via a gate. This allows them to bring in supplies and park near their concession during the event. Their vehicle may serve as their office and a secure place to lock up important items.

SHOWTIME

On-Site Communications

Find a low maintenance, easy-to-operate mechanism to communicate with everyone on the Organizing Committee before, during and after the event, including members of the Entertainment Committee's Transportation Committee who will spend many hours away from the venue.

Some event organizers prefer to rent phone/radio combinations for the weekend. As a convenience for each Organizing Committee member, have laminated lanyards made with fellow committee members radio/ phone number and other key phone numbers too, for example, non 911 police department phone number, talent transportation, host hotel, trash pick-up, etc.

Remember when using a radio or speakerphone, others may overhear your conversation. Be professional and be discreet if this is the select mode of communication.

If your Organizing Committee members have headsets, it can appear to the general public as if they have no desire to speak to anyone other than themselves – a closed, inclusive group. Ask them to avoid clustering together in one spot and instead urge them to spend time out in the park. Experience the event as your patrons do.

The Good, The Bad and The Ugly

Some Festival Chairmen falsely believe the event will be attended primarily by the target demographic audience plus or minus those who affiliate with that market segment – kids, grandparents and friends or relatives who are in town and coming along to be polite.

So while the hope is the event will be attended by 100 percent of those who are truly connected to the event theme type – cooking, craft beer, wine, music, film, seafood, BBQ or festival du jour – don't kid yourself. Festival attendees are a subset of the overall population. Ask a member of law enforcement and they will paint a different picture of those who follow festivals. Your audience is a target for pick pockets, credit card thieves, passers of counterfeit money, etc. Patrons ranging from those driving without a license to pedophiles will attend.

If an event is fenced, less of an opportunity exists for a perpetrator to escape. A visible presence of law enforcement and watchful volunteers also deters criminals.

Don't assume criminal activities only occur during the event; these individuals come early to scope out the situation. Just ask the mom who brought her daughter to a city park after visiting a nearby library. She noticed a man following at a distance. Fortunately, she commented to an Organizing Committee member who alerted the police. The man, a sex offender, was detained and removed from the premises. This was caught early but could have been much worse.

Before the event, key players – the Event Chairman, the Public Relations and Publicity Committee Chairman, Site Services Chairman and Security Chairman – should have an important conversation with the lead police officer assigned to cover the event. Find out if any incidents can be handled off the event grounds. In this way, an event spokesperson can state, "We've been in contact with the police department and the officer in charge advised there were no incidents reported at the event." Yes, a fine line but information that gets buried in a reporter's story rather than an incident being the headline or lead story in the evening news.

That's not to say someone wasn't found to be intoxicated or using illegal drugs or got into a fight; it just means these individuals were walked off property before law enforcement took the next step.

Trash Talk

If using a public venue, like a city or county park, most likely the governing agency will provide the trash cans or cardboard boxes, because this is much less costly than the labor hours to manually pick up trash. Double check if plastic bags are provided, as those may be an expense to the event. If the event is elsewhere, you may need to cover the cost of trash receptacles and liners.

Hopefully, your patrons will take their trash to the receptacles. Then it's the Site Services Committee's job to move them to the dumpster using dollies and hand carts. Speak to your city's sanitation department or your waste management vendor as to how many dumpster pick-ups it feels the event will need. Usually trash pick-up occurs in the early morning hours, so the event will need to allow them access if the venue is locked down overnight. Make early morning security aware who will be at the venue and for what purpose. Otherwise, the phone will be ringing.

In the age of recycling, the event may want to ask the concessionaires to use recyclable products. Instead of using a single receptacle, consider two – one for trash and another for recyclable items. Check with your waste management authority to determine if all recyclables can be put together, or if each product – plastic, paper, aluminum, etc., – needs to be sorted.

Recycling may be an opportunity for a local group, perhaps a Boy Scout troop, to raise money and/or provide a community service. Ask for their assistance in moving trash and, in exchange, let them have the recyclables to sell.

How do you know how many trash receptacles and liners the event may need? Again, your sanitation department may have some experience with other events and be able to assist. The answer to the equation involves: 1) how many people the venue will hold; 2) the number of pounds of trash waste an average person creates per day; 3) the number of event hours each day; 4) the size of the trash receptacles; and 5) how many pounds of trash fit into one yard of trash with or without recyclables.

The Marketing Services Committee's stage announcement script should include periodic requests for assistance – "please pick up your trash and deposit at any nearby receptacle." Just like "last call" at your favorite watering hole, the script should include one final mention each evening. It really works and will make the clean up the following morning much more manageable.

Port-o-Lets or Johnny-on-the-Spot®

If this is your first year, rely on the expertise of the port-o-let vendors who are bidding. If they have been doing this for a number of years, they will know how many attendees it takes to fill one of their units. That number can be affected by the weather and beverage consumption, if concessions are available, or if people can bring their own food and drinks into the venue.

The vendor can also help with the proper ratio of regular units to Americans with Disability Act (ADA) compliant units. Many now include hand sanitizer in addition to toilet paper. The Site Services Committee Chairman should schedule routine visits to each unit throughout the event to ensure enough toilet paper is stocked and that the units are kept clean as the day wears on. Otherwise, don't be surprised to find a social media post of a dirty unit or an empty toilet paper roll.

Typically the pumper truck will come each morning to remove contents, clean and refresh supplies. Have a member of the Site Services Committee ask how many people the vendor estimates attended the event the day before based on outbound waste. Share this information with the Event Chairman and Public Relations and Publicity Committee Chairman so they can compare against their projections.

Daily Clean Up

If the event is held at a city or county park, it's possible their regular maintenance staff will be enlisted to clean the event site each day. However, there may be a charge for the manpower and equipment. If your event is held indoors, anticipate a maintenance charge for clean up.

IMPACTING OTHERS – BE A GOOD NEIGHBOR

Organizing Committees are often so busy planning for an event that they forget how the event may negatively impact the community. The Event Chairman and all committee chairmen should be asked if any of their activities would affect neighboring businesses and residences. Will traffic impede travel to and from points 360° around the event?

If the potential exists, the Event Chairman should reach out to these individuals or businesses and provide a mechanism to be contacted should the worst occur. It may also be possible to extend a special invitation to those affected.

Imagine how residents of a nearby nursing home or assisted living facility would feel if the event deters family and friends from their regular weekend visit. Turn a negative into a positive. Invite the residents to come and be your guests during the early hours of the event by letting them sit in the otherwise empty VIP seats. Give them easy access by routing them to VIP parking.

The Big Event

As a former Event Chairman, I can tell you that nothing is more rewarding than standing behind center stage and peering out into a huge crowd of people, many wearing the event's commemorative tee shirts. For me, this is my first chance to breath a sigh of relief. I'm glad no one is watching as I usually smile to myself and do a little happy dance. My next thought is to find every one of my Organizing Committee Chairmen and give each a hug or a pat on the back and say, "Thanks. Together "we" created this."

With every event, an Organizing Committee hopes to positively affect a lot of lives, bring a little bit of joy and great entertainment and make your sponsors happy. Unfortunately, these can't be quantified on a balance sheet.

One Event Chairman shared this story: "Over the years of my involvement, I always had trouble sleeping; so the year I chaired the event, I made it a point to only drink water and avoid the cold caffeine products readily available in the hospitality tent, especially late at night. Yes, I figured out what caused my insomnia. At the after party, a few of my team members came up to me and wondered out loud why I was so calm and relaxed this year. A good night's sleep goes a long way, but a great team goes even further."

Yes, it's magical how an event all comes together. The weather can be comfortable, hot, cold, rainy or windy or perfectly calm. The tone of the event is set by the temperaments of the Event Chairman and the Organizing Committee members. To those who require caffeine as a normal part of your day, go ahead. To everyone else, stay hydrated with water. Remember to eat healthy and take a break. Don't make the days and nights seem longer than they are.

REMEMBERING HOW WE GOT HERE

Thank You, Thank You, Thank You

Unfortunately, many frontline personnel today close out a transaction with "here's your change." When this happens to me, I glance at the person with me, tilt my head and raise my eyebrows. The return expression begs me not to put on a performance that should embarrass the person at the register but certainly won't. It goes like this, "Oh, my goodness! This is my change? I had no idea? I've never seen dollar bills and coins like this before. Are you kidding me? This is my change?"

For me, "Here's your change" is one of the dumbest things anyone can say because it's obvious. What I'm actually hoping for is something that goes like this – "Thank you." That thank you indicates to me that the company appreciates my shopping at their store or using their service. My giving this company my support, my business and my hard–earned money – because I have lots of choices in the marketplace – is reciprocated with those two words. Consumer demand is the reason this company needed to hire a cashier – this person – and I assume results in their sense of purpose as well as a paycheck.

So when I give of my time, money and energy and throw it in the direction of anything or anyone, I want to be appreciated. Wouldn't you?

As such I encourage every Organizing Committee member who is the recipient of someone else's time, money or energy to thank each of them routinely. Not to the point of being fake or not genuine but grateful. Sponsors and patrons should hear it from every volunteer level.

The men, women, boys and girls who are hauling bags of trash to the dumpster need to have their volunteer boss thank them. Other members of the Organizing Committee, as well as the Event Chairman, all need to sing the same "Thank-You" lyrics. Those simple words show appreciation for one of the dirtiest jobs. It may be the difference between them saying, "Those ungrateful so and sos" and "Yes, I want to volunteer again next year!"

If you're fortunate, your sponsors' volunteers have actually volunteered and have not been strong-armed. It's important to thank each of them individually. Let each know how wonderful it is their company has supported the event not only with dollars as well as people. You never know who that person is or whose ear they have. This person might work in the executive office or be a future branch manager. At the end of the day, you can't have enough evangelists promoting the event.

When the Event Chairman first started on this journey, sponsorship packages were one of the early tasks. Now, months later, the Event Chairman will come face-to-face with many of those same people, their bosses or designates during the event. All of these people are considered influencers. Say thank you and let them know how much you and the entire Organizing Committee appreciate their support. Along the way, include a few hard facts, if you'd like:

"Did you hear, we had XXX,XXX festival-goers the last X nights? It took X months in planning, and it would not have been possible without your assistance, Mr. Sponsor, and your company volunteers. Most especially, I'd like to thank you for your allowing your [insert management level employee's name] to serve on the Organizing Committee."

If your Sponsor Services Committee or Organizing Committee worked with more than one sponsor contact – marketing, human resources, community volunteer group, etc. – thank each of them by name. Sometimes company contacts are volunteered to do something that only adds to their normal workload. Thank each one of them for all their support in making the event the success that it is.

As Event Chairman, take a few minutes during the event to disconnect from your communication tools. While in the Sponsor VIP Hospitality Tent, hand them off to a member of your Sponsor Services Committee to monitor, so you can have uninterrupted conversation. If the sponsor VIP you are speaking with isn't familiar with the event, only that his or her company is a sponsor, ask if they have any questions.

You never know who might like to have an autograph of the headliner or photo taken with the event's featured chef. This person might be a wine connoisseur interested in a few minutes with your invited winemaker or may be a home brewer wanting a few pointers from the brewmaster. A simple conversation can result in a pilot or aviation buff's dream being fulfilled – a photo taken with the Blue Angels. Taking the time to listen and engage with people may have long-term benefits for the event in the form of continued sponsorship support.

Experience What Your Customers Experience

To better understand what your patrons are experiencing, put yourself in their shoes during the event.

The Event Chairman should request Organizing Committee members to:

- Walk the perimeter of the venue or stand in the back of the park.

- Walk through the crowd at different times.

- Engage your patrons…a simple "How's it going?" is a great conversation starter.

- Stand in line to use the port-o-lets like everyone else.

- Take off the headsets, giving the impression they are now available to talk to guests.

- Stand in line to buy food and drinks and engage those standing in line.

Team members should give the appearance they are available should a guest want to approach them and ask a question. Make sure the team avoids huddling together or being unavailable or inaccessible in a roped off, exclusive access area.

When team members are out in the trenches, it's possible to discover things like …

- Pesky mosquitoes or no-see-ums. Then schedule to spray before tomorrow's event

- We ran out of toilet paper before 6:00 p.m.

- Concessionaire XYZ is selling bottled water, and it's cheaper than at the event's beverage stands/trailers.

- The sound is not working on the left side of the park.

- A guy is selling glow sticks.

Get out in the crowd. Experience what your patrons experience. You, your team and the event will be better for it.

TAKING CARE OF BUSINESS
ESPECIALLY DURING THE EVENT

Yes, you can count on it. People will call your published event phone number during the event and ask all kinds of questions, like the best place to park, if coolers are permitted, the cost of admission, tee shirt prices, lost items, etc. For some reason, they don't understand everyone is at the venue instead of the office, or how to check the website or social media where much of the pertinent information is detailed.

Anticipate these kinds of calls, emails and posts on social media. Ask your Public Relations and Publicity Committee Chairman to arrange for the calls to be forwarded to an available committee member or picked up (calls, emails and Facebook conversations) periodically during the event.

One of the challenges is it is difficult to hear phones ring or vibrate and callers when on the line due to event sounds. Plus, those calls can come at the most inopportune time. An alternative is to disconnect the answering machine during the event or to clearly indicate in the outgoing message no calls will be returned until the start of the business week and direct the caller to Facebook or the event's website.

EXPECT THE UNEXPECTED

The R Word – Rain

You know where this is going – rain, and in some cases, the H word – hurricane. Completely and totally unpredictable, the weather impacts events in many different ways. For more details, see SITE – Insurance.

With any amount of research, it's possible to pull up historical weather models – rain, temperatures, sunshine, cloud cover and more. No matter what has happened in the past, nothing compares to the present conditions. If it's going to rain, it's going to rain. Just make sure the Organizing Committee has discussed all the viable scenarios and has a Plan B in place.

At some point water and electricity do not mix, as when a wet and slick floor puts your talent and concessionaires or vendors in a precarious situation; as when music, sound and lighting equipment needs to be covered and removed from the elements; as when your guests are in harm's way because of a potential lightning strike; and/or as when your sound and lighting personnel need to come off the scaffolding tower.

Everyone needs to know who is responsible for making the decision to stop the activities and wait it out when inclement weather arrives. An Event Chairman may defer to the area most impacted by the rain – the Stage Manager. That call should be made in consultation with the Event Chairman and the Public Relations and Publicity Committee Chairman unless the weather turns quickly. Again, Plan B needs to be anticipated. Once announced, the dominoes fall for every other area.

Be prepared for your guests, if outside, to seek cover and shelter. See if neighboring buildings can be opened temporarily to bring people out of the rain or you may find patrons huddled under the front porches of nearby homes. The Event Chairman needs to make sure patrons are taken care of before they seek shelter.

Picketers

While unions control some venues, parks are typically not affected unless city workers who are union members are involved.

As an Event Chairman, it's important to keep your ear to the ground and ask innocent questions when taking the helm. "Are there any city employee unions that will negotiate a contract this year?" "Are there any sponsors negotiating contracts with its personnel this year?"

While attendees seem more focused on the event, picketers on a city street near your audience can be a distraction. Regardless of which side of the fence you support, the picketers are hoping to garner sympathy from your audience but, instead, may do more harm than good. After all, the entire event should be about having fun.

Concessions/Vendors

An Event Chairman once remarked, "My uncle and godfather was bigger than life. Among his many talents was that he ran a catering business and specialized in fried chicken. Everyone loved him and he could fix or make anything. When I needed someone to handle my concession area, I searched for someone who captured his spirit and was fortunate to have found someone very special."

Breaking bread with family and friends is what creates a sense of community. As such, concessions – food, wine, beer and beverages – are an important part of any festival. Often, it's the focal point and, for other events, it complements everything else. Food can set the tone for the entire experience.

KEY INGREDIENTS

Decisions. Decisions.

If this event is a first-time event, you'll need to weigh the pros and cons of food vendors be it food trucks, traditional self-contained carnival-style vendor trailers or local restaurants and nonprofit organizations under a concession tent. Each can add a completely different flavor – bad pun intended – to an event.

The Site Services Committee's Concession Committee has the choice of creating an online registration or a paper application form. Check with the event Treasurer to determine if the event is using, or plans to use, an online ticketing system. That system may also offer a registration/application component. From the Treasurer's perspective, using a single system would keep everything in one place. Once the banking piece is in place, it should be easy to set up.

Below are a few of the benefits of an online registration/application:

- The concessionaire registration/application process can be inserted into the event's website.

- It eliminates sending concessionaire or vendor registration/application packets via mail or email and then re-sending when they are lost. With all the information on the website, it greatly reduces follow-up phone calls, voice mails and emails.

- Everything is in one place, including reporting, so you know exactly where the event stands from one minute to the next, providing the online system offers real-time reporting.

- The Concession Committee will no longer need to chase down a concessionaire for a promised check. The registration/application and concessionaire payment occur at the same time.

- If the event is set up to be its own bank and is not paying the online ticketing/registration system for this service, the money can be released to the event as it comes in rather than after the event is over.

If the Concession Committee members are not tech savvy, assume someone on the Treasurer's Committee or Site Services Committee is and can assist in getting the registration/application online. The benefits far outweigh someone painstakingly creating lists of concessionaires and products from scratch. The concessionaire, as part of the online registration/application process, can enter all of this information. It then displays in the reports, can be exported to a spreadsheet and adapted to a new report or for a master list. No data entry, just re-ordering existing information.

If using an online system, once the registrations/applications have been reviewed and concessionaires have been selected or finalized, use the system to cancel each of those not selected. A cancellation email can be sent, along with an email indicating a refund has occurred. Make sure the cancellation email can be edited to soften their not being selected.

There should also be a way to communicate within the online system. If that's the case, send a new online registration form to the selected concessionaires asking them to indicate the number of security credentials or passes needed, whether they want to purchase tablecloths – and how many – and/or an overhead banner, among other items.

Because the concession area should be a secured area, the number of people allowed here is limited. Because workers are rather fluid based on who can work when, it's normally easiest to ask the concessionaire to provide the number of security credentials or passes desired or needed. Give this quantity to the Site Services Committee's Security Committee Chairman who can prepare and issue them to the Site Service Committee's Concession Committee Chairman. In turn, they will distribute them to the concessionaires in advance of set up or on set-up day.

Below are a few things the Concession Committee should consider:

Inclusive or Non-Inclusive – What elements will the Organizing Committee include with the registration/application fee? ... health department permit, tents, string lights, tables and chairs, signs, electricity, water, trash cans or trash pick-up?

Patrons – Will they be permitted to bring in their own coolers into the event? If they bring in liquor, how does that affect your insurance? Will allowing coolers negatively impact the sales of food, beer and wine? Will the decision to allow or disallow coolers be clearly stated in promotional material? What security measures need to be put in place if coolers are or aren't permitted?

Tents – When food, wine and beer are not under large tents, the event should rent individual tents and include as part of registration/application fee. This allows the event to have a more cohesive appearance. The event can better control where the tents are placed and by what time they are set up. Confirm with the local health department if cooking is permitted under the tent.

Menu Items – Any variation of a menu item prepared by a concessionaire should be considered a new item, requiring it to go through the full approval process including review by the health department. Such changes made after approval should not be permitted because it can create a domino effect among all concessionaires. Whatever a customer slathers on a food item after it's sold doesn't count.

Foods – Consider asking vendors to feature foods having a healthier bent – organic, locally sourced, gluten free, dairy free, etc. Can food be prepared in an off-site, health department approved kitchen and brought to the event or will all food need to be prepared at the event? Require each vendor to post its complete menu with prices large enough to be easily read from a distance.

Beverages – Some events will secure a beverage sponsor. In doing so, food concessionaires may be limited as to what beverages they can sell. When the event is limited to local restaurants and not carnival trailers, the event may only permit drinks to be sold that are featured on a concessionaire's regular menu such as ice or hot tea, coffee, lemonade, hot chocolate, etc.

The Environment – In the age of recycling, the Concession Committee may want to require or request vendors, when possible, use recyclable packaging.

The Registration/Application Process

As part of the online registration or paper application process and so that no one can say they didn't know, the Concession Committee should incorporate all event or health department rules and regulations governing the concession area. List what the event will provide – tent, tables, chairs, lighting, power supply, access to water, etc. – and what the concessionaire is responsible for bringing – proof of insurance, equipment, for example, grills, sinks, ice chests, grease traps, chaffing dishes and warming burners; furnishings; decorations; supplemental power or extension cords; supplies, like hand sanitizer, and fixtures; etc. Spell out who pays for the health department license; what infractions can get the concessionaire thrown out; if alcohol is permitted; or if only beverages from a sponsor's product line can be sold.

Highlight the selection criteria so each applicant knows the basis by which they are being considered. This should serve to minimize the chance of someone crying foul later when a Concession Committee member's brother's fraternal organization is accepted. Below are some examples of selection criteria:

1. Quality food product.

2. Food product as it relates to variety of all concession applicants.

3. If a new concessionaire – reference checks with other festivals or similar events on: a) quality; b) cleanliness; c) speed of service; d) adaptability to a special event; e) cooperation with volunteers or staff; f) ability to meet deadlines; and g) ability to follow instructions.

4. If a former concessionaire – the committee will review and verify file notes from previous years.

5. Suggested prices.

6. If a former concessionaire – adherence to previous rules, regulations and concessionaire agreement.

7. Will your products be distributed in recyclable containers and/or with recyclable utensils and napkins?

Reinforce the need that menu items be easy to prepare. Some events require menu items be approved by the event as well as the health department.

Wrap the official Concession Agreement into the application process and require it be signed (an original or via electronic signature) and returned with the deposit or fee in order to be considered. Once all concessionaires are confirmed, a master list with the concession name, contact person and phone number should be shared. This will allow each to coordinate efforts with others if you desire.

Reviewing the Applications/Applicants

A point system seems to provide the fairest and most equitable way to select concessionaires or vendors. The criteria promoted with the application must be the same during the review process. To further reduce the possibility of bias, some Concession Committees remove the vendor's name when reviewing applications.

While not every concessionaire may have a history with the event or any event, the Concession Committee can use this system in three different ways. If the applicant has:

1. No history with the event or any event, two committee members should visit the restaurant separately, and then complete the survey. They may opt to make several visits together rather than one.

2. No history with your event, but history with other events, contact at least three (3) references, scoring points for each and then take the average.

3. If history with the event, one or more members of the committee should be familiar with past performance and should complete the form.

Notification of Selected Vendors

It's best to prepare in advance a "congratulations you've been selected" and a thanks-but-no-thanks letter or email. All correspondence needs to be sent at the same time.

Use an acceptance letter as the opportunity to remind participants about certain requirements or an upcoming meeting, to reconfirm the concessionaire's name and contact information and to say thank you.

Rejection letters can be a bit stickier. Make them brief, revisiting the criteria and indicating where they did shine. In some cases you may want to encourage a vendor to try again. Let them know when and how their application fee will be refunded, if appropriate.

Anticipate being contacted by those non-approved wanting to know why. Sometimes, the mere fact that they are asking is the very reason why they were not selected.

Concessionaire's Pre-Meeting

After the concessionaires are selected, a mandatory pre-event planning meeting should be scheduled with all participating concessionaires. Arrange to have the following attend: health department inspector, an electrician, a representative of the venue, the Concession Committee Chairman, Site Services Committee Chairman and the Event Chairman.

These key contacts should be able to address electrical or power sources and limitations, health department requirements, water and sewer access, garbage collection, vehicle access before the event, parking and parking permits, concession area security credentials or passes, availability of event tee shirts for concessionaire volunteers, etc.

KEEPING IT COOL: BEVERAGE SALES

Beverage Stands/Trailers

The Beverage Stands Coordinator can travel down one of three different roads with beverages: 1) bottled water, teas, juices and sodas (soft drinks or pop); 2) portable trailers with dispensers for syrup and CO_2 tanks and cups and possibly lids and straws; or 3) a combination of bottled and dispensed. The latter two options may require more cleanup effort. All methods require ice.

Comparing profit potential may drive the event's decision as to which option and to what size bottle or cup. Your local beverage distributor and its competitors may be the best resources. They should be able to share what is the most popular size. Armed with information and a matrix of scenarios, the Beverage Stands Coordinator should sit down with the Site Services Committee Chairman and Treasurer, review the options and jointly make a decision.

The Site Services Committee's Beverage Stands Coordinator should also attend the pre-event meeting with all the concessionaires. Much of the information shared will be helpful. They will be working closely with the concessionaires, as this person will be responsible for delivering ice during the event to the concessionaires. This gathering provides the perfect opportunity to get to know everyone.

The information below addresses beverage stands/trailers with syrup and CO_2 tanks.

Your local beverage (soda, soft drinks or pop) distributor may maintain self-contained trailers and coolers to assist in beverage sales. Assuming this is the case, the Beverage Stands Coordinator will need to order them in advance to assure they are available.

On set-up day, the distributor will be asked to bring the trailers or beverage stand supplies to the event's parking lot or closest street. The Beverage Stands Coordinator should have arranged in advance to borrow the forklift (used by the sound and lighting crew) to move the trailers, if used, into the venue versus risking the landscape and turf being damaged if in a park-like environment. If in a tight area, a forklift may be easier to maneuver the trailers into position than the beverage distributor's vehicle.

Once in place, the Beverage Stands Coordinator should inventory the products and supplies and take a photo of all four sides of each trailer or cooler before accepting the units and their contents.

Fountain soda dispensers use a syrup concentrate available in 2.5, 3 or 5-gallon BIBs (bag in box) and will vary based on the product. A self-contained trailer is usually stocked with a starter set of BIBs, once know as figals (5-gallon tanks). The syrup is mixed with carbonated water (CO_2). Use the distributor's recommended ratio of syrup to water for the optimum product. Ask for a quick lesson if you are unfamiliar with how the tap valve or connectors work. Any one of the event's concessionaires who has dispensed soda, soft drinks or pop can probably provide assistance otherwise.

Depending on expected crowds and if your concessionaires are also selling beverages (bottled or dispensed), smaller events should anticipate at minimum two CO_2 tanks per day per beverage stand/trailer, with one serving as a back up. Anticipate some loss of syrup as volunteers get familiar with changing out equipment and perfecting the mix.

Cups can be ordered by the case. At one time boxes came with 1,000 cups in each. Ask that volunteers only open one case and one tube at a time because unopened and undamaged cases and tubes should be able to be returned for a credit.

Anticipate a minimum number of pounds of ice will be needed. Temperatures may affect the inventory. Ask the beverage distributor how many pounds of ice are typically needed per BIB, based on a specific temperature. All ice delivered to the beverage stands/trailers should be tracked and a receipt signed as delivered. The beverage stands/trailers should be charged for ice like other concessionaires.

The Beverage Stands Coordinator should double check with the distributor if supplies can be replenished during the event if they run low. Also ask when final payment is due to the distributor and alert your Treasurer.

With each shift change or cash skim, the Beverage Stands Coordinator should count the cups to match sales with sold product. For more details, see MONEY MATTERS – Money Handling Procedures and ATMs, Robberies, Hold-Ups and Counterfeit Money.

The Beverage Stands Coordinator should also inventory the syrup, CO_2 tanks, cups and ice used each day and provide this information to the Treasurer or their designee in the on-site office. For more details, see MONEY MATTERS – The Toolkit – Cash Handling Supplies and Concession Tickets.

The Toolkit

If the event is operating a concession, like a beverage stand/trailer, most likely this area will need supplies. Here's a brief list of some of those items:

Beverage Specific Supplies:

- Health permits.

- Ice scoops – Check to see if the health department will permit plastic or if stainless steel is required. Cold plastic can chip. While stainless may be more expensive, it will provide years of service.

- Pickle buckets – Ask any restaurant in town if it has extras. Use this to hold hot water and bleach, a common health department requirement.

- Plastic coated paper cups, lids and/or straws for soda, soft drink or pop ordered from the beverage vendor.

- Phone number of the beverage company contact in the event supplies need to be replenished.

- Two dollies to transport ice – when ice is needed, everyone wants it at once.

- Receipt book – The Treasurer should provide receipt books for the ice sales to concessionaires as well as to the beverage stands/trailers.

For more details, see MONEY MATTERS – Toolkit – Cash Handling Supplies.

AVOIDING LAST MINUTE GLITCHES

Pre-Event Reminder

A week or so before the event, send out a reminder to each of the concessionaires by email with a bullet list of key points. Those that are organized will continue to be organized and those that aren't ... will pull things together at the last minute. No one will know but the Concession

Committee Chairman and health department personnel because this concession will likely be the last one inspected.

After Hours Security

While an event may likely arrange for after hours security, it can only be responsible for its property. A concessionaire or vendor's contract should clearly state equipment brought onto the premises is "at their own risk," especially those items left overnight.

No one likes to walk into his or her concession booth the next day and find equipment has been stolen, so a little common sense is required. Every concessionaire should take simple precautions.

For this reason, if a concessionaire has valuable, irreplaceable equipment, urge them to bring in a trailer or van for overnight storage and move those items inside. If a trailer, remember to bring locks with short U-shaped necks (harder to cut off with a bolt cutter) and lock not only the trailer doors but the hitch as well. Alternately block in the hitch end of the trailer so it can't be maneuvered and moved off site. Make sure to have arranged for back-up keys for your locks if lost, stolen or misplaced.

With cameras readily available on smartphones, encourage each concessionaire including the Beverage Stands Coordinator to take photos after set up – inside and outside views. Also take quick shots each night before leaving. The next morning, if questions, the answer will be as close as the phone.

NOW A WORD FROM OUR CONCESSIONAIRES

It's important to have input from the public, sponsors and concessionaires regarding their event experience. Nowadays, it's easy to create online surveys to gather comments. They take less time than sending the "pre-paid return envelope is enclosed for your convenience."

Reach out to the Marketing Services Committee Chairman who can probably recommend an online survey system, like SurveyMonkey®, Survey Gizmo or Responster, that they have vetted and are using. They may also offer to review the questions you propose be included to make sure they are not leading questions and may ask to add a marketing question or two. If the survey is fairly short, they may offer to set it up within their chosen service in order to keep all event surveys in one place.

Surveys such as this should be prepared in advance, and anyone being sent one should be given a heads up. "Hey Bill, about the middle of next week, we're emailing all the concessionaires a short survey asking for their feedback."

Don't expect responses from everyone. Like all surveys, really happy people will respond as well as those who have nothing nice to say. It's much like the Laffer Curve we read about in economics class. Watch out for those 10 percent at either extreme. The 80 percent in the middle are not likely to respond because they are content.

Don't send out a survey for the sake of sending one. Have a purpose. Realize when you ask for people's input about making a change, they believe one will come. Once a survey is completed, share the results internally, but then also share them with the respondents.

Lastly, make the online survey instrument easy to take – simple yes or no questions, multiple choice selections (check boxes) or single answers (radio buttons) and maybe throw in a fill-in field at the end for comments. Make it short. Let those taking the survey know how many questions and/ or how much time it will take. Don't waste someone's valuable time.

Post Event

A festival committee chairman reminisced, "Every time the houselights came on and the crowds headed for the doors or the parking lots, the song "The Party's Over" started rolling around in my head. You work so hard all year long to bring an event to life and before one knows it, it's over, ... or is it really just beginning again?"

All the energy has been focused on "the" festival. Afterwards, it's that strange empty feeling when it's ended.

LEAVE NO FOOTPRINTS

Closing Down the Event Site

The Event Chairman and Organizing Committee have spent months in building an event. A huge amount of energy was directed at creating the event and now it's over or, so some may think. If this is a workday, many committee members are returning to their regular day jobs, leaving a skeleton crew to handle closeout duties. It's important for your Volunteer Services Committee Chairman to staff closeout and to double the staffing needs, because many will be a no show. For some reason, the need for physically strong individuals is always greater at closeout.

While the end may appear to come to an abrupt halt, a number of things need to now roll out in reverse order. All of the things brought into your venue/location need to be removed – fencing and barricades, tents, port-o-lets, banners, sound and lighting equipment, scaffolding, recreational vehicles, tables and chairs, etc.

The day after is about hanging out while waiting for delivery trucks to arrive and pick up various items. Make sure to sign for each of these items as it is loaded and removed. Take it a step further and photograph all four sides just to protect yourself. It's not unusual for a piano to leave the premises in perfect condition and then to arrive at the retail store scratched. Make sure the delivery receipt, signed days ago, also has photos to back up its condition and any concerns are notated on the signed receipt.

Keep an old-fashioned phone book or a fully recharged phone or laptop handy so you can more easily chase down people or vendors when they don't arrive on time. Most of the materials will be returned by those who brought them or picked up by those who delivered them. However, there will be a number of items that belong to the event needing to be transported back to the office or to a storage facility.

It's important that storage boxes are not accidentally destroyed during the event. Consider storing them in someone's vehicle. It's also important to do a full inventory of everything moved into storage and to diagram the approximate location. Leave an aisle down one side so items can be accessed mid-year. Invariably, something stored in the deepest and darkest area will need to be retrieved.

Once the event site is cleared of all these temporary objects, the barricades can come down and roads can be opened. The Site Services Committee Chairman should have a contact to call when the appointed hour occurs or have pre-scheduled it to occur. Much like unpacking a suitcase immediately after a trip, the same should occur at close out. Do as much the day after the event as possible. As the days drag on, it's too easy to have every day life get in the way of taking care of those few strangling things.

On closeout day, always staff the office. People will call asking about lost items. Vendors will call to make sure the check is waiting for them when picking up their leftover product. Any number of calls could come in and should be handled promptly.

Post-Event Details

- Make sure all final invoices and expenses are in by a specific date so the Treasurer and Event Chairman can announce to the Organizing Committee whether the event made a profit or not. Expect the media to also want to know the answer.

- Explain how the thank-you letters and notes work – letters should be sent out with the Event Chairman and Committee Chairman's signature.

- Remind all the committee members when the post-event meeting is scheduled.

- Prompt each as to what they need to bring to the wrap-up event.

- Advise all Organizing Committee volunteers that they WILL resign after each event so the new Event Chairman can make their own appointments.

THE IMPORTANCE OF SAYING THANK YOU

Thanking Those Who Gave So Much to Organize the Event

An amazing number of volunteers give of their time and energy to the community and numerous nonprofit organizations. Many do not do this for awards or accolades but rather because they enjoy helping others and making their community a better place to live, work and play.

The Event Chairman should consider offering every team member a memento to thank them for their commitment and sweat equity in making the event so successful. Some may go into the actual event not knowing what to give, but before it's over, someone's clever expression or action becomes the team's mantra. Perhaps that mantra is printed on a tee shirt for everyone as a gift.

Two thoughtful gifts options are: 1) a small photo album with the event logo embossed on the cover with event photos unique to each person, or 2) a very nice pen with an etched or stylized event logo. The gift needs to be personal and so unique it is something only this prized group of people will receive.

The Event Chairman may also offer Organizing Committee members, too caught up in running the event, the ability to purchase at a discounted price additional quantities of signature merchandise for holiday gifts.

Post-Event Wrap-Up

If all has gone as planned and the weather cooperated, it was a perfect event.

Your meeting calendar should include a wrap-up session within two weeks of the event. This allows your team members' lives to return to normal, but the euphoria of the event remains fresh in their memory. Every member should plan to attend and be prepared to bring:

- Any [Event Name] materials they would like put in file storage. Specifically, ask them to turn in a binder (digital versions are fine too) with copies of all contacts and correspondence.

- Anything that needs to be put into the storage facility.

- Any outstanding invoices or bills and copies of receipts.

- Any extra security credentials or passes, holders, wristbands, etc.

- Any written recommendations for next year. Start with "If I could do over." This should include any items each would like to see purchased (assets of the event) or items needing to be repaired or replaced.

- A list of who have been sent thank-you letters or notes and a list of those needing to be thanked.

- A funny/humorous incident that happened during the event.

Things to remember:

- This meeting is less about business and more about socializing. Involve food and drink because it further solidifies the communal experience you can only achieve after living multiple days in identical outfits (event shirts or uniforms).

Without being asked, team members most likely will bring photos and want to share.

This is also a place for the Event Chairman to give each member of the Organizing Committee a small gift of appreciation; and, if time permits, make a brief comment, share a funny story and offer gratitude and appreciation about each. The Event Chairman's job is almost finished, all but sending thank-you letters and notes and closing out the financial paperwork. For more details, see POST EVENT – Thanking Those Who Gave So Much to Organize the Event.

The Organizing Committee members have now earned this time; let them enjoy it and the friends they've gained along the way.

Thank-You Ad

For more details, see MARKETING – Advertising.

Event Chairman Thank-You Notes – Personal

Some individuals who may not be involved in the event also deserve a small note to let them know how much they are appreciated. These potentially are your boss for allowing you the time, co-workers who carried a heavier load, a spouse who rarely saw you, children who spent more time with your spouse, parents who listened to your stories, mentors who inspired, dear friends who encouraged you to be the Event Chairman and former Festival Chairmen who provided support.

Volunteer Thank-You Letters

A month before the event, the Volunteer Services Committee Chairman should have presented to the Organizing Committee their recommendations for a thank you or memento for each on-site volunteer. These may feature the year's logo or play to the theme of the poster or tee shirt design. These should be readied for distribution by mail within seven to 10 days of the event's ending or at a special post-event gathering. Those not attending would receive their copy by mail.

Thank-You Letters and Notes

Now is the time to show your appreciation to all those who helped make the event such a success. Take the time to recognize everyone regardless of the size role they played. Today the guy who volunteered in the beverage stand/trailer may be a mid-level manager at a local corporation. Ten years from now they may be serving on their company's community allocation committee and remember someone took the time to thank them for a three-hour shift on a hot Sunday afternoon.

If appropriate, send a letter to your local law enforcement agency citing the names of the officers who served your event. In some cases, these will land in their personnel file. What may seem as a trivial sign of appreciation can actually help strengthen the relationship between the event and those who help make it a reality.

Your local newspaper may be interested in running a re-cap of the event; this may be your last opportunity for free publicity with a plug for your event sponsors.

A letter to sponsors thanking them should emphasize continued support to indicate you plan to return again next year.

Thank everyone from the event's talent to concessionaires.

The Event Office

E ven if your event office is a cardboard box in the trunk of the Event Chairman's car, it's so important to recognize the value of saving event "firsts" and placing them in an archive of some type. Make sure to pass along a copy of your poster or brochure or a tee shirt to the local heritage museum so the event can reserve its place in history.

WHY AN OFFICE IS SO IMPORTANT

Event History

While Columbus is credited with discovering the world was round in 1492, it was actually Eratosthenes of Cyrene who lived from 276 to 194 B.C., a Greek astronomer, who scientifically came to this conclusion long beforehand. So, too, with events; many Festival Chairmen choose to ignore an event's history. The Event Chairman and Organizing Committee members should be careful when suggesting something they are doing is a "first-time ever" activity. Quite often, it's really not the first time. Statements like this are actually disrespectful of previous volunteers who were the Eratosthenes of their time.

Having served with the individual who actually created the "first-ever event survey," it was interesting to read about it again in a newspaper article a number of years after we were no longer involved. The same thing occurred with two grant applications completed and submitted to a state agency and a local destination management organization (DMO)

20 years before the "first-ever event grant" was recently announced.

Early on, set a standard for what information is maintained in your historic files. Establish a filing system and document the contents. Then distribute this each year to the Event Chairman and Organizing Committee. This should be provided along with the clear understanding that each Committee Chairman will be required to provide copies of their records to go into the files at the end of the event and added to this list.

While many chairmen are more concerned with survival, a member of the community with an archival background may agree to serve over a number of years to assure certain materials are maintained. In some cases, this may be a member of the local library staff or a member of the local history museum. Always set aside two posters, programs, tee shirts, etc., to donate to the library and/or history museum and keep for the event's time capsule. In many years to come, a special exhibit may feature all area events or highlight the event at a significant anniversary.

Maintaining the Files

For many events run by volunteers, event files can be found in file boxes and binders and scattered among computers around town.

Today your organization may only have a virtual office rather than a physical location, but it's important for the event Secretary to keep tabs on who has what files and to make sure the (virtual) office has been copied in on all final files, executed contracts, etc. This can be done at the end of the event or throughout the year.

I recall one event when the rising Vice Chairman had been copied in on all the correspondence by the Event Chairman throughout the year. When assuming the position of Event Chairman, they indicated the now past president had not given them any files. If only they'd taken the time to read their emails and many, many copies and memos given to them throughout the event. Communication is key. Clearly explain in advance how the sharing process will work.

IT TAKES A LOT OF PEOPLE

Beyond the Founding Fathers

If the event has passed its 10th year, it's time to give less credit to the people who started the event and instead thank all the other Festival Chairmen who have carried it forward. Sometimes those early event creators are concept people who dream up ideas impossible to turn into reality even with a significant budget.

Idea people have a place, but it's the future Festival Chairmen and Organizing Committee members who deserve all the credit and respect. They've either found a way to make bizarre ideas functional or have had the courage to kill off illogical and unrealistic activities. For instance, a small Organizing Committee holds pre-event parties and fundraisers all over town in the days leading up to the signature event and spreads the team too thin while taking their focus off the main event. With each year's passing and news story after story spotlighting the idea people, it further rubs salt in the wounds of those who actually make a "thought" into a successful business.

Past Chairmen

As mentioned in the Committee Volunteer Types, a former chairman can take on the role of The Meddler, but these are the exceptions. Most will serve their time and then move on to other community events or take a back row seat and accept the assigned duties and nothing more.

Regardless of your personal feelings about an individual, a Past Chairman assumed the leadership in creating the event. In doing so, this person probably gave up a year of their life. While that year's event may not be of the magnitude it is today, each successive year built upon a previous chairman's stepping stones making the event what it is today.

Do not discount Past Chairmen. Maintain a list of each former chairman and, on significant anniversaries, invite them to the event, giving them the opportunity to attend or decline and be recognized during the event. Any person who says they can't track down a Past Chairman hasn't searched too hard. Tap into that year's Organizing Committee and someone will know how to reach them because friends do stay in touch.

Treat Past Chairmen with respect and admiration because, without them, the event would not be what it is today. In many cases, the cash in the event's bank account is because of their efforts and saved a later chairman when the rains came pouring down.

Keeping tabs on all past Organizing Committee members is a wonderful thing, too. Each of them made a significant contribution and laid a foundation that is built upon each year. Including all past Organizing Committee members is a great goodwill gesture.

GATEKEEPING NOW AND FOR FUTURE EVENTS

Passwords

This topic probably needs to be addressed with every committee; but because it has value and needs a gatekeeper, it is included in this section.

The use of generic email addresses will prove to be invaluable when it comes to passwords. It's best if the Event Chairman and the Secretary pre-create and distribute approved user IDs and passwords for all possible uses. Few people realize how easy it is for a hacker to breach a website and email accounts. Fortunately, a number of systems nowadays require passwords be X number of characters, a mix of upper and lower case letters, a number plus a special character. The latest directive is to avoid dictionary words that can easily be churned using hacking software. Some experts even recommend a system for passwords such that no password is used twice.

SplashData, which studied 3 million leaked passwords in 2014, released its annual list of the worst passwords. (Go to: http://www.splashdata. com/press/releases.htm.)

SplashData offers these simple tips to be safer from hackers online:

- Use passwords of eight or more characters or more with mixed types of characters.

- Avoid using the same username/password combination for multiple websites.

- Don't use a favorite sport as your password – "baseball" and "football" are in the top 10, and "hockey," "soccer" and "golfer" are in the top 100. Don't use a favorite team either as "yankees," "eagles," "steelers," "rangers," and "lakers" are all in the top 100.

- Don't use your birthday or especially just your birth year – 1989, 1990, 1991, and 1992 are all in the top 100.

- While baby name books are popular for naming children, don't use them as sources for picking passwords. Common names such as "michael," "jennifer," "thomas," "jordan," "hunter," "michelle," "charlie," "andrew," and "daniel" are all in the top 50.

Also in the top 100 are swear words and phrases, hobbies, famous athletes, car brands, and film names.

Few realize the ability of hacking software to data mine words, especially pet names and addresses found on Facebook to drill right into your accounts and make your life miserable.

It may also be possible (storage limits permitting) to maintain all the event emails on the server, thus having access is important should someone leave the organization.

Legal Advice

If you are fortunate, your Organizing Committee may find a local attorney who has an affinity for your type of event and is willing to review your contracts pro bono (for free).

In general, having worked with numerous lawyers over the years, I know that if you want your documents to be reviewed quickly, the Organizing Committee should invest some time and energy in reviewing them beforehand. While a member of your local community may offer free legal services, they may have no or minimal experience with your type of event or the language of your industry. It may take some time and a bit of effort but include point-by-point concerns and explain why. Offer suggestions, such as to how to remedy each concern.

This publication is presented for informational purposes only. The publisher and the author are not offering any legal, tax, accounting, financial, insurance or other professional service or advice. If readers desire such services or advice, please consult a competent professional. Content contained herein may be affected by relevant laws which vary from state to state. Please consult an attorney before using any sample documents. The contents

Related Events and Activities

As the years pass, other groups may come forward and ask to be involved with your event. One such case was a Downtown Development Association whose board was very pleased with the foot traffic the event brought to the downtown core and the exposure the area and member businesses received. To show their support, they asked if they could host the kick-off event the night before the official event began. The Organizing Committee voted with an enthusiastic "Yes. Absolutely. Thank you."

The official event may need to develop criteria in order to sanction these kinds of additions. It can be a simple application form which, once approved, allows the related event to be promoted on the master event schedule and to use the event logo.

Types of related events can be a luncheon cruise featuring music of the same genre as the event, a wine dinner, a children's story hour, poetry reading, wine demonstration, children's band concert, after-hours jam session, kick off party, etc.

SHINING THE SPOTLIGHT

Economic Development

It's important for any event to have the respect of the business community. A well-run event with a solid line-up of talent can garner a prestigious reputation and enhance the community's quality of life.

The Event Chairman should seek opportunities to keep and promote the event as a must-do activity by creating exclusive opportunities where sponsors, business leaders, elected officials and talent can rub elbows with one another.

The economic impact of an event can be more significant when it draws visitors from the outside area. Whenever possible, work to make the travel industry aware of the event in order to increase its draw and brand name recognition beyond the local community.

Business and Industry

Government and nonprofit groups, like economic development councils (EDC) and chambers of commerce, work to entice potential businesses to relocate to their community. As one might suspect, these leads are kept confidential so as to stop other cities and regions from stealing them by offering (tax) incentives and/or other enticements. The EDC maintains an inventory of available land and buildings, statistics on the work force and a laundry list of items contributing to the overall quality of life – educational institutions, medical facilities, housing and cultural opportunities.

Relocation inquires are sometimes made with the condition of anonymity so the requester is not inundated with information. Instead, the EDC compiles all the materials and sends a single package. Visits are then made by business representatives to see for themselves. The visit or weekend can include spouses who can also influence decisions.

An Event Chairman should reach out to the local EDC immediately after being named Event Chairman to determine if the EDC would be willing to organize a familiarization (FAM) trip weekend around the event. Because these are VIPs, the EDC most likely will want access to a private room or location to host a catered meal function, VIP seating and admittance to the Sponsor VIP Hospitality Tent, and souvenir items for gift bags (tee shirts and posters). The Sponsor VIP Hospitality Tent will provide potential businesses wanting to relocate the chance to get to know other community leaders and (cross your fingers, perhaps a future sponsor) maybe have a photo taken with the event's featured talent.

Work closely with the EDC during the planning stages but don't expect them to share the names of those coming.

The Travel Industry

FAM trips are a tool used by the travel industry to introduce airline personnel and travel agents to a destination. Airline personnel may travel during non-peak times when flights are more available, although travel agents may visit over a long weekend to minimize out of office time.

The visiting destination typically has a department which promotes leisure travel. Its responsibility is to develop an itinerary or agenda that highlights the area while giving fair and equal play to the entire destination. This schedule can include stops at museums; time on the slopes; beach time; or a visit to an award-winning park, well-known winery or craft brewery, a theme park, garden or attraction.

Members of the local community host these groups and provide complimentary meals and admission in the hopes of receiving exposure or being promoted. With each hotel that hosts a meal, site inspections are given of the hotel's guest rooms. This is a working trip and the price paid for a complimentary getaway. The itinerary is full from morning to night.

If travel agents attend your event, see if one of the Organizing Committee members can meet the group when they arrive. As an added perk, provide each one a tee shirt, because they are much easier to transport than a poster.

COMMUNITYWIDE SUPPORT

Many events are held downtown as a means to benefit this part of the community, driving attention to an area residents might not otherwise visit.

A taxing district may fund your downtown agency. Make time to meet with its board of directors or paid staff to determine if there may be a win-win activity or event which would benefit them as well as the event.

To lend support to a major event being held downtown, some downtown organizations will host a kick-off party featuring similarly themed local talent or offer to place event-provided posters in downtown store windows welcoming attendees. Yet others have a promotional budget and will help underwrite colorful street light banners showcasing the event. If designed correctly, the graphics are timeless, so they can be used for several years forward. These types of relationships and events lend themselves to pre-event publicity and solidifying a strong bond between businesses, neighbors and the event.

Resources and Notes

FESTIVAL & EVENT ASSOCIATIONS
by STATE and REGION

Arizona
Festival Event Association of Tucson and Southern Arizona
http://featsaz.com

Arkansas
Arkansas Festivals and Events Association
http://www.arfea.org

California
California/Nevada Festivals and Events Association
http://www.calfest.org

Colorado
Colorado Festivals and Events Association
http://coloradofestival.com

Florida
Florida Festival and Events Association
http://www.ffea.com

Greater Miami Festivals and Events
http:// www.FestivalsMiami.com

Illinois
International Live Events Association
http://www.ileahub.com

Indiana
Indiana Festivals
http://www.indianafestivals.org

Kansas
Kansas Fairs and Festivals Association
http://www.kansasfairsassociation.com

Kentucky
Kentucky Festivals and Events Association
http://kfea.com

Louisiana
Louisiana Association of Fairs and Festivals
http://www.laffnet.org

Michigan
Michigan Festivals and Events Association
http://www.mfea.org

Minnesota
Minnesota Festivals and Events Association
http://www.mnfea.com

Missouri
Missouri Association of Fairs and Festivals
http://www.mofairs.org

Nevada
California/Nevada Festivals and Events Association
http://www.calfest.org

North Carolina
North Carolina Association of Festivals and Events
http://ncfestivals.com

Ohio
Ohio Festivals and Events Association
http://ofea.org

Oregon
Oregon Festival and Events Association
http://www.oregonfestivals.org

South Carolina
South Carolina Festival and Event Association
http://scfea.com

Texas
Texas Festivals and Events Association
http://www.tfea.org

Utah
Utah Association of Fairs and Events
http://www.utahfairsandevents.org

Washington
Washington Festivals and Events Association
http://www.wfea.org

West Virginia
West Virginia Association of Fairs and Festivals
http://www.wvfairsandfestivals.org

Southeast U.S.
Southeast Festival and Events Association
http://www.southeastfestivals.org

International
International Festivals and Events Association
http://www.ifea.com

Canada
Festivals and Events Prince Edward Island
http://www.festivalspei.com

Festivals and Events Ontario
http://www.festivalsandeventsontario.ca

Ottawa Festivals
http://www.ottawafestivals.ca

Ireland
Association of Irish Festivals and Events
http://www.aoifeonline.com

United Kingdom
The Association of Festival Organisers
http://www.festivalorganisers.org

National Outdoor Events Association
http://www.noea.org.uk

FOOD, BEER, WINE & SPIRITS ORGANIZATIONS

American Brewers Guild
http://abgbrew.com

American Homebrewers Association
http://www.homebrewersassociation.org

American Institute of Wine and Food
http://www.aiwf.org

Brewers Association
https://www.brewersassociation.org

National Food Truck Association
http://www.nationalfoodtrucks.org

National Restaurant Association

http://www.restaurant.org

Wine and Spirits Wholesalers of America

http://www.wswa.org

WineAmerica

http://wineamerica.org

Wine Institute

http://www.wineinstitute.org

Wine Market Council

http://winemarketcouncil.com

World Food Travel Association

https://worldfoodtravel.org

ORGANIZATIONS

Main Street America™

http://www.preservationnation.org/main-street

MUSIC LICENSING

Broadcast Music, Inc.® > Music Users > Licensing

http://www.bmi.com 877-264-2137 888-689-5264

The American Society of Composers, Authors and Publishers (ASCAP)

http://www.ascap.com

SUPPLIERS

American Pyrotechnics Association
http://www.americanpyro.com

Drum Corps International
http://www.dci.org

International Amusement and Leisure Defense Association
http://www.ialda.org

Mid America Horse Show Association
http://www.midamericahorseshow.org

National Fireworks Association
http://www.nationalfireworks.org

National Independent Concessionaires Association, Inc.
http:// www.nicainc.org

Portable Sanitation Association International
http:// www.PSAI.org

NOTES

ApplePay is a trademark of Apple Inc., registered in the U.S. and other countries.

QR Code is a trademark of DENSO WAVE INCORPORATED CORPORATION JAPAN in the U.S. and other countries.

SurveyMonkey is a trademark of SurveyMonkey Inc. and its affiliates and is used under license.

TWITTER, TWEET, RETWEET and the Twitter logo are trademarks of Twitter, Inc. or its affiliates.

Wikimedia Wordmark is a trademark of the Wikimedia Foundation and is used with the permission of the Wikimedia Foundation. We are not endorsed by or affiliated with the Wikimedia Foundation.

Acknowledgments

An enormous thank you to my husband for his love and encouragement. To our boys who remind me daily when it's time to leave my office and go home.

With deep appreciation to those:
Who have inspired: Gertrude Brainerd, Joann Dumont, Irene Obrecht Estes and Mary Ann Young.
Who saw promise, mentored and inspired: Nancy Kaylor.
Who has led, made footprints, allowed me to walk in them and add a few of my own: Nancy Kaylor.
Who were always up for a challenge and said yes when asked: Fred Boscarino, Bruce Boyers, Dale Kleine, Claude Miranda, Valarie Nussbaum-Harris, Victoria Scotti and Deborah Vincent. Plus a host of others too numerous to mention.
Who have never said no: Anne Adams, Ron Bortolini and Ebe Bower.
Who were always there ... Anthony & Julia, Cathy, Cheryl, Dale, Ebe, Francis, Joseph & Deb, Nancy & Steve, Nancy & Ray, Patrick and Todd.

To my family ... dad, mom and my siblings, especially my brother John, Cousin Barb and Aunt Mary, Aunt Adrienne and Uncle Ralph for the foundation of love and support they have given me and continue to do so today.

Index

About the Author

Throughout her career, Lynn Fuhler has successfully organized and promoted numerous festivals as well as corporate and community events and leadership programs and activities. The former Tourism and Convention Director of Clearwater and Clearwater Beach, Fla., currently the #1 beach destination in the United States, has worked extensively with the hospitality industry to market destinations, festivals, events and visitor activities throughout the world. She is the former Event Chairman of the all-volunteer Clearwater Jazz Holiday, then the largest free jazz festival in the Southeast U.S.

Lynn Fuhler is a consultant, speaker and publisher of a blog which focuses on all aspects of festival and event planning. A native of Illinois and the greater St. Louis area, Lynn holds a B.S. degree in transportation, travel and tourism from St. Louis University's Parks College. Based in North Carolina, Lynn is the co-founder of Flying Compass, Inc. a hospitality marketing company.

A Midwesterner at heart, Fuhler resided in Florida for many years before heading to the Carolinas. Travel is her avocation, along with studying maps, people and places. She credits newspaper advice columns she read while growing up with helping her hone her problem solving skills. She has fond memories of camping which laid the foundation for festival and event management.

www.lynnfuhler.com
www.festivalexperts.org

Made in the USA
Charleston, SC
29 November 2016